INDIA'S ORGANIC FARMING REVOLUTION

India's Organic Farming Revolution

*What It Means for
Our Global Food System*

Sapna E. Thottathil

UNIVERSITY OF IOWA PRESS, IOWA CITY

University of Iowa Press, Iowa City 52242

Copyright © 2014 by the University of Iowa Press

www.uiowapress.org

Printed in the United States of America

Design by April Leidig

The University of Iowa Press is a member of Green Press Initiative and is committed to preserving natural resources.

All photographs were taken by the author and are in her possession.

Printed on acid-free paper

Library of Congress Cataloging-in-Publication Data

Thottathil, Sapna E., 1982–

India's organic farming revolution: what it means for our global food system / Sapna E. Thottathil.

pages   cm

Includes bibliographical references and index.

ISBN 978-1-60938-277-3 (pbk)

ISBN 978-1-60938-301-5 (ebk)

1. Organic farming — India. 2. Organic farming — Law and legislation — India — Kerala. I. Title.

S605.5.T56   2014

631.5'84095483 — dc23   2014010225

To the organic farmers of Kerala
and their supporters

CONTENTS

ABBREVIATIONS AND ACRONYMS

ACT	Organic Agriculture Certification Thailand
AOA	Agreement on Agriculture
APEDA	Agriculture and Food Products Export Development Authority
ASEAN	Association of South East Asian Nations
CBD	Convention on Biological Diversity
CESS	Centre for Earth Science Studies
CPI	Communist Party of India
CPI(M)	Communist Party of India (Marxist)
CSA	Community Supported Agriculture
DDT	dichlorodiphenyltrichloroethane (pesticide)
EPA	Environmental Protection Agency (US)
FAO	Food and Agriculture Organization
FiBL	Research Institute of Organic Agriculture
GDP	Gross Domestic Product
GMO	genetically modified organism
HDI	Human Development Index
HYV	high-yielding variety
IADP	Intensive Agricultural District Programme
ICA	International Coffee Agreement
ICAR	Indian Council of Agricultural Research
ICS	internal control system
IFOAM	International Federation of Organic Agriculture Movements
Indocert	Indian Organic Certification Agency
INFAM	Indian Farmers Movement
IOFPCL	Indian Organic Farmers Producer Company Limited
ISO	International Organization for Standardization
IUCN	International Union for Conservation of Nature

KAU	Kerala Agricultural University
KSSP	Kerala Sasthra Sahithya Parishad ("People's Science Movement")
KVK	Krishi Vigyan Kendra
LDF	Left Democratic Front
NAFTA	North American Free Trade Agreement
NCOF	National Centre of Organic Farming
NGO	nongovernmental organization
NPOP	National Programme for Organic Production
NSOP	National Standards for Organic Production
PDS	Public Distribution System
PGS	Participatory Guarantee System
PL-480	Public Law 480 (US)
POP	persistent organic pollutant
SDP	State Domestic Product
SECO	State Secretariat for Economic Affairs (Switzerland)
SHG	self-help group
UDF	United Democratic Front
UNCTAD	United Nations Conference on Trade and Development
UNEP	United Nations Environment Programme
USAID	United States Agency for International Development
USDA	United States Department of Agriculture
WHO	World Health Organization
WTO	World Trade Organization
WWF	World Wildlife Fund

From India to My Plate

WHEN THE BRITISH government announced in 2000 that it would cut 60 percent of its greenhouse gas emissions by 2050 to mitigate climate change, no one expected that this plan would conflict with sustainable development and poverty alleviation in countries like India. Unfortunately, development agencies, nonprofit organizations, and religious groups soon found themselves working at cross purposes with each other. The problem was "food miles."

As consumers, activists, and policy makers began to realize that the distance that food travels to reach us could increase its "carbon footprint" —the amount of energy required to bring food from seed to plate— importing fresh produce and dry goods from afar seemed increasingly like a bad idea. Several organizations therefore advocated that British consumers only buy local food. The logic went like this: if everyone were to lower their food miles by consuming smaller amounts of imported goods and greater amounts of local produce instead, less air, ship, and rail transportation would be needed to bring imported foods into Britain. The consumption of fewer fossil fuels and less energy in shipping would lead to a smaller amount of carbon dioxide being released into the atmosphere, and climate change's disastrous effects could potentially be forestalled.

Organizations dedicated to development, on the other hand, found themselves conflicted about this announcement from the British government. Oxfam, for example, had been promoting organic and Fair Trade farming in the developing world as a sustainable development strategy for years.[1] It hoped that connecting poor, organic farmers in places like Africa and India to premium export markets (typically in countries that formerly colonized them) would augment farmers' incomes and improve their livelihoods. But Oxfam was also committed to mitigating climate change and supported the goals set by the British government.

Meanwhile, British consumers concerned about these issues were becoming confused about which products they could ethically buy from grocery stores. For example, when given the choice between local British apples *or* Fair Trade apples from South Africa (produced with minimal chemical inputs), what were they supposed to select? This is precisely a choice I encountered at a store in Oxford, England, in 2005. At the time, I was not sure which to purchase. I hemmed and hawed, oscillating between the selections, and then eventually bought both, using my research as justification.

Between 2005 and 2006, I studied the trade-offs between Fair Trade and local foods while earning a master's degree from Oxford University. To gauge consumer attitudes, I interviewed 460 shoppers at retail food outlets in England. I discovered that many people grappled with similar concerns about their food.

Said one customer to me, when given the choice between an organic apple from abroad and a local apple produced conventionally: "I personally never, ever buy a foreign apple. They taste disgusting. They are revolting. If you can get them banned, I'd be for it. They are disgusting." Another consumer expressed less scorn and more anxiety: "[I] tend to buy local . . . food rather than imported, although I then worry that by not buying and supporting [developing] economies, I condemn the Third World to continuing poverty." And yet another shopper told me, "I am often unsure whether to buy organic."

Through these interviews I unearthed a diversity of feelings—mixtures of doubt, disdain, and even paternalism toward countries like India that export food to the United States and Europe. While I found that several consumers focused on questions of taste and provenance, whereas others emphasized farmers' livelihoods, I also found that most people were uncertain about how to make sense of competing arguments while shopping. Further, I began noticing that these consumer opinions echoed growing debates about the place of organic agriculture in our global, industrial food system.

Soon after I conducted these interviews, Michael Pollan's *Omnivore's Dilemma* (2006) hit bookstores. Exasperatedly, he described difficulties —much like those I had encountered—in determining the merits of various ethical products in a Whole Foods grocery store in California. The answer to "what to eat for dinner," he concluded, was not simple.

THIS BOOK IS actually not about consumers, but organic producers.

Asking myself "what to eat for dinner" prompted me not just to think about what I was buying but to study farming practices hundreds of miles away from Oxford, England, as well as from my home in the United States. I wanted to explore how the food I bought was produced, to find an answer to the dilemma I had identified in 2005: Is there an inherent conflict between sustainable agriculture and a globalized world?

My interest in this question wasn't purely intellectual. As a first-generation Indian American whose family historically engaged in farming, the issue of sustainable food imports and exports piqued my interest. I'm the daughter of farmers who chose to leave their home in Kerala, a state in southern India, and their agricultural roots, to work in other professions in the United States. As a child growing up in America, if I happened to express any hesitation over finishing the vegetables on my dinner plate, my father would often say sternly that poor children were likely going hungry in India at that very moment. While parents may frequently scold their children for neglecting their vegetables, my father's reprimands had a personal meaning. Although he grew up on a farm in Kerala, surrounded by family with extensive knowledge of agriculture, he experienced hunger on a regular basis. His parents and siblings often did not have enough money from their agricultural work to buy food. The oldest child in his family, my father was born a few years after World War II, when a combination of global, political, and ecological factors caused the newly formed nation of India to experience severe food shortages.

In moments of reflection and reminiscing, my father would sometimes share with me his strategies for combatting hunger while he was young, including drinking a lot of water "so I would feel full." Eventually, both my father and mother pursued another strategy to lessen their agrarian hardships: they left farming and India to pursue occupations with fewer risks and more rewards halfway around the world.

To understand the global economic system that structured my parents' choices, as well as the contemporary food system, I decided to continue my research on food and agriculture through a PhD program in geography at the University of California at Berkeley. When it came time to do my fieldwork, I went back to my parents' former home in Kerala, spending fourteen months there between 2009 and 2011, studying farming practices and access to global markets. These two years were an exciting time to be in Kerala, because in 2010 the state promulgated a policy to convert its entire agricultural production to organic practices within ten years.

While in Kerala, I spent time with farmers in their fields, attended organic agriculture training sessions and conferences, interviewed policy makers and government officials, and traveled throughout South India to study and analyze its emergent organic farming sector. Close to nine thousand farmers were farming organically in Kerala by the time I left. They had diverse and complex reasons for doing so, reasons that American and European scholars and journalists had largely overlooked.

From my time in India, I discovered that the politics of our contemporary food system are intertwined with a complex history of colonialism, free trade agreements, and exchange between local and distant cultures, flora, and fauna. Food and agriculture in one place are intimately interconnected with food and agriculture in other places. Therefore, the question of what to consume or produce in any country has global implications. Muddying this picture, however, is the fact the agro-food system is not a level playing field. Its multifaceted history has produced a world where millions of people remain malnourished, even though the overall global acreage devoted to agriculture has increased and produces enough food for everyone alive today. Much of that food is left to rot or is diverted for fuel, or it remains unavailable or too expensive for those who need it because of financial speculation in commodities, the inadequacy of distribution networks, and poor wages. Many people just cannot afford to buy food in today's world. Moreover and ironically, the growing footprint of agricultural production is contributing to several health-related and environmental problems, from pesticide poisonings to a decline in global biodiversity.

In this book, I examine the place of South India's organic farming movement in our contemporary, globalized food system. My aim is to complicate the conversations about food imports and the role of sustainable agriculture in places like India. Stories from Kerala's organic producers illustrate the fact that the debate around organic agriculture must move beyond taste and whether consumers should purchase local food. As a political movement, organic agriculture can be much more—in fostering grassroots political empowerment, in protecting the health and well-being of farmers and their families, and in constructing mutually beneficial trade relationships. Organic farming in India represents one positive step toward reforming industrial agriculture and ensuring a healthier, more sustainable future for all of us, producers and consumers around the world alike.

ACKNOWLEDGMENTS

OVER EIGHT YEARS of research and thought went into writing this book, which emerged from my PhD dissertation work at the University of California at Berkeley. I am indebted to the many people who gave me extensive time and resources to conduct my research and then write about it over these years. This book would not have come to fruition without their support.

Foremost, my PhD dissertation committee at Berkeley—Michael Watts, Jake Kosek, and Nancy Peluso—oversaw and guided my research and writing. Michael and Jake helped structure my ideas into something concrete, and I learned much from them both. At Berkeley, I also benefited from conversations with Nathan Sayre, Gillian Hart, Ananya Roy, and Julie Guthman. Diana Liverman, my former master's adviser at Oxford deserves thanks as well, not only for bringing me into the field of geography but for inadvertently introducing me to the world of food politics.

I owe immense gratitude to Usha and Sridhar from Thanal, as well as several staff at the Kerala State Biodiversity Board (especially V. S. Vijayan and R. V. Varma), who spent much time with me and without whom I would not have been able to conduct this research. Thanal's work continues to be inspiring to this day. A. K. Sherief, Bhaskaran, George Thomas, and several others at Kerala Agricultural University invited me to observe classes and workshops in Kerala's agricultural extension. Faculty and students in agricultural extension took time to have several hour-long chats with me, and they opened up my eyes to Kerala's political scene in productive ways. Similarly, Bijoy Nandan at Cochin University of Science and Technology shared much of his own research with me so that I could better understand Kerala's organic farming projects. Many officials in Kerala's Agriculture Department also spoke candidly with me, and their insights helped significantly in the development of my arguments.

In Wayanad District, P. J. Chackochan, K. M. George and Organic Wayanad, and M. P. Joy welcomed me like family into their homes and their workplaces; I hope my research and writing does justice to their great work on organic farming. The M. S. Swaminathan Foundation staff and board members, as well as Thankamani at Greens, contributed greatly to my understanding of agriculture in Wayanad, and were rays of light in my days during the heavy monsoon rains.

I owe much thanks to many of the informants throughout Kerala who gave me their time, as well as tea, biscuits, and several organic fruits, which my husband and I happily shared. Several of these people, some of whose names I've changed throughout this manuscript to protect their identities, greatly contributed to my thinking, research, and writing. I hope that I have been a collaborator and partner to all my informants, and that our time and conversations together were mutually beneficial. Most important, I hope that I have successfully conveyed why, despite my parents' departure from agriculture and India, sustainable food systems in Kerala remains a significant, worthwhile, and inspiring topic of inquiry.

The American Institute for Indian Studies (AIIS) in Kerala was like a second home to me while I was there. At AIIS, Dr. V. K. Bindu ("Bindu teacher") and Arun both went above and beyond their duties to help settle me into Kerala, fill out complicated paperwork, and develop necessary relationships. AIIS reacquainted me with Kerala and Malayalam, and I could not have done this research without its help. Funding for my participation in the AIIS Malayalam school came from a Foreign Language and Area Studies (FLAS) grant through the United States Department of Education. I also owe immense thanks to the Department of Education for a Fulbright Hayes Doctoral Dissertation Research fellowship, which provided me with the support to return to Kerala and conduct research. I truly hope these educational programs continue to receive funding.

The United States-India Educational Foundation took care of several logistics so that I could proceed with my research. In Kerala, the Centre for Development Studies in Thiruvananthapuram did the same and wrote multiple letters of support for me so that I could access various archives within Kerala. It gave me an excellent scholarly base as well. Likewise, the University of Kerala generously shared its resources with me. Sasi, our reliable driver in Thiruvananthapuram, also assisted my husband and me in many ways.

The chapters in this book benefited from discussant comments from presentations at several conferences, including the 2012 Association of American Geographers Conference, the 2012 Association for Asian Studies Conference, and the Eighth International Conference on Sustainability in 2012. I also enjoyed presenting my research at the Institute for Policy Studies (IPS) in Washington DC, thanks to Beth Schulman. In fact, it was the presentation at IPS that caught the eye of my editor at the University of Iowa Press, Catherine Cocks. Catherine and editors at the University of Iowa Press have been a pleasure to work with. Constructive comments from anonymous reviewers on my manuscript have also strengthened the text and my arguments.

Annelies Goger, Laurah Klepinger-Mathew, and Jennifer Sarrett remained extremely supportive of me both during and after my field research. Annelies, Laurah, Sonja Thomas, Sarah Besky, Kimberly Kinder, and Jennifer Devine took much time to read and give me comments on my work. I am also grateful for the support and advice of Jennifer Baca, Greta Marchesi, Glenna Anton, Xochitl Marsilli, and Pablo Palomino— as well as several other Berkeley colleagues. Ted Steck, my former undergraduate adviser at the University of Chicago, provided me with extensive and constructive comments on early chapters of this book. Eli Zigas also commented in detail on early versions. Additionally, colleagues at Health Care Without Harm and Physicians for Social Responsibility were very understanding about the time I needed to take off to complete this book and have confirmed my commitment to sustainable food systems. Conversations I had with coworkers like Kendra Klein helped focus my thinking around the relationship between the consumption of food, human health, and the environment.

Finally, I owe a large thank-you to my family in the United States and India for helping me make several logistical arrangements, feeding me, and supporting my research in general. It was wonderful to be around my aunts, uncles, cousins, and grandmother in Wayanad District. A thank-you to Mom, Dad, Sherry, and Somy; you helped me figure out how to balance two worlds. Somy, especially, thanks for being a sounding board. Mom and Dad, thank you for sharing your stories. And last, but certainly not least, a thank-you to David—this was fun but stressful, and yet you maintained good spirits all along. And best of all, you learned Malayalam!

INDIA'S ORGANIC FARMING REVOLUTION

Globalization and Organic Food Systems

When Christopher Columbus discovered America, it is said he was disappointed, for the place he was really seeking was this, the coast of Malabar, India's fabled spice coast, linked by intricate waterways to a hinterland of unimaginable riches. The Romans and Phoenicians, the Arabs, Chinese, and Europeans all came here in search of ivory, silks, and gold. But most of all, they came for the spices of India: cardamom, ginger, cinnamon, and black pepper—or black gold.—Narration from an Indian Ministry of Tourism *Incredible !ndia* video

IN THE SOUTH OF India is a land of coconuts—Kerala, as it is called in Malayalam, the local language. Several sizes and varieties of coconut trees fill every possible corner, swaying behind train stations in groves and along city streets, lining the sides of every canal and waterway, and ranging from the Malabar Coast to high into the foggy mountain ranges of the Western Ghats. When you look down from rooftops or out of the window of an airplane, everything is green—a verdant landscape extending to the horizon.

Kerala has enchanted travelers for centuries with its natural resources and geography. Marco Polo sought its spices, and colonial empires fought for control of its teak forests and medicinal plants. Today, the southwestern Indian state is the "torchbearer" of the Government of India's Incredible !ndia, a marketing campaign designed by the Indian Ministry of Tourism.[1] Images of Kerala's greenery, from its rolling hills of spice gardens to its coasts lined with coconut palms, dominate promotional posters and videos for India.

"Don't be fooled," warned Sugathakumari, an environmental activist born and raised in Kerala. "You can't even drink our coconut water without getting sick." She did not see a mythical landscape of spices and coconut palms. Instead, when she looked at the state's landscape, she saw mono-crops of pineapples, rubber, and other cash crops, all regularly sprayed with the pesticides furadan and endosulfan, two poisonous chemicals leaching into the watersheds.[2] Promotional images of the state for travel and tourism belied how its greenery was produced.

It was the year 2010. The Kerala Forest Research Institute had just released a study documenting that the fingernails of pineapple pickers in Kerala were falling off after they had been exposed to an unknown cocktail of chemical pesticides. This was not an unusual story, Sugathakumari emphasized to an audience gathered for the 2010 Indian Biodiversity Conference in the capital of Kerala, Thiruvananthapuram. She reminded the crowd that, earlier in that same decade, several children in a northern agricultural district of the state had been born with severe physical deformities after their parents had been exposed to endosulfan, a harmful chemical classified as a persistent organic pollutant by the scientific community, because of its ability to linger in the environment for years. For over a quarter of a century, these agrarian communities had been repeatedly sprayed aerially with the chemical to control pests on nearby cashew plantations. Kerala had become a toxic place: its lush greenery was now drenched in poisonous pesticides, bad for human health and the environment.

Sugathakumari was one of the keynote speakers at the 2010 conference, which had attracted environmentalists, students, government officials, and farmers from throughout the state to share research and news about environmental issues. While conversations and panel discussions were often somber, in response to recent news stories about pesticide poisonings and agriculture's threats to biodiversity, another news item cheered up the gathered people and dominated the speeches: Kerala's recently issued organic farming policy. Internationally renowned environmental activist Vandana Shiva was so impressed with the state's policy that she spoke of it at length at the closing ceremony. "Kerala is and can be a model," she insisted, suggesting that the state could be a "torchbearer" again, this time in the organic farming sector. Shiva continued: "The world needs more models."

THE POLICY THAT so delighted the people at the conference on biodiversity was an official plan put forth by Kerala's government leaders to convert the entire state to organic farming within ten years.[3] State officials claimed that organic agriculture—farming with limited use of synthetic inputs such as chemical fertilizers and pesticides—could be the solution to the innumerable agrarian problems the state was facing, from farmer suicides to poisoning by pesticides such as endosulfan. The policy's announcement signaled a momentous political step and indicated that an ever-increasing amount of land in India was being set aside solely for organic production. While Kerala is geographically one of the smallest states in India, its 2010 policy initiative is the equivalent of designating an area greater than the size of Maryland as an organic zone.[4] Over thirty million people living in the area would be covered.

Estimates as of 2013 suggest that over fifteen thousand farmers in Kerala are already or in the process of being certified organic for export to the United States and Europe; that is, they meet the legal standards that define organic farming on a national level, as determined by a third-party certifier.[5] According to the International Federation of Organic Agriculture Movements (IFOAM), a nonprofit umbrella organization promoting sustainable agriculture globally, certified organic products are "those which have been produced, stored, processed, handled and marketed in accordance with precise technical specifications (standards) and certified as 'organic' by a certification body."[6] In India, these technical specifications are called the National Standards for Organic Production (NSOP), which are set by the Agriculture and Food Products Export Development Authority (APEDA) of the Ministry of Commerce.[7] APEDA has accredited twenty-four institutions in India to carry out organic certification, many of which are located outside of the country.[8] The first indigenous organic certification body in India, Indocert (Indian Organic Certification Agency), is based in Kerala, indicative of the leadership role Kerala is playing in South India's organic farming movement.

Throughout the rest of India, organic agriculture is also growing. Between 2003 and 2010, the area under certified organic agriculture grew by almost 2,500 percent, totaling more than four thousand square miles.[9] While this area represents less than 1 percent of India's cultivable land area, over half a million organic farmers live in the country, the highest number of organic producers of any country in the world.[10] For the sake of comparison, the rate of growth for the area under certified organic production in the United States was just 12 percent between 2008 and 2011.[11]

Twelve Indian states are currently either discussing or have organic farming policies in place.[12] As part of its Tenth Five Year Plan, the national government earmarked millions of dollars for the promotion of organic agriculture throughout the country and has allocated funds for organic farming ever since.[13] Several states are setting up research and training institutions to assist farmers with organic methods of growing food. Nongovernmental organizations, foundations, and development institutions are financing the rollout of organic farming in many villages.[14] Furthermore, India's growing middle class and urban populations increasingly express interest in purchasing organic produce. Some estimates suggest that organic retail within the country may even be growing at a rate of 100 percent per year.[15]

Indian organic farmers also rely on foreign markets, having sold over $100 million dollars' worth of organic goods such as rice, spices, and fruit to Europe, the United States, and other countries in 2009.[16] Market estimates forecast this amount doubling by 2014, if not earlier.[17] Today one can find organic Indian products such as vanilla, black pepper, and tea in the aisles of many American and European supermarkets. Many of these food items hail from Kerala.

Globally, organic food sales are around $60 billion and growing, in spite of the economic downturn.[18] More and more land is being converted to organic farming, now totaling 37.2 million hectares worldwide.[19] Big-box retailers like Walmart have even begun to supply organic products for their shoppers, and the United States now represents the largest market for organic goods (worth almost $30 billion), with Europe close behind.[20] This rising demand means that organic foods are often in short supply, spurring the growth of organic exports from developing countries like India.[21]

Alongside the rapid global growth in the organic food market and exports, however, have come cautionary and sometimes farcical tales. Recent editorials have called organic food elitist because of its high prices and limited availability, headlines have suggested that organic produce from China is contaminated with chemical pesticides and fertilizers, and scholarly research has documented labor abuses occurring on large organic farms in California.[22] Some activists have even claimed that the food miles of organic food can be "catastrophic" and have suggested that imported organic products be denied organic certification.[23] It is no wonder that, as several popular books have claimed, consumers are regularly confused about what to purchase at the grocery store.[24] My own research in England revealed widespread consumer disdain and confusion around organic products from the developing world.

Yet, as a result of the growing market for organic foodstuffs, as well as the premium prices that such products can fetch, Kerala's organic farming initiatives could be considered a wise economic move that may bring greater income and development benefits to farmers. On the other hand, the state's new policy could be considered risky and shortsighted. Current trends in the organic sector lead to the following questions: Are Kerala's farmers venturing into a fickle international market? Are they avoiding the pitfalls of organic agriculture—the elitism, the chemical contamination, and the labor abuses? Are they able to make meaningful connections with consumers who may be located in other countries? Two issues are intertwined here: organic food and the globalization of our food system.

BROADLY, PEOPLE have three basic criticisms regarding organic food systems.

The first critique is that organic food offers limited nutritional benefits, even though it costs a lot more at the grocery store than conventionally grown food. The former issue gained traction with the release of a 2012 Stanford University School of Medicine paper entitled "Are Organic

Foods Safer or Healthier Than Conventional Alternatives?" After reviewing over two hundred English-language studies of nutrient and contam-
inant levels in organic foods from January 1966 to May 2011, the authors
concluded that "the published literature lacks strong evidence that organic foods are significantly more nutritious than conventional foods."[25]
Subsequently, social media and news outlets buzzed with discussions
about the benefits and drawbacks of organic food consumption. A *New
York Times* article ran with the headline "Stanford Scientists Cast Doubt
on Advantages of Organic Meat and Produce."[26] National Public Radio
aired a segment titled "When It Comes to Buying Organic, Science and
Beliefs Don't Always Mesh."[27] Roger Cohen, an Op-Ed columnist for the
New York Times, welcomed the Stanford study, calling organic food elitist
and equating it with "paying to send your child to private school."[28] Web
commentary for these and similar media included statements by consumers who no longer wished to buy organic food.

There are several reasons why organic food is usually more expensive
than its conventional counterparts in a grocery store. One is that the
limited supply of organic foods can drive their price up. Furthermore,
the cost of organic production can often be higher, given factors such as
the increased reliance by farmers on manual weeding by laborers (as opposed to relying on chemical pesticides that can be applied fewer times
with lower labor costs). Price premiums vary, though, depending on the
season, crop, and marketing venue. Sometimes organic and nonorganic
foods actually cost the same. Nevertheless, the higher price of organic
food is an oft-cited reason that consumers shy away from purchasing organic products.[29] As for the nutrition aspect of this argument, there are
contradictory studies about the nutritional profile of organic foods. Even
the controversial Stanford study pointed out that organic products were
likely to have fewer chemical residues—many of which can be linked to
negative health effects.[30]

The second criticism frequently leveled at organic agriculture is that
it cannot feed the current population of over seven billion people. This
claim is based on the fact that yields can indeed be lower in organic agriculture, especially during the conversion period from industrial to organic farming. Typically, the pesticides and synthetic fertilizers used in

industrial agriculture strip soils of beneficial microorganisms and nutrients. As a result, soils take several years to recover from the "shock" of chemical input withdrawal. Microorganisms return only slowly, and consequently the land does not produce as much food during this transition.

In today's world, when industrial agriculture continues to be dominant and the organic market small, the Food and Agriculture Organization (FAO) estimates that nearly nine hundred million people, mostly in developing countries like India, are undernourished.[31] The existence of nearly one billion undernourished people and the initial lower yields of organic farming have led several scientists to denounce organic farming as a viable agricultural method. Some, like those in a 2012 article in *Nature*, argue that to compensate for yield loss under organic farming, more and more land would have to be dedicated to agriculture, which would only enlarge agriculture's environmental footprint as it encroaches into areas of high biodiversity, like forests. Furthermore, land is a limited resource, increasingly needed around urban areas as they expand.[32] "Organic farming is rarely enough," ran another recent headline in *Nature*.[33]

The other element in this argument against organic turns on population growth. Often, fears that population growth will lead to food shortages evoke the eighteenth-century scholar Thomas Malthus's vision of an overpopulated world, filled with misery and vice, with not enough food to go around. Malthus argued that because population grows at a faster rate than food resources, food shortages are inevitable. Malthusian thought exerts a strong influence on environmental circles and in the scientific community, contributing to a fixation on yields as the utmost priority in agriculture.[34]

While there is no scientific consensus on the relationship between yields and organic agriculture, claims that global grain yields are already decreasing, thereby threatening the food supply, have bolstered skepticism around organic food. A 2012 *Economist* article, for instance, insisted that consumers need to support the large-scale companies that have historically developed and promoted the use of chemicals in agriculture, to counter yield declines and combat hunger in a world of seven billion people.[35]

The third broad charge against organic agriculture has to do with its scale and long-term trajectory: some believe that it has come to be very much like globalized industrial agriculture. This perspective emerged in the 1990s, when scholars began to examine the political economy of organic production, with a focus on California. The authors of one seminal 1997 study concluded that "despite . . . countervailing tendencies, organic agriculture is beginning to resemble conventional agriculture."[36] Specifically, the authors found that organic farmers were beginning to adopt more intensive and possibly unsustainable agricultural practices such as monocropping, so as to remain competitive in the marketplace and to minimize economic losses. These farmers were also relying more and more on large agribusiness for investment capital and employing undocumented workers or paying lower than living wages for laborers. Rather than solving the ills of industrial agriculture, the critics argued, organic agriculture in California was instead maintaining and perpetuating the status quo of an economic system that exploits nature and workers.[37]

Similarly, others point out that as the organic movement grows, corporations are becoming increasingly interested in obtaining a share of the organic market. Corporate involvement has led to a watering down of organic standards in the pursuit of profit.[38] Food activist Raj Patel and journalist Michael Pollan have called this phenomenon "organic-industrial" farming.[39] Others highlight the fact that organic standards and production constrain and produce tensions for organic producers and their communities in the developing world when they grow for export markets. For example, illiterate farmers have found that organic certification requires extensive and written farm-level records that are burdensome and time consuming to create. Some communities have also found the certification process to be cost prohibitive and therefore inaccessible for poorer farmers.[40] Another scholar even went so far as to call organic certification a form of "neocolonialism," the reassertion of the power of former colonial powers over their former colonies, as producers in the developing world come to rely on export markets for their livelihoods.[41]

On a larger scale, many claim that neoliberalism—the economic liberalization of the world's national economies since the 1970s—is exacerbating these trends toward inequality and corporate control of organic agriculture.[42] Organic farming is increasingly top down and subject to the whims of the free market, suggest these critics. Many of the original proponents of organic farming now argue that globalized organic agriculture has strayed far from their original social vision of organic agriculture as more democratic, small scale, and an alternative to globalized industrial agriculture. Globalization thus appears to be a foe to organic farming.

ALTHOUGH ALL of these critics raise important questions about the feasibility and sustainability of organic agriculture, it remains a distinct improvement over industrial agriculture. To understand why, we need to look at the way our current food system works—and the ways that it doesn't.

Industrial agriculture is fossil-fuel and energy intensive, highly dependent on artificial inputs of fertilizers and pesticides. Farmers rely on machinery and grow monocultures on large plots of land; livestock operations are concentrated; and much of the labor is low wage. In countries like the United States, some farm laborers are undocumented workers who are paid meager wages and have no guarantee of job security or benefits. One of the main goals of such agriculture is to produce high yields, ideally for greater profits. The scholar Michael Bell has deemed this "monologic," that "cheap food is all we should ask of agriculture."[43]

Unfortunately, profit margins tend to be thin in industrial agriculture, as unpredictable weather can destroy crops, and since unpredictable global markets and free trade agreements can depress commodity prices. Boom-and-bust cycles are the norm. As such, farmers are constantly under pressure to extract profits where they can, whether through cheaper labor or by cramming livestock into smaller and smaller areas. The intensification of farm operations has increased nutrient waste runoff into watersheds, led to inhumane practices toward farm workers and animals, and prompted many families to leave agriculture. Corporate entities now control larger shares of agricultural operations around the world.

Industrial agriculture mushroomed in the mid-twentieth century, due to factors such as the increase in plant biotechnology research at universities, the overproduction of (and subsequent need to consume) chemicals resulting from the discovery of nitrogen-based explosives and biological warfare around World War II, and the greater pressure on farmers to produce cheap food while competing in international markets. Agriculture became globalized in an unprecedented manner, as the adoption of several multilateral and bilateral trade agreements among countries allowed for the freer import and export of agricultural products across national boundaries. Intricate food chains now cover thousands of miles and involve many middlemen, particularly because many processes that used to occur on farms now occur downstream. Agricultural activities currently have among the largest environmental footprint of any human enterprise.[44]

In places like India, agriculture has become ever more industrialized since the Green Revolution, a system of agricultural intensification that the government launched in the 1960s to escalate domestic food production. This intensification involved introducing technologies such as irrigation, heavy machinery, high-yielding varieties (HYV) of seeds whose progeny did not produce viable seeds, and chemical inputs. Abandoning the free or cheap technologies and methods they had been using, farmers began to buy more and more of these commercial inputs with the hope of obtaining higher yields. To encourage this transition, the Indian government subsidized farm inputs such as fertilizers.[45] Many farmers in states like Kerala became completely reliant on the annual purchase of these new inputs in order to grow their own food.

Globally, as a result of the increased use of chemical inputs and new farming technologies, yields of agricultural staples have grown faster than the world's population. Unfortunately, this triumph of technology has brought with it serious problems. Industrial agriculture today is rife with environmental and social abuses and inefficiencies around the world. For example, as mentioned previously, for about thirty years a public sector company aerially sprayed the pesticide endosulfan over Kerala's cashew plantations and neighboring areas—about forty-five hundred hectares —to control agricultural pests. As Sugathakumari reported at the 2010 biodiversity conference, this spraying, and similar efforts by other farmers in the area, contributed to the birth of several children with developmental defects, as well as a significant decline in biodiversity. Pesticide use also caused severe health problems in adults.

At the same time, the rising yields of staple crops, the main goal of industrial agriculture, has not lessened the number of people without enough to eat in India. In 2010, several million tons of food grains, worth millions of dollars, rotted in Indian silos. Meant as buffer stock to stabilize food prices, these grains were never distributed and went to waste, in spite of the fact that millions of people in India are malnourished.[46] The situation repeated itself in 2011 and then again in 2012.[47]

More disturbingly, over a quarter of a million Indian farmers have committed suicide since 1995, due to unbearable debt burdens they built up while trying to industrialize their agriculture. In a bitterly appropriate gesture, most of these farmers took their lives by drinking pesticides.[48]

The list goes on, and it is hardly limited to India: dead zones in the Gulf of Mexico, deforestation in the Amazon, E. coli outbreaks from fresh vegetables, and biodiversity loss in Southeast Asia can all be linked to globalized industrial agriculture. And yet, as Eric Holt-Gimenez of the nonprofit Food First points out, "We already grow enough food for 10 billion people . . . and still can't end hunger."[49] Indeed, it is estimated that, on an annual basis, we produce four billion tons of food globally, yet up to two billion tons—half of all the food produced—are not consumed by people because of factors such as poor distribution and waste.[50] Our agricultural status quo is leading to social and environmental degradation, while still failing to feed the world's population.

IS IT POSSIBLE for organic farming in India to remedy some of the ills of modern food production without becoming similar to industrial agriculture in its financing, labor practices, and focus on monocultures? Can Kerala's organic farming movement and its 2010 organic farming policy ameliorate the social and ecological problems of the state's agrarian sector? After having spent a year and a half with farmers and policy makers in Kerala, I believe the answer to both questions is yes. More than that, Kerala's growing organic farming movement illustrates that farmers and their communities in the developing world are recognizing that the way our food system is structured must change. Organic agriculture is providing one concrete and immediate avenue for reform.

During my fourteen months in India, I witnessed many examples of civic engagement, farmer empowerment, and positive changes in agriculture—all the result of the organic farming movement. One middle-aged organic farmer in northern Kerala told me that he and several other organic farmers now felt politically confident enough as a group to lobby for their interests at the state capital, in the south of Kerala. In the previous year, they prepared and delivered a memorandum of understanding to the Chief Minister, the highest political official in the state, requesting remuneration for losses they had suffered while converting to organic agriculture or in farming organically.[51] This farmer did not consider himself to have been active politically before he became engaged in organic farming, but the new agricultural practices had empowered both him and his community. Moreover, as a beneficiary of the state's organic farming policy, he used government funds to convert his paddy fields to organic farming methods.

On another occasion, during a training session promoting alternative agricultural methods, a young organic farmer tearfully revealed that his cow had saved him from death, implying that he might have committed suicide or been forced off his land if he had continued to farm conventionally. Reverting to organic agriculture and utilizing cow-based inputs had revitalized his farm and his assets. This farmer is now part of a network of other organic farmers in Wayanad District of Kerala, and regularly speaks at training sessions and showcases his organic farm.

Similarly, K. M. George, a leader in Kerala's organic farming movement, adamantly declared to me in an interview that he would never return to chemical-based agriculture.

"Why?" I asked him, intrigued by his defiant attitude.

He explained that his family's health had dramatically improved after switching to organic food production and consumption, cutting down on their need for medical services. He also added, "If you enter my farm, there's a peace."

He continued: "If you go onto our soil during the rain time, there's a lot of life, a lot of life. . . . You can see the earthworms, their peace. Every time you look at the trees, as they grow, there's a mental satisfaction. Last evening, I was working on my beans and tying them. In a few days, when I see some beans start growing, I'm going to think about picking them and making a curry. That's satisfying." George explained that he was happy to no longer be relying as much on local markets to purchase pesticide-laden produce from unknown farms, since his own farm was producing a significant amount of organic fruits and vegetables. George is now the coordinator of Organic Wayanad, a group of organic farmers in northern Kerala, and actively organizes local farmers to join the organic "family" to act as advocates and reinforcements for one another in their everyday lives and in local politics.

These stories suggest that organic farmers in South India have joined in a strong countermovement opposed to chemical-dependent, market-driven, industrial agriculture.[52] This countermovement is producing positive political, ecological, and health outcomes for farmers and their communities. These are outcomes that consumers can't see while at the grocery store, and that reports skeptical of organic farming's promises have largely ignored.

IN THE NEXT FEW chapters, I examine the emergence of organic farming in South India and its impact on the people who earn their living by growing the food we eat. I also reflect on the criticisms of organic agriculture using evidence from India. I take this place-specific approach to analyzing organic farming because I'm committed to understanding the relationship between nature and culture as dynamic and open-ended.[53] The global organic farming movement does not have a predetermined future. What is happening in India and elsewhere, in the United States or Europe, isn't the only way organic agriculture can develop. I show that alternative farming movements can take a variety of uneven and place-specific trajectories, influenced by government policies, natural disasters, existing institutions, social movements, and global dynamics. These particular circumstances create unique opportunities for substantively criticizing chemical-dependent agriculture and building viable alternatives to it. In Kerala specifically, its history of radical politics and social movements, legacies of land redistribution at the state level, and existing cultural politics are contributing to the growth (and transformative potential) of organic farming in the state.

In the following chapter, I explain why and how industrial agriculture came to India, a place that has historically battled famines and food shortages. I then detail how industrial agriculture and the Green Revolution created an ecological and social crisis in India in general and in Kerala in particular. This crisis included what the activist Sugathakumari bemoaned at the 2010 Indian Biodiversity Conference: pesticide poisonings, hundreds of farmer suicides, and massive crop loss from diseases and pest outbreaks. These events mobilized Kerala's government and civil society into forging an organic farming movement.

In the third chapter, I introduce Kerala in detail, a place long called a "model for development" because of the relatively high life expectancy, income, and levels of education of its citizens, including almost 100 percent literacy despite widespread poverty. Kerala's Human Development Index (HDI) has consistently been the highest of any Indian state and is close to that of Western European countries. This achievement is the result of many factors, including active social and environmental movements, as well as extensive involvement by Communist political parties in creating a state government system that prioritizes education, welfare, and the redistribution of wealth.

I tell the story behind the making of Kerala's 2010 organic farming policy in the fourth chapter. The dynamics that produced the new policy illustrate the kind of structural change that is possible when and if activists, farmers, and policy makers collaborate and mobilize. The state's history of social and environmental movements and progressive politics has been integral to this most recent change. I show that now organic farming is becoming an alternative form of development—one that promotes local planning around agriculture in place of earlier, top-down programs.

I then turn to the implementation of the new organic farming policy in the fifth chapter. I also introduce the experimentation with third-party organic certification for export among farmers in districts like Wayanad. Exploring both the state policy and organic certification demonstrates the benefits that organic farming is providing to Kerala's farmers and the environment. For example, the creation of a state-based certification body, staffed by individuals who share cultural practices and histories with the farmers they are certifying, is allowing organic farmers in Wayanad to better understand organic production requirements.

The sixth chapter examines the contentious issue of exports and explores the relationship between Kerala's government, its organic farming movement, and agrobiodiversity. The state's organic farming movement is divided between those who advocate growing staple crops (like rice) for Indian consumption and those who advocate growing cash crops (like coffee) for the global market, to earn price premiums that can improve their livelihoods. Debates over food security and yields, certification difficulties, free trade agreements, food miles, market prices, caste, culture, and several other issues complicate this divide. This extensive list of contentious subjects contributes to the unevenness of the development of organic agriculture even within Kerala.

To illuminate these complex questions, I focus on the Syrian Christian communities of Wayanad and their historical ties to export markets. Using this case study, I question the food movement's overall fixation on "local food" as the ultimate good in our globalized food system and illustrate why such thinking misunderstands how people are interconnected through political, economic, and historic forces. It also overlooks how different practices of agriculture contribute to the heterogeneity of agrobiodiversity conservation. Given Kerala's historical interconnectedness with the global spice trade since the time of Marco Polo, and farmers' current familiarity with cash crop agriculture, there is no easy resolution to the debates over what role organic farming exports should have in the state's agricultural economy.

In the last chapter, chapter 7, I address some challenges to Kerala's organic farming movement and the future of its organic farming policy. I also discuss the potential role for organic farming in the national and international economies, and I suggest that the organic farming movement more fully embrace the concept of "food sovereignty."

By the time I reach chapter 7, I hope to have shown that organic agriculture in developing countries is demonstrably worthwhile, because in Kerala, and in places like it, it has become a sustainable alternative to industrial agriculture. Kerala proves that it is possible not only to envision, but to create a food system without toxins dripping from trees. While Marco Polo and Christopher Columbus sought Kerala just for spices, the world today has much to learn about organic farming's possibilities from watching this torchbearer forge ahead.

Crisis in Indian Agriculture

BANANAS, particularly salty, deep-fried plantain chips, have become an increasingly popular snack and gift in Kerala. People eat them during afternoon teatime, bring over bags of freshly made chips when visiting the homes of friends and family, and regularly snack on them while on the go.

These and other snacks are so popular that environmental activists complain that the growth in banana consumption has turned one of the northern districts of Kerala, Wayanad, into Vazhanad, translating into "land of bananas" in English. Since 1961–1962, the cultivated area devoted to bananas in the state has increased by close to 40 percent.[1]

At a class on food safety for new organic farmers, K. M. George, coordinator of the organic farmers' group Organic Wayanad, remarked cynically that the district deserved a different name; he called it a "doctor's Dubai" as a result of anecdotal evidence documenting a surge in cancer rates and the great need for doctors in the area. While many people from Kerala were emigrating to countries in the Persian Gulf region in the hopes of finding better employment, George contended that Wayanad could be the economic equivalent for medical practitioners, given its increasing number of cancer patients. He believed the district's abnormal incidence of cancer was the direct outcome of greater pesticide use for banana cultivation.[2]

Using a back-of-the-envelope calculation, George estimated that farmers applied several hundred metric tons of furadan to banana fields in Wayanad's 2,131 square kilometers of land in 2009. Furadan is a chemical pesticide and neurotoxin. Carbofuran, its active ingredient, is so toxic that the United States Environmental Protection Agency (EPA) is slowly phasing it out of use.[3] However, furadan is widely used in the developing world.[4] Many farmers in Kerala have relied on it to prevent crop losses, and rumor has it that they frequently apply more of it than the state's agricultural extension offices recommend, particularly to combat ever-evolving pesticide resistance.

After condemning the use of furadan, George asked the trainees: "Who ends up eating these furadan bananas?" He pressed them: "When you go to someone's home and bring a gift, when you want to buy a little child a snack, maybe your nephew, what do you buy?" He paused for effect and then answered, "Banana chips, right? These poisons are coming right back into our homes!" George—a farmer himself—decried the fact that farmers were poisoning fellow Indians, their own brothers and sisters.

IF FURADAN is so poisonous, why is it used in India? Why are any pesticides, meant explicitly to kill a variety of organisms, used at all? I asked these questions of many farmers I interviewed during my fourteen months in India. The answers were not simple, and they ranged from "I have no other choice" to "The Agriculture Department gives them away sometimes." One study estimated that farmers in Kerala apply over 462 metric tons of chemical pesticides, including insecticides, fungicides, herbicides, and rodenticides on an annual basis to their crops.[5] And every year, over three million cases of pesticide poisoning in humans are reported.[6] Farmers can't help being aware of the cost of their practices, as they are the most at risk for being exposed to these chemicals, but they often complain of being on a "pesticide treadmill," unable to grow enough food or make ends meet without using greater and greater amounts of chemical inputs.[7] As pests become increasingly resistant to the chemicals used to kill them, and as agricultural output suffers from pest outbreaks, the only solution seems to be to use more.

Chemical-based agriculture is a recent phenomenon in India, initially promoted by the national government in the 1950s and 1960s as part of the Green Revolution, a system of agricultural technologies and chemical inputs intended to increase food grain yields. Government officials, international development organizations, and scientists championed the Green Revolution as a solution to India's ongoing problems with famines, food shortages, and dependence on foreign food aid. This effort to industrialize farming also aligned well with the shift toward market-based agriculture that British colonial rule had imposed on India between the mid-nineteenth and mid-twentieth centuries. While yields initially improved, over forty years after India's Green Revolution began, incidents of pesticide poisoning, farmer suicides, and even reports of yield declines in crops other than staple grains also increased, leading to an agrarian crisis in India.

Kerala's agricultural community acutely experienced this agrarian crisis in the late 1990s and 2000s. The state suffered hundreds of farmer suicides, fungal diseases in black pepper vines, deteriorating coffee production, and endosulfan poisoning. All four of these problems were the outcome of intensive chemical use encouraged by market-driven agricultural policies at the state and national levels.

IN PROMOTING the Green Revolution, India's government was trying to solve a long-standing problem of food insecurity. Famine has been a common occurrence in the country's history. Between twelve and thirty million people are estimated to have died of starvation in India from 1876 to 1902. Crop failures caused by erratic monsoon rains contributed to the widespread hunger and malnutrition during these years. However, historians have argued that British colonialism exacerbated the effects of these environmental conditions.[8]

The Indian subcontinent, which includes modern-day Bangladesh, Pakistan, and India, was a British colony from 1858 to 1947. The British colonial government imposed several social and economic changes in the region that led to food insecurity and famines during El Niño years around the turn of the twentieth century.[9] To transform the subcontinent's agrarian economy into one oriented toward markets and exports, British officials used taxation, debt, and enclosure (the privatization of lands previously held in common) to force locals to grow wheat and cotton on a large scale, instead of growing a diversity of staple food crops such as pulses, as they had before.[10] Thus, the structure of agriculture changed so that farmers in India no longer produced traditional food for local consumption but cash crops or monocrops for the world market instead. Food became a commodity that people had to purchase. As such, communities in India had to sell their agricultural outputs to earn money to buy food and to pay taxes to the colonial government.

This new economic system exacerbated the problems caused by changing weather patterns. Normally, India experiences two monsoons, or tropical rainstorms, one from the southwest from June through September, and another from the northeast before the year ends, around October. During El Niño, a global climate phenomenon that occurs every three to six years, the Indian monsoons deliver less rain, often producing drought. When the El Niños brought drought to India during British rule, most Indians found themselves ill equipped to deal with the consequences. If a wheat crop failed one season, a farmer would earn no income and would therefore be unable to buy food.[11] Millions found themselves in this situation at the turn of the twentieth century.

The problem was not that there wasn't enough food to feed the hungry. India as a whole could have fed itself during these droughts, as it was producing millions of tons of wheat and grain throughout these historic famines. Some argue that annual grain exports from India actually increased in these years, from three to ten million tons, enough to feed twenty-five million people.[12] Colonial officials may have deliberately maintained exports to support the economy of Britain instead: Indian farmers produced and supplied raw materials to sustain the industrialization of Britain and its extensive global empire.[13] For example, grains grown in India fed the English working class, and Indian timber built the ships of the British navy.

Similar processes happened throughout the world in other colonies: they began producing primary commodities for export on the world market and turned away from subsistence agriculture intended to feed local people. Colonial powers justified these changes in agriculture by arguing that their tropical and southern colonies had a "comparative advantage" in growing monocrops and in cash crop production—that is, that these countries could produce certain goods at a lower cost because of their cheap labor and climatic conditions. Communities lost local control over their markets as agriculture commercialized, leading to industrialization and the transition to capitalism on the global scale.[14]

As a result, the flow of food changed during the industrial era. This flow no longer responded to local needs but was shaped by free markets, speculation, and even hoarding on the global scale. The world market now set food prices, and food went to those who could afford to buy it from middlemen and traders—not necessarily to those who were hungry. Moreover, food shortages in one region, perhaps due to drought, could elevate prices in another region. When food prices rose, however, farmers predominantly growing wheat and cotton in countries like India would become unable to feed themselves.

During World War II, India experienced another series of food shortages and famines due to a conjuncture of factors that limited foreign and domestic food supplies of rice. In the spring of 1942, Japanese military forces invaded the neighboring country of Burma, cutting off supplies of rice to southwestern India, which had become reliant on Burmese imports. A few months later, a cyclone hit the rice-growing region of Bengal in northern India, destroying paddy fields and the supply of rice to the northeastern parts of India. To make things worse, fungal disease and erratic monsoons further undermined food stocks in Bengal. Speculation and the hoarding of food ensued, leading to the rise of food prices and food shortages all over the subcontinent. Government administrators imposed a ration system throughout the country, yet between one and three million people died in the infamous Bengal famine alone.[15]

Following the war, India gained independence from Britain. Nevertheless, its food shortages continued. Independence also meant the partition of India into two separate countries: India and Pakistan. This political division of the subcontinent left the new country of India with a smaller proportion of land under grain production and a larger population to feed.[16] Exacerbating the situation was the fact that the entire region's existing problems with food shortages were still unresolved.

As a result, ever since its establishment as a sovereign, independent country, India has had to cope with famine and food insecurity. Many of its national policies and planning processes have therefore fixated on food production, and intensifying the political preoccupation with food security were worries of possible uncontrollable population growth. In the years after independence, Indian economists, planners, and policy makers frequently and publicly debated how best to stimulate agricultural production and achieve food security. These debates were also regularly linked with concerns about industrialization and the desire to become a modern, powerful country. Rapid industrialization and economic growth, however, required cheap, abundant food to feed a large, low-wage urban labor force.[17]

The solution to the problem of how to grow more grain to feed India's population of workers came in the form of Public Law 480 (PL-480)—an American law, one sign of how globalized agriculture had become. Enacted in 1954, PL-480 was a program of global food aid by the United States. To beneficiaries, it offered donations, credit to enable the direct sales of low-cost food grains, and the barter of food grains for raw materials. [18] India was one of the early participants in this program. The United States Agency for International Development (USAID) claims that between 1954 and 2004 "the Food for Peace program [as PL-480 is now known] ... sent 106 million metric tons to the hungry of the world, feeding billions of people and saving countless lives. The program depend[ed] on the unparalleled productivity of American farmers and the American agricultural system."[19]

More cynically, however, critics argue that this American program actually increased India's dependency on food imports and promoted agricultural underdevelopment within the rural countryside.[20] As cheap American grains flooded the domestic markets, they rendered the cultivation of local food unprofitable. Indian farmers continued to lose their self-sufficiency and established ways of farming, as they had under the British-led commercialization of agriculture. Farmers left agriculture or converted to cash crop farming. At one point, India was importing over six million tons of wheat per year from the United States.[21]

In the mid-1960s, the PL-480 regime and India's system of food imports started to change. Increasingly, the United States was attaching political and economic conditions to its offer of food aid, and the American government even attempted to use PL-480 as leverage in India during the Cold War. United States President Lyndon Johnson expressed displeasure with the Indian government's criticisms of the American presence in Vietnam and pressured India to devalue its currency to reduce the country's trade deficit. Johnson's "humiliating" tactics, including the withholding of food aid until India met American demands, along with yet another drought in the mid-1960s, prompted Indian lawmakers to pursue a completely different and more internal food strategy.[22]

An influential report published by the Ford Foundation in 1967, entitled *India's Food Crisis and the Steps to Meet It*, affirmed this move. The report blamed India's food aid dependency on its growing population and advised the country to quickly and dramatically increase its domestic production of food. To augment yields, the report recommended that the Indian government and society move away from decentralized agriculture and instead promote an agricultural system based on the use of chemicals (like synthetic fertilizer inputs, pesticides, and herbicides), hybrid seeds, large-scale monocropping, credit, mechanization, and the centralization of decision making. India's Green Revolution was born.[23]

POLITICIANS AND scientists hailed the Green Revolution as a miracle for Indian agriculture. First initiated in Mexico with funding and oversight from the Rockefeller Foundation and the United States Department of Agriculture (USDA), the Green Revolution involved converting farmers to using high-yielding varieties (HYV) of hybrid plant seeds and agricultural technologies that were developed in laboratories with private industry input.[24] With the assistance of organizations such as the Ford Foundation, Indian policy makers and scientists welcomed the Green Revolution to India.[25]

In India the revolution initially revolved around wheat breeding. Scientists experimented with crossing and breeding wheat varieties to discover a type that yielded more per acre. The new plant they created, however, also required more water and pesticides than traditional varieties to grow well. In addition, these new varieties of wheat came from hybrid seeds—seeds that produced a first generation of vigorous, high-yielding plants but whose progeny were unlikely to be healthy or capable of the same productivity as the previous generation. This development, the commercialization of a complicated, hybrid seed, meant that farmers would have to buy new seeds every year.

After years of scientific experimentation, the national government facilitated the spread of Green Revolution technologies throughout India. It subsidized inputs such as fertilizer, funded large infrastructure projects to provide water for irrigation, and promoted the purchase, planting, and growth of HYV wheat.[26] Foundations trained legions of agricultural scientists, and together with the government they set up several agricultural research stations throughout the country, to disseminate scientific knowledge about hybrid seeds, inputs, and farm machinery. Scientists and policy makers encouraged farmers to buy new HYV wheat each growing season (as opposed to saving seeds) so that they could continue to produce high yields of wheat on a regular basis. Indeed, wheat yields in India increased rapidly and dramatically, and they are estimated to have doubled soon after the rollout of the program. By 1972 wheat production in the country had reached twenty-six million tons.[27] Just as officials had hoped, the rate of food production surpassed the rate of population growth.[28] India soon also became one of the largest producers and consumers of chemical fertilizers in the world.[29]

As a system of agriculture, the Green Revolution prioritized maximizing grain yields and increasing agricultural productivity. These political priorities were the outcome of an ever-present worry over how to feed a growing population, as well as the desire of the Indian nation to become independent from food aid. Supporters of the Green Revolution also argued that by increasing agricultural outputs through advanced technology and scientific knowledge, India could develop an international advantage in agriculture and maintain foreign currency reserves as a result of agricultural exports.

The Green Revolution also represented the aspiration to better and more efficiently control nature and natural processes to promote industrialization. As environmental scholar John Perkins notes of similar processes elsewhere: "Higher production efficiencies, in turn, could feed into an ever-growing economy by either 'freeing up' or 'pushing out' labor from agriculture into the new factory system, thus creating further incentives for producing more agricultural produce from less land and less human labor."[30] As predicted, the Green Revolution rapidly transformed India's agrarian society to support economic growth that favored industrialization and urbanization. This process ironically made agriculture itself more factory like: mechanized, homogenized, and large scale. An agricultural system based on chemicals and rooted in the separation of humans from nature became the new norm.[31] Maintaining biogeochemical cycles, preserving cultural and community practices, and conserving agrobiodiversity became less and less important.

The environmental toll of these new agricultural methods has included the growing pesticide resistance of pests, the pollution of waterways from the runoff of fertilizers and other chemicals, and the loss of biodiversity due to the almost exclusive planting of monocrops of HYV plants. Kerala's coastal mangroves, for example, are under threat from chemical contamination and excess nutrient buildup from nearby agricultural sources. Similarly, environmental groups lament the fact that many traditional seed varieties planted by previous generations, some of which have desirable traits such as drought tolerance, may have been lost forever as planting HYV seeds has become the norm in Indian society.

Farming communities have also grown smaller and less autonomous. Because farmers are buying more and more inputs such as seeds and fertilizers from the market, in the hopes of obtaining higher yields (and higher incomes), they have become more reliant on subsidies from the Indian government. Many farmers have also taken out loans from both formal and informal lenders to make these purchases and have gone into debt. Such income insecurity and debt have become common in India's agrarian communities, as farmers are increasingly completely dependent on the annual purchases of chemical inputs in order to grow food. Unfortunately, farmers have found it difficult to repay loans and cover the costs of these inputs, as yields have been less than expected and as the prices for particular crops have fluctuated unpredictably. Those who planted one crop exclusively and relied on buying inputs regularly found themselves extremely vulnerable to crises in global commodity markets. Farmers with smaller plots of land, and consequently less access to credit, found the benefits of chemical agriculture to be even more elusive, and they were at greater financial risk than larger farmers when crops failed. Many farmers left agriculture and more continue to leave.

Beginning in the 1970s and 1980s, environmentalists, activists, farmers, and researchers started drawing attention to these and other shortcomings of the Green Revolution. Environmental activist Vandana Shiva, for example, has written prolifically on this topic. She has also noted that the new agricultural methods worsened the status of women by diminishing their autonomy and control over food systems and their households. Government programs often targeted men, urging them to convert their land to cash crop agriculture and monocrops. As a result, the agricultural priorities of families changed, and the burden of engaging in subsistence agriculture and finding daily food for their households fell to women.[32]

The "success" of the Green Revolution has thus been extensively questioned. As Perkins states: "If success means an increase in the aggregate supply of grain, the green revolution was a success. If success means an end to hunger, then the green revolution was a failure. People without access to adequate land or income, regardless of their country of residence, remain ill fed."[33] Over two hundred million people in India are undernourished today, in spite of the production gains of the Green Revolution.[34] At the same time, similar to the British colonial regime, the Government of India exports millions of tons of wheat and rice, suggesting that production-oriented agriculture alone does not solve the problem of hunger in the food system.[35]

IN THE SOUTHWESTERN state of Kerala, the first Green Revolution technologies and experiments centered on rice, through the government-funded Intensive Agricultural District Programme (IADP) in 1961. This program introduced HYV rice to Kerala, and promoted the use of chemical inputs. While some farmers in Kerala were already aware of and using synthetic chemicals and HYV rice before the IADP, it was only after the advent of this program that most farmers abandoned traditional varieties of rice and adopted and used chemical fertilizers and pesticides in agriculture more widely.[36]

Since the 1960s, Kerala's policy makers have actively promoted market-oriented and chemical-based agriculture for a variety of other crops as well, from black pepper to coffee, signaling widespread state government support for an agricultural system based on Green Revolution principles. Because farmers in Kerala have historically specialized in crops like spices, the state's early government leaders encouraged farmers to grow these agricultural products and promoted their widespread planting. For example, the state's first major planning document after Indian independence, Kerala's Second Five Year Plan, explicitly expressed the importance of commercial cash crop agriculture to the economy. (States in India plan their budgets and activities in five-year cycles, outlined in Five Year Plans.) This plan called for setting up research and production schemes to intensify cash crop agriculture throughout the state. Early policy makers hoped that by improving the agricultural output of commodities like black pepper, coffee, and cashew nuts, the state could earn more revenue through exports.[37]

Today, as a result of these agricultural intensification efforts, Kerala has a predominantly export-oriented agricultural economy. Despite the IADP's initial focus, the majority of Kerala's agricultural production is now comprised of cash crops—grown to be sold, not eaten, by the farmers' families. Between 1961–1962 and 2006–2007, the area under paddy cultivation in Kerala dropped by 65 percent. Eighty percent of the state's agricultural commodities are currently sold to external markets.[38] Kerala is also the leading producer of several of India's commercial crops, including black pepper.

Although scholars debate the reasons for Kerala's shift away from the cultivation of rice—which was also supported by the state's Five Year Plans—one ironic driving force behind the change has been the Green Revolution. While this new agricultural program increased the overall production of rice in India, it lowered the investment return for individual rice farmers in Kerala.[39] As mentioned earlier, people in the state, such as George, the organic farming leader, have now nicknamed districts like Wayanad ("land of paddy fields" in the Malayalam language) as Vazhanad ("land of bananas"), because so much of the state's landscape has been transformed to produce cash crops like spices and fruits instead of staples like rice. During organic farming training sessions in Wayanad, George regularly utilizes this play on words to criticize the change in agriculture in his home district.

Because Kerala's agriculture now revolves around tradable commodities, its agrarian sector is impacted by global prices, international policy, and foreign trade. When India joined the World Trade Organization (WTO) on January 1, 1995, and agreed to the market and export principles of the WTO's Agreement on Agriculture (AOA), farmers in Kerala found themselves vulnerable to global markets in unprecedented ways.[40]

The AOA represents an international effort by several countries and multinational corporations to regulate global agricultural trade more systematically, by reducing domestic agricultural subsidies and eliminating import tariffs on foreign goods. In early AOA negotiations, Indian officials argued that developing countries deserved to have some flexibility in making these changes and regulating their own agricultural sectors, to protect their farmers from international competition. At the time, Indian agriculture was structured in such a way that farmers had come to rely on subsidies for cheap fertilizer inputs and a protected internal market for several of their cash crops.[41]

India's negotiations with the WTO remain ongoing. However, soon after joining the WTO, the Indian government pursued several free market reforms as a demonstration of its commitment to liberalization, including lowering tariffs on certain food imports. Policy makers viewed opening up the market in the agricultural sector as one way of stimulating national economic growth, potentially leading to poverty reduction in the country. Yet removing restrictions on certain foreign goods created stiff competition for Kerala's agricultural products—such as coconut oil, tea, pepper, and coffee—in the domestic market.[42] For example, when lawmakers reduced the national import tariff on edible oil, this resulted in the increase of palm and other oils imported into the country, which then led to the fall of coconut prices in states like Kerala, where coconut oil has been a staple in its cuisine and where production of the oil is a source of traditional labor.[43] Cooks have begun to replace coconut oil with cheaper oil, and other commodities customarily grown in Kerala, such as tea, are now being imported into the state.[44] As a result, cultivating these crops is not as lucrative or financially viable. One estimate claims that Kerala has been losing over $1.1 billion on an annual basis as a result of these tariff changes.[45]

Despite these negative effects, the Indian government has continued to negotiate additional free trade arrangements with other countries.[46] India's activities in this realm are part of a larger international trend, in which several nations are pursuing free trade agreements in the hopes of spurring economic growth. The results of free trade agreements for countries around the world and their citizens have been mixed at best, however. For example, the United States' involvement with the North American Free Trade Agreement (NAFTA) has led to the loss of particular manufacturing jobs in the country and an increase in environmental degradation along the border with Mexico, as several factories have popped up along the Mexican side to take advantage of freer trade, cheaper labor, and weaker environmental laws.

As a result of all these changes in agriculture, at the turn of the twenty-first century India faced a severe agrarian crisis. This time, the crisis involved not just hunger and food insecurity but chemical poisoning, farmer suicides, and declining agricultural productivity and economic returns. For example, chemical-intensive agricultural practices spurred the extensive die-off of Kerala's black pepper crops. Concurrently, the declining price of another commodity, coffee, further strained farmers' finances, impelling many to leave agriculture. Faced with large debts incurred in buying into the Green Revolution, several farmers also committed suicide—many by drinking pesticides.

THE HISTORY OF pepper and coffee cultivation in Kerala sheds light on how the Green Revolution and the marketization of agriculture combined to generate this agrarian distress. Native to the region, black pepper has historically been one of Kerala's major agricultural products, called "black gold" by explorers such as Marco Polo and Christopher Columbus.[47] Over 90 percent of India's pepper is grown in this one state.[48] Black pepper planting guides from the country's commodity boards and agricultural offices frequently reiterate the long-standing fame of the state's pepper crop. The foreword to the 2009 *Black Pepper Guide* from the

Directorate of Arecanut and Spices Development, a department within India's Ministry of Agriculture, describes it thus: "Black pepper or the black gold, the spice of commerce, is one of the most important spices, which brought many seafarers to the shores of India from the ancient times. It was one spice, the trade of which has become an important part of history, which lead [sic] to . . . great adventure, exploration, conquest, and naval rivalry."[49] Such praise of Kerala's black pepper as a cornerstone for economic development and a cause of geopolitical skirmishes is not without basis—European countries and India's maharajas fought to control South India's spice trade for three centuries before the British consolidated power in the subcontinent.[50]

To take advantage of the state's historic competitive advantage in pepper production, the government heavily promoted the crop immediately after Indian independence from the British Empire. Kerala's Second Five Year Plan, for instance, observes: "Pepper is an important spice crop of the State. It is largely exported and is a good dollar earner. India is now subjected to severe competition from some of the South East Asian countries. It is therefore necessary to put the production of pepper in India on solid foundations as to enable it to withstand the growing competition in world markets."[51]

Maintaining Kerala's lead in pepper production was imperative for the early state government. Through agricultural extension offices, it introduced several new HYV pepper vines. Farmers began to rely on these pepper strains as their major source of income. Most of the farmers who came to utilize the new pepper varieties were small to medium landholders, with less than two acres of land, who devoted their pepper cultivation to one or two of the newer HYV varieties only.[52] In contrast to their previous practice of saving seeds, many of these farmers also began to purchase the pepper vines from the Agriculture Department, agricultural extension, and commodity boards, and as the Agriculture Department recommended, began to utilize heavy doses of pesticides in their growing. As a whole, the production of pepper and the outcome per acre increased in Kerala.

In the 1990s, Kerala's pepper plants began to wilt and die off on a large scale. Phytophthora, a fungus that ails the roots of pepper vines, caused

production to collapse in unprecedented magnitude in several areas of the
state. Many scientists are currently convinced that this fungal epidemic
occurred as a result of the disturbance in the natural equilibrium of soils
by the constant application of chemicals. Their theory is that pesticides
and fertilizers killed off useful soil-dwelling microorganisms, including
another fungus, trichoderma, a natural enemy to phytophthora. The absence of trichoderma allowed pepper wilt to proliferate without impedi-
ment.[53] Phytophthora has caused losses equivalent to two thousand tons
of pepper per year, valued at several million dollars annually.[54]

To make things worse, in the late 1990s to early 2000s, pepper prices declined worldwide and especially in India, because free trade agreements
promoted pepper production in and trade with other Asian countries,
such as Vietnam.[55] Whereas pepper sold for 260 rupees per kilogram on
average in 2000 in Kerala, its price dropped to 78 rupees per kilogram in
2004.[56] Pepper was no longer a viable source of income for farmers.

THE COMBINATION of the Green Revolution and the commercial globalization of agriculture affected Kerala's coffee growers as well. The
state's farmers frequently intercrop their pepper with coffee. Pepper grows
as a vine on shade-producing trees, and coffee bushes grow underneath
(fig. 1). British planters introduced coffee into Kerala in the 1800s, and
area farmers, finding that coffee fared well in the state's humid climate,
continued to plant it years after independence.[57] The state government
also encouraged coffee cultivation. As a result, Kerala is now the second
largest producer of coffee in India after Karnataka, a neighboring state.

At the same time that Kerala's pepper production was reeling from the
phytophthora outbreak in the 1990s, coffee yields also started to decline
due to similar factors, including pestilence and weakened soils caused by
farming practices based in chemicals. Coffee farmers began earning less
revenue from their bushes, further undermining already tenuous household finances.[58]

Compounding this difficult situation, in the 1990s the international
price for coffee declined. Researchers pinpoint the origin of this "coffee
crisis" in the collapse of the 1989 International Coffee Agreement (ICA),
which had regulated stocks and quotas of coffee production in participat-

1. The intercropping of pepper and coffee in Kerala.
Photo by the author.

ing countries.[59] As a result of the dissolution of the ICA, coffee production
was deregulated globally, new coffee producers moved into the market,
and low-quality coffee flooded the international markets. The dissolution of the Rupee-Rouble Agreement with the former Soviet Union
aggravated this situation, as Indian farmers were no longer guaranteed
a market in Russia for their coffee.[60] India's share of the coffee market
therefore declined.

Given the concurrent reduction in coffee output and price, Kerala's coffee farmers found themselves earning little to no return on their labor. As
with pepper, coffee no longer provided reliable and sustainable income,
which jeopardized the livelihoods of Kerala's farmers and laborers.

One farmer in Kerala, Neela, explained to me in detail how the waning output of her coffee bushes was affecting her quality of life. She calculated that when she had first started growing coffee on her husband's land after their wedding day, decades ago, she harvested a hundred sacks (weighing fifty-four kilograms each) worth of coffee beans from their four acres of land. In 2011, however, she only collected thirty-five sacks from the same land and plants. Neela speculated that the productivity had declined because of multiple factors, including soil exhaustion.

I asked Neela what she planned to do, given her current situation.

"What will we do?" she repeated musingly, and then answered, "That's why we're not putting work into our land. We just take what we can get." She and her husband had decided that taking care of their coffee bushes was no longer a worthwhile investment. They could not afford to pay several laborers to help maintain their crops or prune their coffee bushes during the short window when the trimming of coffee bushes had to occur.

Neela's story was not uncommon. Several other farmers with whom I spent time in Kerala admitted to neglecting the maintenance of their coffee bushes, to avoid labor costs at a time of low returns for commodities. Another farmer disclosed to me that he cut down all of his coffee bushes in frustration, only to then lose his black pepper to wilt. Unlike others, this farmer was lucky to own several hectares of land, and he was able to receive income from other cash crops, as well as additional income from a side practice of medicinal consulting, which prevented a financial crisis for his family.

Neela, on the other hand, did not have as diversified an agricultural operation to keep her afloat for multiple years. As a result, I asked Neela a few more questions to understand why she had specifically decided to forgo the upkeep of her coffee bushes.

"We don't get enough coffee from our land to pay the costs for a year," she answered, and then listed her expenditures around coffee: sprinklers, wages for laborers, and fertilizers. She added, "We don't get anything to pay for our household costs." She had therefore decided to use any spare money to buy food for herself and her family, instead of on upkeep of her cash crops. Nevertheless, the quality of the food the family ate had declined, since she, her husband, and their only son could not afford to buy vegetables consistently anymore. Even purchasing rice on a regular basis was a struggle. These were not surprising claims, given that the price of grain and food commodities reached record highs in the 2000s and were expected to rise further—more evidence of the effects of the commercialization and globalization of agriculture intersecting with local conditions.[61] Neela lamented that if only coffee outputs and prices were better, she could have a better life and perhaps even repair her dilapidated house.

She worried, though, that she would eventually have to sell her land to make ends meet. "As the years pass, we're getting old. Already, our bodies are weak and becoming weaker. I have that hardship, that fear. We might have to sell our land after a while."

LIKE NEELA, many farmers in Kerala—and India as a whole—found themselves unable to afford food, let alone pay their debts from one growing season to another. Thousands of these farmers resorted to suicide. In 2006, one of the worst years for this phenomenon, over one hundred thousand Indian farmers committed suicide.[62] Journalist P. Sainath, who has extensively documented India's agrarian crises, claims that close to a quarter million farmers committed suicide in India between 1995 and 2010. Many of these individuals were cotton growers—farmers who specialized in commercial crops, as opposed to subsistence crops.[63]

At one point, Kerala had the third highest suicide rate in India, despite being one of the smallest states in the nation.[64] Between 2003 and 2007, close to one thousand farmers took their lives in the state. Many were deep in debt and food insecure. They possessed less than one acre of land, which they used mostly for the cultivation of commercial cash crops, such as coffee and pepper. Several of these farmers had also taken out loans to purchase agricultural inputs, like HYV seeds and chemical fertilizers. Farmers in areas of Kerala such as Wayanad District had become extremely dependent on loans for agricultural activities: in fact, one study found that all of the farmers who committed suicide in this region had outstanding debt.[65]

Environmental activists such as Vandana Shiva blame these suicides on the marketization of agriculture in India, which was accelerated by the Green Revolution. India's economic restructuring of the 1990s—during which the national government eliminated subsidies on fertilizer and other products while simultaneously opening up India's markets to international competition—aggravated the financial situation of many farmers. Faced with high prices for agricultural inputs and low prices for their crops, many smaller farmers found themselves trapped by heavy debts they could not see a way to repay.[66] Because they had turned to growing cash crops, formerly self-sufficient farmers and families had become wholly dependent on markets for the food they ate as well. As the price of grain and other staple foods soared in the 2000s, these families became increasingly vulnerable to hunger.

The majority of farmers in one study ended their lives by drinking liquid pesticides. The researchers suggested that this may have been a popular method of ending one's life because of the widespread availability of chemicals such as furadan on farms and in agrarian areas.[67] The World Health Organization (WHO) has noted that pesticide consumption is not an uncommon way of committing suicide in rural areas of the developing world.[68]

EVEN DISREGARDING suicide, Kerala has had a contentious history with pesticides. From 1976 to 2002, the Plantation Corporation of Kerala, a public sector company, sprayed the pesticide endosulfan aerially over its cashew plantations and neighboring areas in the northern district of Kasaragod, totaling over forty-five hundred hectares.[69] In the late 1980s and early 1990s, community members, farmers, and local agricultural officers began noticing a high number of birth defects, developmental disabilities, and abnormal deaths among young people in the district. These defects were soon linked to endosulfan.

Endosulfan is a persistent organic pollutant (POP), a chemical compound that resists breaking down easily, thereby persisting in the environment for years and even decades, long after it is initially applied. POPs can travel through the air and water, and they have been found in places as remote as the Arctic. Since they do not degrade quickly, they accumulate in food systems and in human and animal bodies, slowly amplifying health risks over time.

The chemical pesticide dichlorodiphenyltrichloroethane, colloquially known as DDT, is one well-known example of a POP that was widely used in American agriculture. DDT entered the national spotlight with the release of Rachel Carson's *Silent Spring* (1962), which raised concerns about the long-term environmental health consequences of its use. A former United States Bureau of Fisheries scientist, Carson documented the pesticide's toxicity and its negative effects on wildlife.[70] After the release of her book, subsequent public outcry, and mounting scientific evidence against DDT, the United States banned it. Other countries soon followed suit. One hundred seventy countries have also since ratified the Stockholm Convention, an international treaty banning the use of DDT in agriculture.

Unfortunately, DDT isn't the only POP. Endosulfan, like DDT, is a toxic chemical that remains in the environment for weeks and months after it is introduced. EPA studies have indicated that it may disrupt the human endocrine system and negatively affect the nervous system as well. The EPA has also found that exposure to the chemical causes reproductive and developmental problems in birds, fish, and mammals.

In Kerala, endosulfan was widely used. For a quarter of a century, Kerala's growers of cashew nuts relied on endosulfan to protect their crops. The state has historically been the largest producer of these nuts in India, and it currently remains one of the biggest producers. Cashews are a significant part of Indian food, utilized in its rice dishes, curries, and desserts and thereby a thriving commodity market. To take advantage of this market, the Government of Kerala promoted the use of chemical inputs to enhance the cultivation of cashew nuts beginning in the 1960s. Kerala's Second Five Year Plan, for example, introduced a state-led scheme to improve cashew production in the state. As described in the plan:

Cashewnut industry is a very important one in southern Kerala and employs several thousands of labourers. . . . It is therefore proposed to step up the production of cashewnut in this country so as to meet the full requirements of this industry.

At the present time, cashewnut is grown in the poorest soils and no attention is devoted to this crop. The scheme envisages the improvement of the cultivation of cashewnut . . . also by taking the necessary steps for controlling the diseases and pests of cashewnut.[71]

As noted in the early Five Year Plan, pest control was a top priority.[72] Early in the state's history, the national government and its Agriculture Department recommended the use of endosulfan to control mosquitos and other pests breeding around or attacking cashew trees.[73] Farmers of other crops, such as cardamom, also used the chemical to protect their plants and maximize their returns.

Endosulfan's negative effects on the environment have not gone unnoticed. Several countries are currently phasing it out. In May 2011, delegates at the international Stockholm Convention on POPs "agreed to add endosulfan to the list of POPs to be eliminated worldwide."[74] The Indian government initially opposed the move, citing the hardship a ban would impose on Indian farmers—an opposition that illustrates how dependent Indian agriculture has become on chemicals. Later in the year, the Indian Supreme Court banned the use of endosulfan in India but allowed for its continued export from the country as a way of dealing with existing stocks of the chemical.[75]

In Kerala, the Pollution Control Board had stepped in years earlier, in 2004, to suspend the aerial spraying of endosulfan, and in 2010 the state officially banned any use of the pesticide in agriculture.[76] However, the effects of endosulfan continue to make headlines on a weekly basis in Kerala. The press alone had identified almost three thousand endosulfan victims by 2010, many of whom had experienced headaches and nausea after being directly exposed to the pesticide. Many other victims, however, have been small children, who have experienced problems including abnormal weight gain, delays in reproductive organ development, and skeletal deformities.[77]

Endosulfan's residues have been found in the soil, homes, and drinking water of many communities in Kerala. Research by the Salim Ali Foundation has recorded a decrease in aquatic diversity in areas where the aerial spraying of endosulfan occurred, which has threatened the area's endemic biodiversity.[78] The use of this POP has resulted in the poisoning of Kerala's agricultural lands, environment, biodiversity, and human bodies for the long term.

Complicating matters, however, is the pervasive notion among farmers that pesticides are a necessity in their business. At one meeting that I attended at the M. S. Swaminathan Foundation Centre in Wayanad, farmers revealed that they themselves either used or knew of others in the area who indiscriminately used endosulfan to prevent crop losses to pest outbreaks. As Neela, the coffee farmer I interviewed, put it pessimistically: "If you want to know my opinion, farmers need pesticides to survive." She acknowledged that pesticides were harmful, but then she said, "This endosulfan, if Kasaragod [District] doesn't get it, there won't be cashews. If a disease comes . . . we absolutely need chemicals . . . we need it. . . . We're farming to live, after all."

As Neela opined, farmers in India now depended on chemical inputs like endosulfan to produce food, especially because crops were becoming more and more vulnerable to pests. This frame of mind and the situation that causes it have been likened to being on a treadmill that keeps speeding up but remains stationary: As the natural fertility and pesticide resistance of soils and soil-dwelling organisms progressively weaken because of constant chemical applications, farmers need more and more artificial inputs to augment soil fertility and prevent pestilence. Meanwhile, their incomes remain stagnant or decline. This pattern repeats and even accelerates. In the past, if and how farmers could ever step off the treadmill has not been clear, but obviously a break from chemical-dependent farming is necessary.

KERALA'S agrarian crisis exemplifies hardships that farmers throughout India have encountered in the past twenty years. The problems are the result of the marketization and industrialization of agriculture—a process rooted in British colonialism, intensified by the Green Revolution, and influenced by more recent trade policies. As farmers have come to rely on markets to buy and sell food, their livelihoods have become more tenuous. Environmental degradation, from pesticide runoff into waterways to a loss in biodiversity, has also increased as agricultural processes have intensified and as food production has come to prioritize expanding yields over other outcomes. Pesticide use, from furadan to endosulfan, has also taken its toll on the health of many people in India. As George noted during his training session for organic farmers, farming with chemicals is a toxic, poisonous business. Yet, despite the intensive use of chemicals, many Indians continue to go hungry. The Green Revolution has not solved the country's problems of food insecurity.

In recent years, sustainable food advocates have drawn on the writings of the political economist Karl Polanyi to think about these and related changes resulting from the globalization of agriculture.[79] In his book *The Great Transformation* (1944), Polanyi describes how processes of marketization and the commodification of the environment devastated England during its industrial revolution in the nineteenth century. This devastation ranged from "the denudation of forests" to "the deterioration of craft standards [and] the disruption of folkways."[80] As the economic system changed, industries became profit driven, and land and other natural resources came to be regarded simply as inputs for industrial progress and growth. In other words, in this process of marketization, natural resources became atomized, seen simply as commodities with only an economic value. This economic transformation increased the vulnerability of the environment to unregulated exploitation. From a Polanyian perspective, the four agrarian tragedies in Kerala—suicides, the proliferation of fungal disease in pepper, the deterioration of the coffee sector, and endosulfan poisoning—epitomize the contemporary destruction resulting from the commodification of agricultural inputs and outputs, the move toward chemicals and cash crops, and the prioritizing of yields throughout India.

Despite this grim history, Polanyi saw hope in the way that communities and societies historically responded to environmental and social crises. In England, a "countermovement" emerged to protect the environment and community groups from complete annihilation. According to Polanyi, countermovements are forms of social protection for the environment and society. They intervene in the free market to enact protective legislation, to restrict environmental and social destruction. Polanyi wrote about how trade unions, various classes, churches, and individuals banded together in countermovements to regulate and monitor the free market to protect their livelihoods from the detrimental effects of commercialization.[81]

Just as Polanyi would have predicted, India's agrarian crisis has stimulated various countermovements, including a turn to organic farming in states like Kerala. The state government passed an organic farming policy in 2010, which led to the ban of several pesticides in the state. Moreover, several key organic farming bodies, such as India's first organic certification organization, are now based in Kerala. The state's contemporary organic farming movement is very much a Polanyian countermovement— a reaction by farmers, activists, consumers, and policy makers to problems in India's farming sector and globalized agriculture. Organic farming, and the rejection of chemical inputs that must be purchased, have the potential to transform Indian agriculture once again and take farmers off the chemical treadmill.

The Third World's Model
for Development

IN THE 1990S, famed environmentalist Bill McKibben penned that Kerala was "weird—like one of those places where the *Starship Enterprise* might land that superficially resembles Earth but is slightly off."[1] He went on to laud the South Indian state as "the Mount Everest of social development," a place that stood out in the developing world.[2]

In writing these words, McKibben joined a crowd of development practitioners, scholars, and politicians who had been praising Kerala for decades as a "model for development." As early as the 1970s, the anthropologist Joan Mencher had described how increased educational levels and the politicization of people in Kerala positively affected local communities to demand better health care.[3] In the 1990s, another anthropologist, Richard W. Franke, along with sociologist Barbara Chasin, wrote for the food policy think tank, Food First: "Kerala is an experiment in radical reform as a modern development strategy."[4] Later in that decade, riding the momentum of the international United Nations Conference on Sustainable Development in Rio de Jainero, the scientist Govidan Parayil cheered the state's performance in "sustainable development."[5] Well into this century, researchers, writers, and Kerala's politicians have praised Kerala's ongoing achievements in the realm of social development.[6]

This pile of accolades pivots around Kerala's high Human Development Index (HDI), which measures education, life expectancy, and income. The state's HDI has consistently been the highest of any Indian state and close to those of Western European countries. Literacy is almost 100 percent, and education is universal.[7] It has the highest female-male sex ratio in India, since infanticide of girl children is rare here (but common in other states). In fact, Kerala is one of the few Indian states where women outnumber men. Its population growth rate is also lower than the Indian average. Unlike most other states in India, Kerala achieved low birth and death rates (known as a "demographic transition") in the 1980s. The current fertility rate is below the replacement rate, at 1.7 children per woman. Kerala's mortality rate is low as well, as life expectancy is close to seventy-six years for women and seventy-one years for men.[8]

It is these high social indicators—in a country struggling with hunger and poverty—that have bestowed upon Kerala its reputation for being a model for development. Moreover, the state attained this high HDI without corresponding economic growth and the high consumption and environmental degradation that often come with such growth. This level of development contradicts what economists and environmentalists predict: that social development and a demographic transition can only occur after a country obtains a certain level of economic development. In our globalizing world, where developing countries prioritize economic growth as the chief policy priority—often at the expense of social development—Kerala's achievements are noteworthy.

Furthermore, communities in the state are actively involved in labor and environmental movements, as well as local and state politics. One of India's first anti-dam movements occurred in Kerala, for example. In the 1970s and 1980s, the Save Silent Valley Campaign successfully defeated a plan to construct a large, 120-megawatt dam in the Western Ghats mountain range. The national government subsequently turned the area into a national park. This sort of vibrant political life has contributed to Kerala's status as a model for development.

How exactly did Kerala come to be a model? And how is this important to the story of organic farming in South India? Another way to phrase these questions is to ask, How did the state's sociopolitical factors and environmental conditions influence its development decisions, particularly around sustainable agriculture?

My interest in Kerala as a place and its status as a model—or, more precisely, the foundational history behind the latter—is rooted in my efforts to explain why it became one of the first and is still one of the few states in India to cope with its agrarian crisis by turning to organic farming at the state level. This state-specific focus follows the lead of other researchers specializing in the food system who have shown that there are local and regional variations to global agricultural changes.[9] Globalization—in the form of free trade agreements like the WTO's AOA, for example—is not effacing social and ecological dynamics at the local level. Instead, local communities and state governments are reacting in various ways to global pressures to create countermovements. As I mentioned at the end of the previous chapter, the political economist Karl Polanyi theorized that societies respond to the marketization and destruction of their environments and communities through countermovements.[10] In the case of Kerala, the state has responded to the Government of India's implementation of free trade agreements and economic liberalization policies, which have so distressed the country's farmers, by pursuing strategies such as state-sponsored organic farming.

The specific shape of Kerala's organic farming countermovement is the result of the state's history of redistributive reforms, a socially mobilized populace, substantial spending on human and social development, and prior environmental movements. These have been previously fundamental in the development of Kerala's high HDI and its reputation as a model as well. Much of this agenda was first initiated by Kerala's Communist parties just after independence and then sustained by various political coalitions over the past fifty years. The subsequent intersection of this political tradition with a growing local environmental movement has created a society ready and willing to experiment with alternative social development and reforms—now an environmental transformation as well.

GEOGRAPHICALLY, Kerala is a small state in southwestern India. Close to the equator, its climate is tropical, and its agriculture relies on the two annual Indian monsoons. These geographic conditions have made it an ideal place for the cultivation of several warm-weather crops year round, including spices such as black pepper. Farmers in South India have traded many of these spices for centuries with various countries and explorers, and these valuable commodities have at times been at the center of trade wars.[11] Throughout the state, rice has also been a traditional agricultural crop, as well as a dietary staple.

Kerala is bordered by the Arabian Sea to the west and the Western Ghats mountain range to the east. Ecologists consider these mountains one of the world's twenty-five biodiversity hotspots.[12] Almost nine thousand feet in elevation at its highest peak, the range is home to many large fauna, including Asian elephants and Indian tigers. Biologists estimate that 30 to 40 percent of the plant and animal species found in the Western Ghats are endemic to the area.[13] As a harbor of biodiversity, the mountains have become a key policy concern for the state government.

Kerala only recently came into existence as a state. The newly independent nation of India forged Kerala along linguistic lines (the Malayalam language) in 1956, seven years after independence from the British Empire. Like other states, it was set up with a parliamentary system, comprised of an elected assembly of representatives. The political party that wins the majority of votes after elections assumes executive power over the Assembly, organizes a coalition of allied parties in a "front," and selects a Chief Minister for the state until the next elections. In 1957 the people of Kerala democratically elected a majority of Communist Party representatives to the Assembly. This election was momentous because it meant that the new state and political institutions were then designed by the Communist Party to prioritize welfare reforms and the redistribution of wealth. Various political coalitions over the following thirty years, led by the Communist Party—the Communist Party of India (Marxist), in later years—went on to implement a series of reforms to improve health care, workers' rights, and education. Over two million acres of land were also distributed to tenants under the state's land reforms in the 1970s.[14]

The Communists' successful political mobilization and their ascendance to political power early in Kerala's history have roots in the previous societal structures and social protests of the region. The area that is Kerala today covers three main historic regions: Malabar, the northernmost area, which experienced direct British rule under the Madras Presidency; and the two southern territories of Travancore and Cochin, which remained independent kingdoms that maintained close ties with the British. The three regions upheld rigid feudal caste-relations until just after independence and the Communist-led reforms.[15] For example, prior to statehood, higher-caste Hindus owned land, while lower-caste communities of various backgrounds were regularly barred from land ownership, government jobs, and even government-funded schooling.[16]

In Malabar, landlords called *janman*, composed of higher-caste Hindus, owned vast tracts of land that were farmed by tenants. These tenants were often from the Mappila, or Muslim communities, and they had no guarantee to the land they tilled; they could be kicked off at any time. Additionally, they regularly paid rents and other levies to their landlords. Colonial officials maintained these pro-landlord policies in their quest to collaborate with the powerful elites in the area, to gain access to Malabar's timber and spices, which intensified the inequalities of feudal society. Some of these resources were grown on plantations farmed by tenants.[17] As a result, taxation and oppression in Malabar's feudal system increased under colonial rule.

Around the turn of the twentieth century, many Mappila communities revolted against landlordism and the British. The Mappila groups had initial support from the Indian National Congress, one of India's major political parties. This party, led by Mahatma Gandhi, lobbied for Indian independence from British colonial rule. In 1921, Kerala's land revolts culminated with the Mappila Rebellion, which led to the arrest and deaths of several people in the mostly Muslim movement. These events left an important political legacy: they spurred the introduction of several land reform policies in Malabar and then in the nascent state of Kerala.[18]

In the south, in the Travancore region of Kerala, lower-caste communities (such as Ezheva Hindus) experienced daily discrimination prior to statehood. They could not attend government-run schools and access other government services, were banned from entering several Hindu temples, and were forced to practice many humiliating lower-caste pollution rituals (such as leaving one's breasts uncovered). Even members of Kerala's Syrian Christian community, although they occupied a higher caste stratum than Ezheva Hindus, were denied government jobs and access to government-run schools, as these places were reserved entirely for higher-caste Hindus. To combat these societal restrictions, Hindu reformers such as Sri Naryana Guru created associations and schools for lower-caste Hindus, so that they could collectively learn about and organize against Kerala's caste system. In 1936, this lower-caste movement culminated with the announcement of the Temple Entry Proclamation by the maharaja of Travancore. The proclamation abolished the ban on lower caste people entering Hindu temples in the south.[19]

Upon statehood, Kerala's branch of the Communist Party of India (CPI) utilized the momentum from the movements in Malabar and Travancore to bring further societal reforms to the entirety of the new state.[20] Specifically, the CPI mobilized and created alliances between poor tenants and landless laborers and took up the cause of anti-casteism to change the feudal social and economic structures. In 1957, E. M. S. Namboodiripad of the CPI became the first democratically elected Chief Minister of Kerala. Subsequently, left-leaning coalitions introduced several reform bills into the Assembly, including the famous and highly scrutinized Land Reform Act of 1963. The eventual enactment of this bill abolished Kerala's contentious land relations of the past by creating a cap on landholdings and redistributing excess land to tenants. As the political economist Ronald Herring observes: "The Kerala reforms emerged from the organized demands and decades of agitation of the peasantry, articulated through electoral victories of the Communist Party (later parties) in the state."[21] Kerala's Left, therefore, successfully united Kerala's civil society across caste, class, and religious lines, to prioritize education, welfare, and land reforms in legislation at the state level.

Such alliance building was not without extended struggle and dissent from various groups, though. The early years of Kerala's state history were tumultuous. For example, many of the Syrian Christian communities opposed the Communist reforms within the state. They protested vigorously against efforts that allowed the state to appoint teachers at private Catholic schools and that imposed a ceiling on family landholdings after the land reforms (originally five acres for unmarried individuals cultivating certain crops).[22] Many Syrian Christians refused membership in Kerala's Communist parties and instead joined the other dominant party in the state: Congress, which has tended to be more economically conservative. Due to the resulting political agitation between Syrian Christian communities and other groups in Kerala, in 1959 the current Indian Prime Minister at the time, Jawaharlal Nehru, imposed "President's Rule" in the state. The national government dismissed the Communist-led state government and placed Kerala under direct federal rule for several months. When another election was held in early 1960, the CPI lost the majority of its seats in Kerala's Legislative Assembly to the Congress party, and state rule was restored. Despite this defeat, and attempts by the Congress party and its supporters to alter Kerala's land reform bills, Kerala's Communist parties continued organizing and mobilizing citizens around redistribution. They and their allies won the majority of Assembly seats again in 1967.[23]

The implementation of Kerala's Communist-driven Land Reform Act of 1963 began in earnest in the 1970s. This revolutionary "land to the tiller" policy endorsed a society where cultivators could finally become the owners of their land and their agricultural outputs—and ideally become self-sufficient as a community of small farmers. Over one million tenants benefited from these reforms, and in excess of two million acres of land were transferred to new farmers.[24] During this process, the government created new property rights and transitioned the economy from feudalism to capitalism.

As with other reforms, implementation did not occur without struggle. Several vested interests preferred maintaining the status quo of land relations in the state. According to Herring, it took the Left several years to build support for Kerala's land reforms, and what was eventually passed in 1963 was a watered-down version of the Communists' earlier vision.[25]

However, Kerala's early government coalitions agreed that feudal land relations had contributed to the stagnation of the agrarian economy. Agriculture had become inefficient and yields low. The Communist and coalition governments also agreed with the British colonial regime about the importance of commercial farming for export, as a source of needed revenue for the nascent state government. As the early series of official Five Year Plans from Kerala shows,[26] the state Assembly therefore encouraged the new landowners to plant cash crops in order to bolster exports on the global market. As explained in the last chapter, the state government ushered in new technologies and chemicals, such as HYV seeds and endosulfan, to assist with increasing agricultural outputs throughout the state. Early state leaders were enthusiastic supporters of India's Green Revolution. Given the importance of cash crops to the economy, the state government also exempted several plantations from the new landholding ceilings imposed by land reforms. Coffee and tea plantations, for example, were among the exceptions to the five- to twenty-five-acre ceilings of the 1963 act.

After building momentum for land redistribution, the Communist-led coalitions focused on workers' pensions and labor rights, education, and health. Herring argues that today the outcome of these reforms and actions "is an interventionist and welfarist political economy that attempts to keep the market in its place."[27] The Communist-led mobilizations and reforms created new norms and institutional structures that continue to prioritize redistribution to this day. Several studies have documented that Kerala's radical leftist activity, such as its land reforms, has improved the quality of life for people across the state.[28]

IN SHORT, Kerala's social movements and progressive past have been major contributors to the state's high HDI, as well as its exceptionalism in development.[29] Yet the state's social and political orientation could not prevent the government's fiscal crisis in the 1980s and 1990s, when the economy stagnated. Compared to the rest of India, Kerala's share of national exports fell, agricultural output declined, and growth in its manufacturing sector slowed. Unemployment also increased.[30] Said former state finance minister Thomas Isaac, in an article with a colleague: "Kerala is one of the states that did not share in the acceleration of the national economy from the late 1970s. Not only was the growth rate of SDP [state domestic product] markedly lower than the national average but it was also significantly lower than the SDP growth rate achieved during the previous decade."[31] Kerala's economic slowdown led several scholars of economics to question whether the state was a true and comprehensive model for development and whether or not it could continue to prioritize redistribution.

People offered a number of explanations for the economic slowdown. Some political leaders and academics contended that Kerala's Communist parties fostered labor militancy, with the result that laborers would regularly and freely stop business to protest anything, crushing entrepreneurialism and undermining the state's market leadership. As a result, the state was scaring away high wage jobs, forcing many Keralites to emigrate while creating an economy dependent on remittances.[32] Other scholars criticized the state and its welfare programs as unwieldy and overly dirigiste—that is, heavy handed, bureaucratic, and anti–free market: "The inefficiencies of the state's apparatus—arising out of an over-centralized, over politicized, and corrupt bureaucracy—have been the bane of Kerala, retarding its development," said one.[33] Several others accused the government and political system of being top down and unresponsive to the economic and political needs of people in the state.[34]

As a rejoinder to the economic enervation, charges that the state was bureaucratically inefficient and top down, and other political and social changes underway since the state's founding, Kerala's Communist-led coalitions launched the People's Campaign for Decentralized Planning in 1996. The Communist Party of India-Marxist (CPI[M]), which emerged from the CPI), led its allies in the broader Left Democratic Front (LDF) in implementing "the People's Plan," as it was popularly known. The CPI(M) described it as "democratic decentralization," intended to better involve the people of the state in planning processes in a bottom-up manner.[35]

The People's Plan gave local village communities called *grama sabhas* control over 35 to 40 percent of the state's annual planning budget. These individual communities now decide how to use state funds within their constituency.[36] The LDF also built several local-level institutions to empower Kerala's populace to get actively involved in this new process. For example, the front fostered the development of women's neighborhood groups, known as Kudumbashree, as subsets of grama sabhas, to increase women's participation in political and economic matters. In meetings of grama sabhas, attendees regularly discuss the state's annual and Five Year Plans, development issues, and how to manage the health, education, and transportation sectors in their communities. Significantly for the turn toward organic agriculture, they also discuss environmental management, because the People's Plan required local communities to map and document their natural resources, to better assist with planning. As a part of natural resource management, the plan also decentralized agricultural decision-making in the state.

The LDF's decentralization transformed Kerala's politics by creating more opportunities for direct democracy, so that people could become even more active participants in the political and economic realms. Local-level officials now determine a significant portion of state economic and political activities.[37] Some claim that the People's Plan represents an alternative to traditional forms of development—a "new model" for development that harnesses the energy of the state's vibrant political life.[38]

THE PEOPLE'S PLAN had several roots in the environmental movements of Kerala, and it incorporated existing environmental mapping projects into its activities. One significant connection was with the Kerala Sasthra Sahithya Parishad (KSSP), a social organization of respected scientists and leftists committed to disseminating science in the Malayalam language.[39] In the 1990s, the KSSP was already working with the state government on environmental planning, resource mapping, and participatory engagement in both of these processes.

The KSSP first garnered national and international acclaim through its protests during the Save Silent Valley Campaign of the 1970s and 1980s, which I mentioned earlier as an important victory for Indian anti-dam activists. Silent Valley is in the mountains of eastern Kerala, on the border with the state of Tamil Nadu, in the southern part of the Western Ghats. In 1973, the National Planning Commission approved plans that were over fifty years old for a 120-megawatt hydroelectric dam in the valley. The Kerala State Electricity Board, the main proponent of the Silent Valley Dam, claimed that the state's growing electricity needs required the construction of such a large-scale hydroelectric power generator in the region. This news immediately caused an uproar among the state's environmental advocates, who claimed that because the valley was located in the biodiverse Western Ghats, it must be preserved.

Members of the KSSP, many of whom previously had not been environmental advocates, visited Silent Valley.[40] The KSSP reviewed the Electricity Board's plans, and performed a scientific and environmental assessment of the dam and the proposed site. The results of this study led the organization to condemn the dam as unscientific and unnecessary for electricity needs within the state. It criticized the Electricity Board for selling surplus electricity to neighboring states instead of supplying power to the people of Kerala. The KSSP argued that the dam would not only submerge the biodiverse forests of Silent Valley but bring little economic benefit to Kerala. Members of the KSSP simultaneously engaged in mass campaigns to convince the public and international groups to oppose the dam, and they agitated against the state and national governments. Prominent international conservation organizations, such as the International Union for Conservation of Nature (IUCN), supported the KSSP and even wrote letters to national officials, pleading with them to halt plans for dam construction.[41]

Due to the KSSP's efforts, the proposal for the dam was ultimately defeated. Then, in 1985, Prime Minister Rajiv Gandhi turned Silent Valley into a national park. The Save Silent Valley Campaign was one of the first successful anti-dam movements in India, and it propelled Kerala's environmentalism into the spotlight.[42] It also stimulated and laid the groundwork for action around other environmental issues in the state, from protesting against Coca-Cola for excessive groundwater use and pollution to shutting down the Gwalior Rayons factory for polluting the air and water with industrial chemicals.

The success of the Save Silent Valley Campaign also thrust the KSSP into the limelight, earning it "global acclaim as a flagship civil society organization in India and the third world,"[43] and its growing fame soon drew the attention of the LDF-led state government. But first the organization itself underwent a few changes, turning it into an ideal partner to assist with decentralization. Specifically, the Save Silent Valley Campaign radicalized the KSSP.

I had the opportunity to hear about these changes directly from M. K. Prasad—a leader in the Save Silent Valley Campaign, self-identified Marxian, and member of the KSSP since 1967—who was instrumental in starting an environmental activist wing within the organization.

"What led you to join KSSP?" I asked him on one occasion in his Thiruvananthapuram office.

Prasad answered: "I was fascinated by [KSSP], because this KSSP originated as a science-writers' movement.... This was ... the first people's science movement in India."

Prasad was referring to the fact that members of the KSSP wrote about science in the Malayalam language, so that communities in Kerala could have access to scientific knowledge about the world in their native language. Prasad had always been of the opinion that a sound scientific education was important for people to possess. "And they should ... use this science for their improvement in livelihood," he declared adamantly in the interview.

Yet the KSSP had not been satisfied with sticking to science writing alone. "After some years, the group found merely spreading science [through writing] is not going to help," observed Prasad. "So this society resolved to use science as a tool for social revolution."

The KSSP reevaluated its purpose as an organization, particularly after the Save Silent Valley Campaign, and made the decision to expand its activities beyond writing and translating science for Malayalam speakers, to engage in the state politics of development more broadly. As a result, its members also became more involved in environmental advocacy. They began actively training people in scientific methods and providing them with skills that would demonstrably help them to improve their livelihoods within their communities.

For example, in the late 1980s to the early 1990s, the KSSP engaged in the Total Literacy Programme, a local-level planning and development intervention to educate Keralites. Yet this initiative was not solely aimed at teaching people to read and write about science and nature. "Science for social revolution," a phrase Prasad used during our interview, is the KSSP's official slogan, signaling that its efforts have a purpose beyond just education. KSSP's members hoped that instilling literacy skills in a community's people would empower them to become actively involved in social movements, politics, and development in Kerala.

By teaching literacy through environmental education, and mobilizing educational volunteers at the local level, the Total Literacy Programme brought the state's literacy rate to over 90 percent. Later in the 1990s, the KSSP then turned its attention to resource mapping, to foster "land literacy" and political action focused on environmental issues.[44] Collaborating with local governments and the Centre for Earth Science Studies (CESS), the organization trained people how to identify and inventory watersheds and water bodies, various plants, land boundaries, and other natural resources.[45] The KSSP and CESS envisaged that gathering this information would inform contingency planning and other resource management efforts by local governments and communities.

In 1996, the KSSP's environmental programs crossed paths with Kerala's decentralization reforms, the People's Plan. The newly elected LDF government claimed that the inspiration for the People's Plan came from the grassroots successes of the KSSP—its Total Literacy Programme, mapping campaigns, and its bottom-up approach of empowering people to revolutionize society. The KSSP's leaders, many of whom were card-carrying members of LDF parties, were pulled into implementing the People's Plan, as well as developing the LDF's local self-government institutions.[46] This is precisely what happened to Prasad; his current job is networking and computerizing local governments in Kerala. Many other volunteers who had participated in the KSSP's literacy and mapping programs were also called upon to assist with statewide decentralization projects.[47]

As a result of the marriage between Kerala's environmental movement and its local-level politics, environmental issues became formally implanted in state-level discussions. Some scholars hailed the state's decentralization reforms as a "new model" with considerable potential to engage Keralites and their governments in sustainable development.[48] Natural resources now play a more prominent role in various government departments and their programs. For example, the Department of Tourism regularly features Kerala's mountains and seascapes in its marketing materials, to draw visitors to the state. It has even nicknamed Kerala "God's Own Country," to promote the idea of Kerala as Eden, perfect in its natural landscapes.[49] In 2010, LDF finance minister Thomas Isaac delivered the first ever "Red and Green" (*Pachayum Chuvappum*) annual budget to the state's Legislative Assembly—the first budget, in Isaac's view, to foreground the importance of the environment in Kerala's politics and economic plans alongside civil welfare.[50] In the state's 2013–2014 budget, Kerala's current finance minister, K. M. Mani, reiterated the importance of environmental sustainability in the state.[51]

The entwining of Kerala's political model with sustainability and environmentalism produces what scholars may call a particular "imaginary" of the state. An imaginary is an abstraction and ideal, "a way of imagining nature [or society], including visions of those forms of practice which are ethically proper and morally right."[52] The imaginary of Kerala depicts it as a place not only worthy of emulation for development but also as a place filled with fecund nature and stunning, Eden-like landscapes. A utopian understanding of the state's environment and environmental politics now persists in a variety of realms, such as in the Department of Tourism's advertising materials.

Fueling the spread of this imaginary has been environmentalists' increasing attention to the world's biodiversity hotspots—including that of the Western Ghats, which runs along Kerala's spine. The Save Silent Valley Campaign and the formation of Silent Valley National Park have drawn greater attention to the mountain range. Global and high-profile conservation organizations like Conservation International now advocate additional measures to preserve biodiversity in the Western Ghats, especially given that "less than fifteen percent of the [total] Western Ghats is protected in twenty national parks and sixty-eight sanctuaries. ... The protected area network is far from complete."[53] Because of these concerns, biodiversity conservation is taking new forms in the area, including organic farming. Kerala has begun experimenting with the latter, especially as the state's environment becomes synonymous with "biodiversity hotspot."

IN SPITE OF these activities directed at improving the environment and social development, the Kerala model—its reforms, politics, management of natural resources, and HDI—has come in for some criticism. As in the 1980s and 1990s, economists, scholars, and politicians still worry about the performance of the state's economy today, as well as the fact that Kerala's per capita income remains lower than other states. The global economic downturn and the central government's ongoing adoption of free market policies in agriculture have reinforced these worries, particularly as the agrarian sector has faced losses. Kerala's 2013–2014 fiscal budget runs a deficit, for instance.[54]

Furthermore, economic inequality is increasing in the state. As agricultural occupations have become increasingly risky due to the Green Revolution, and as Kerala's per capita income remains low, much of Kerala's labor force has been migrating to countries in the Middle East, Europe, and North America for jobs. Meanwhile, lower-skilled laborers from other parts of India have been flocking to Kerala's urban areas for jobs in sectors such as construction. Kerala's slums, filled with impoverished people, are rapidly growing in size. Workers in industries such as the hotel and tourism sectors earn just under 2,000 rupees per month— almost the equivalent of a dollar a day.

Several scholars have argued that the Kerala model actually perpetuates pockets of social exclusivity, despite claims by the Communist parties that they embrace secularism and equality. Many women, lower-caste communities, and groups from minority religious backgrounds still remain marginalized in Kerala's politics.[55] Several of these political and social divisions were apparent in the early days of the state, such as when President's Rule was imposed within Kerala by Prime Minister Nehru, yet they still remain today.

Just as alarming have been the statistics revealing Kerala's agrarian crisis, which I talked about in the previous chapter. In spite of the state's reputation as a model, and its history and politics, the 1990s and early 2000s were years of farmer suicides, pesticide poisonings, and a decline in agricultural output in many crops. This agrarian crisis was partly the result of policy decisions by Kerala's political leaders, especially right after state formation. Critics argue that the Land Reforms Act of 1963 and related leftist policies have led to ongoing economic and agricultural stagnation. For instance, they contend that land reform, by breaking up large estates and handing land over to small farmers, made agriculture less productive per acre. This situation encouraged farmers to cultivate crops such as spices that are not labor intensive, so they could avoid paying high labor costs when not receiving good returns on their land.[56] Others have disagreed, arguing that restrictions on the size of land holdings have actually benefited people, and that the switch from labor-intensive crops to less intensive ones is the result of other factors, including changes in foreign and national investment in agriculture.[57] All agree, though, that the amount of cash crop cultivation in Kerala has indeed increased. In contrast, the production of staple crops, such as rice, decreased in the late twentieth century.[58] These trends feed into the debate among Kerala's organic farmers over whether they should grow staples for local consumers or cash crops for foreigners, as I detail in chapter 6.

Additionally, several environmental problems plague Kerala: deforestation, soil erosion, and clean water shortages due to pesticide-intensive agriculture.[59] As Sugathakumari complained at the 2010 biodiversity conference: "You can't even drink our coconut water without getting sick." Many environmentalists also worry that Kerala's biodiversity is severely threatened by a range of factors, from human encroachment to climate change. Illegal sand-mining, the destruction of wetlands, rapid urbanization, and poaching are among the other environmental troubles facing the state today.

Kerala's political parties are reacting to the state's environmental and agrarian problems. For instance, concerned by widespread shrinkage of paddy fields and the resulting decrease in state self-sufficiency in rice production, the LDF-led government enacted the Kerala Conservation of Paddy Land and Wetland Act of 2008, "an Act to conserve the paddy land and wetland and to restrict the conversion or reclamation thereof, in order to promote growth in the agricultural sector and to sustain the ecological system, in the State of Kerala." This act builds on laws promoting land reform from the 1960s and 1970s.

More notable, however, were the unveiling of the state's organic farming policy in 2010 and the state's growing organic farming movement. Both grew out of Kerala's history of political mobilization, as well as from the openness of the state government and society to direct democracy, institutionalized in programs like the People's Plan. Kerala's organic farming initiatives now have the potential to ameliorate the agrarian problems facing the state.

While Kerala's contemporary social life and politics are more complicated than its reputation as a "model" suggests, years of social movements, and the institutions and norms built by Kerala's Left, have created a society that is responding to the globalization of agriculture in unique ways. The state's political history provides the key to understanding how and why organic farming has emerged as such a powerful movement here, one that critiques an agricultural system that prioritizes yields, chemicals, and the marketization of agriculture over social development and environmental health.

Forging a Statewide Organic
Farming Policy in Kerala

AT THE TURN of the twenty-first century, Kerala's agrarian crisis was reaching its peak. The Green Revolution was taking its toll throughout the state. Many farmers found themselves without substantial income from their pepper and coffee gardens because of pesticide-induced diseases. Endosulfan-related birth defects were making national news, and NGOs and government officials began investigating the occurrence of farmer suicides. By the end of the decade, however, the state's agricultural sector showed signs of improvement, and visitors like me started to come from afar to learn about Kerala's organic farming policy.

I met some of the other visitors one Saturday morning, when I found myself in rural Palakkad District, one of Kerala's rice-growing regions, stirring a mixture of five products from a cow—dung, urine, milk, yogurt, and ghee (fig. 2)—in a large drum. I had just disembarked from an overnight train, eager to greet the Kissan Swaraj Yathra, a group of farmers and activists touring India to raise awareness of the agrarian distress in the countryside.[1] The group decided to stop in Palakkad to highlight the activities of its Kerala-based partner, the nonprofit named Thanal, an organization that had been conducting several organic farming experiments and educational activities in Palakkad.

The chartreuse-colored and foamy slurry I was stirring emitted a putrid odor, yet everyone gathered closely around it. We were in the garden of an organic farmer, learning about *panchagavayya,* a homemade organic

2. *Panchagavayya*. Photo by the author.

pesticide and fertilizer prepared wholly from the excretions of cows. Despite the smell, plants love panchagavayya, we were told.

One of the founders of Thanal, S. Usha, explained to us how this stinky liquid promoted plant growth while also repelling pests organically (the latter definitely did not surprise me, given how bad it smelled). Plants treated with panchagavayya were healthier, she preached fervently to the crowd. She then proceeded to explain how to make panchagavayya over several weeks, including how often to stir it, and when and how to apply the final concoction to plants.[2] According to her, panchagavayya was a traditional fertilizer and pesticide but was now regaining popularity, as many organic farmers used it in place of synthetic fertilizers and pesticides. Usha, who had been trained as a scientist in Kerala's agricultural extension system, was also a former bureaucrat in the state's agricultural offices. She was well versed in farming practices, chemical and organic.

Having already been on the road for several days in other Indian states, the travelers in the Kissan Swaraj Yathra were impressed with the pancha-gavayya mixture and the alternative farming efforts they saw and learned about in Kerala. As we walked away from the panchagavayya, one member of the group told me he couldn't believe the extensive organic farming activities in the state, the likes of which he had not seen during any previous leg of his journey.

"Kerala is amazing," he said enthusiastically.

"How so?" I asked, curious.

"Here you have a progressive, leftist government that is anti-GMO [genetically modified organism], anti-endosulfan, and pro-organic farming."

"So, you've heard about the organic farming policy?" I asked further.

He nodded, saying that this policy was what had attracted the members of the Kissan Swaraj Yathra to the state. He could not wait to learn more about it from Thanal and then tell other farmers and government officials about Kerala's organic farming policy (and panchagavayya) on the next legs of the tour. He also praised Thanal in particular and Kerala's civil society in general for being instrumental in pushing an organic farming agenda at the state level.

KERALA'S ORGANIC farming policy was unveiled to the world in 2010. At a gathering of organic farmers, environmentalists, and officials from the Agriculture Department, the state's Chief Minister publically announced and endorsed the final version of the State Organic Farming Policy, Strategy and Action Plan (organic farming policy). The Chief Minister, head of the Communist-led LDF coalition in Kerala's Legislative Assembly at the time, promised the crowd that the Agriculture Department would assist with training and inputs—including making panchagavayya. Organic farming was now officially a part of the Agriculture Department's mandate.[3]

The organic farming policy, originally the brainchild of the Kerala State Biodiversity Board and Thanal, vows that the entirety of Kerala will be organic within ten years. The introduction boldly states:

Many farmers have realized that they are fighting a losing battle with the "high yield variety fertilizer-pesticide pack" of [the] Green Revolution. They have also realized that the degradation and disruption of the fragile ecosystems of the "God's own country" are the chief culprits for the water scarcity, nutritional insecurity, loss of primary productivity and agrarian crisis being faced by the State.

The farmers in Kerala are convinced that the only way is to return to the traditional sustainable ways of cultivation without harming the ecosystem, . . . [through] organic farming, a system with the broad principle of "live and let live" . . . recognized nationally and internationally.[4]

Agreeing on this language and forging the policy, however, was no easy feat, and it took four turbulent years to come to fruition, with back and forth debate between Kerala's Agriculture Department and the Biodiversity Board. A large cast of characters participated in these debates—LDF politicians, scientists from Kerala Agriculture University (KAU), NGOs like Thanal, and farmers—and a listing of the main players follows:

POLITICAL PARTIES AND COALITIONS
- Left Democratic Front (LDF), led by Chief Minister V. S. Achuthanadan (2006–2011)
- Communist Party of India (CPI)
- Communist Party of India (Marxist) (CPI[M])
- Campaign: The People's Plan

AGRICULTURE DEPARTMENT
- Minister for Agriculture Mullakkara Ratnakaran (2006–2011)
- Agricultural Production Minister K. Jayakumar

KERALA AGRICULTURAL UNIVERSITY (KAU)
- Teacher's Association of KAU
- George Thomas
- J. Nair (also a member of the Biodiversity Board; not his real name)

BIODIVERSITY BOARD

- V. S. Vijayan, chair (2007–2010)
- R. V. Varma, chair (2010–2011)
- M. K. Prasad (also a member of the KSSP)
- Program: People's Biodiversity Registers

NGOS

- Thanal (S. Ushakumari and R. Sridhar)
- Kerala Sasthra Sahithya Parishad (KSSP) (M. K. Prasad)

FARMERS

- K. V. Dayal

In this chapter, I tell the story of how the Government of Kerala came to adopt an organic farming policy at the state level. This policy and the state's organic farming movement are part of an alternative form of development—development that involves the input of civil society and promotes local-level planning on agriculture and the environment. Kerala's organic farming movement owes its shape and its success in part to the state's history of bottom-up politics and social movements and reforms. In the case of the 2010 policy, Kerala's Biodiversity Board leveraged this political history and mobilized civil society to forge a coalition of NGOs, agricultural bureaucrats, and farmers to delve into the state's agrarian morass of death—poisonings, diseases, and suicides. Utilizing the cause of biodiversity, the Board responded to Kerala's agricultural distress and pushed back against what had become the norm: the Green Revolution.

THE CAMPAIGN started in 2007, when the Kerala State Biodiversity Board began to intercede on behalf of agrarian issues.

Dr. V. S. Vijayan, a retired ornithologist, had recently been appointed by the reigning LDF government to chair this board. Disturbed by the links between pesticide use and toxins found in human bodies and the environment, he led the board into establishing Kerala's organic farming policy, a process that took four years of statewide consultations with farmers, activists, and government officials. The board and its allies championed organic farming as one of the solutions to Kerala's agrarian crisis, and by 2011 the board and its leader had become celebrity figures in the organic farming movement in India.[5]

Oddly for a celebrity, Vijayan is a soft-spoken man whose main hobby is bird watching. Framed pictures of birds fill his house, and his sitting room contains a clock that chimes on the hour with bird songs. A picture of Salim Ali, one of India's prominent ornithologists, hangs on one wall.[6] Vijayan is retired from the Biodiversity Board now, but he still acts as a spokesperson for the state's organic farming policy.

As we sat sipping tea in Vijayan's sitting room one afternoon, I asked what had prompted him, as chair of the Biodiversity Board in 2007, to make organic agriculture the board's priority.

"If you look at the biodiversity in general, you will find that the biodiversity loss is the worst in agrobiodiversity . . . the reason is the Green Revolution and use of chemicals," he began. "I have evidence for this, with birds, because I started observing birds from 1969. And in those days, from Palakkad to Thrissur, if you travel[ed] by any ways, you would see on any road or lane, hundreds of baya nests."[7]

"Hundreds of baya nests?" I asked, not knowing what a baya was.

"Baya. It's a weaverbird. They make their nests with straw, and they make a long spiral thing. . . . It is a tubular nest, very beautiful . . . hundreds of them you could see from the road," he explained. Then his tone turned somber. "Now you don't see a single one. The whole thing has gone," he said, waving his hands. "And nobody needs to tell me the reason. It is very clear; it coincides with the use of pesticides, right? It's not only the baya. . . . So my agenda is very clear."

Spurred by Vijayan's concern for the disappearance of these beautiful birds and the impoverishment of agricultural ecosystems in the state, the Biodiversity Board's main agenda item became the conservation of biodiversity by tackling chemical inputs.

The Kerala State Biodiversity Board does not have any regulatory authority. It is only a statutory body that advises the state government. Yet it succeeded in making its organic farming policy officially part of state's regulatory structure in the Agriculture Department—and in getting it funded. How was the board able to implement its vision for Kerala? And how did biodiversity and organic farming become embedded in state institutions? State political history has answers.

In the recent past, the Biodiversity Board has had direct connections to the LDF and the state's Communist parties, which have significant political sway among Kerala's citizens and over the government. At the same time, the LDF's decentralization efforts, known as the People's Plan, deeply influenced the board's priorities.[8]

The board's institutional history shows how it came to have these connections with the LDF, the People's Plan, and even the KSSP. The Government of Kerala set up the board in 2005 in response to the requirements of the National Biodiversity Bill of 2002. The federal government had enacted the national bill to implement the mandates of the international Convention on Biological Diversity, which India had ratified in 1994.[9] As a signatory, India was required to develop a national strategy to promote biodiversity, identify and monitor conservation efforts, and participate in information exchange. The 2002 bill decentralized biodiversity conservation efforts and mandated that each state create a biodiversity board. Kerala was among the first states to fulfill this requirement.

The Chief Minister of Kerala, the highest-ranking official in the state, presides over the board. Every five years he or she appoints the chair, five nonofficial expert advisers, five ex-officio members, and a member secretary to direct the board. The Biodiversity Board, therefore, is an advisory body comprised predominantly of political appointees. One member even openly admitted to me in an interview that not only was he heavily involved in party politics but he was deliberately put on the board by the CPI(M) to protect the party's interests in all matters relating to biodiversity in the state.

When voters in Kerala put the LDF back into political power in 2007, the board was only two years old, in an inchoate stage, and barely staffed; it didn't even have a chair. The LDF appointed the ornithologist Vijayan as the new chair, only the second in the board's short history. The governing party also appointed several scientists who are members of the KSSP and who were instrumental in implementing the People's Plan. At a crucial juncture, the Biodiversity Board found itself dominated by LDF sympathizers and therefore in a position to carry out and support the party's ongoing decentralization reforms, with an environmental focus.

The Biodiversity Board's activities became formally tied to the People's Plan through one of its main projects: People's Biodiversity Registers. Since its inception, one of the board's core activities has been to set up projects throughout Kerala to collect information about the history and uses of plants and animals, as well as any traditional knowledge about them, while fostering local participation in the government management of resources.[10] Teachers and students from local schools and colleges, NGOs, and villagers produce these registers, and similar biodiversity boards throughout the country are also engaged in developing them, an activity mandated under the National Biodiversity Bill. Kerala, however, has produced the second largest number of registers in India, despite being one of the smaller states geographically.[11]

The initial development of these registers dovetailed with the goals of the People's Plan, which was already being implemented. Not only had several members of the Biodiversity Board supported and had direct experience executing the LDF's decentralization reforms, but the People's Plan had even previously supported a similar inventory process, to assist people at the local level with planning and environmental management. The plan had advocated mapping natural resource information in partnership with NGOs such as the KSSP. The development of Biodiversity Registers therefore aligned perfectly with existing government initiatives.

The People's Plan was first implemented by the Kerala State Planning Board, a state agency. Consequently, the planning board also oversaw the development of the state's first Biodiversity Registers in the late 1990s, with technical assistance from the KSSP. These registers directly received funds allocated to the People's Plan under Kerala's Ninth Five Year Plan. When the state officially established the Biodiversity Board in 2005, the board assumed control over the creation of the registers.[12] To this day, the Kerala State Planning Board and the People's Plan remain influential institutions backing the Biodiversity Board.[13]

I had the opportunity to look at several of Kerala's Biodiversity Registers. Many are stored in the board's main office in Thiruvananthapuram, the capital of Kerala. Dr. R. V. Varma, who succeeded Vijayan's position as chair of the Biodiversity Board when the ornithologist retired and oversaw the finalization of the organic farming policy, once walked me through a completed register for a northern district of Kerala, Kasaragod. "We have the Herculean task of preparing the Biodiversity Registers," he explained at the time. "What we are trying to do is empower."[14]

Varma flipped through the register, a large, heavy book with glossy photos, pointing every now and then to the images of plants and amphibians on the pages. "This has all been collected by the people," he said admiringly. "It is very hard work. This contains information about the crops they grow, what they had earlier, what happened to them."

"This is a lot of work," I admitted, in disbelief that ordinary people in Kerala were actively documenting every animal and plant possible.

Varma repeatedly emphasized to me that the purpose of creating and keeping the Biodiversity Registers was to empower local communities to manage and protect their resources—goals that aligned with the LDF's redistributive and participatory reforms. Most important, though, he explained, creating the registers allowed the Biodiversity Board staff to meet with farmers, environmentalists, politicians, and community members throughout the state. Through these interactions, the Biodiversity Board developed relationships that strengthened its capacity to achieve its aims.

Indeed, given the task of creating Biodiversity Registers, the Biodiversity Board quickly established partnerships with members of civil society, from panchayats (villages) to NGOs from across the state. Therefore, when the chair at the time, Vijayan—moved by declining biodiversity, pesticide use, and the disappearance of baya weavers in the Western Ghats—decided to pursue a statewide organic farming policy, the board already had access to networks of NGOs, farmers, and local politicians who were concerned about conditions in the agricultural sector as well.

One such NGO was a Thiruvananthapuram-based environmental group, Thanal, the same group I came across educating farmers about panchagavayya in Palakkad. Since the early 2000s, it has been heavily involved in anti-endosulfan and rice-saving campaigns throughout Kerala and has developed partnerships with a variety of farmers. The organization pioneered the creation of a weekly organic bazaar selling local produce in Thiruvananthapuram. The bazaar has grown so successful that consumers line up for over an hour in advance to purchase goods, and it is now open every day of the week.

Thanal was formed in the late 1980s by Usha and her husband to promote education about and advocacy on behalf of natural history in the state. Formerly a KAU-trained bureaucrat at a local Agricultural Department office, she left her post to participate in environmental advocacy through Thanal. She explained to me that the intense focus on science and chemical agriculture in the Agriculture Department made her very uncomfortable.[15] She had been deeply influenced by Japanese farmer Masanobu Fukuoka's natural farming book, *One Straw Revolution*, which was published and translated into Malayalam in the late 1980s.[16] Fukuoka's emphasis on chemical-free agriculture created ripples within environmental and farming circles in Kerala. Soon after Usha read the book, Thanal expanded its educational activities to include Fukuoka's principles of sustainable agriculture. Illustrating the close links between Kerala's environmental advocates and the state's Left, many of the staff and leadership of Thanal are advocates of the LDF, and I would typically run into them at CPI(M)-organized conferences and events.

In 2007, Vijayan invited Thanal and other organizations to draft the Kerala State Biodiversity Strategy and Action Plan, the precursor to the organic farming policy. This document is in many ways the bedrock beneath the Biodiversity Board—it defines its direction and its policy priorities.

During a visit to Thanal's office, R. Sridhar, a former engineer who joined Thanal's staff to be active in environmental advocacy, explained to me how he and other members of the nonprofit came to work with the Biodiversity Board to formulate this action plan and the organic policy. The process was very simple: "Vijayan sent us a letter . . . asking us to join on a consultation on the State Biodiversity Strategy and Action Plan," he said. Vijayan and his organization, intensely committed to the LDF's decentralization plan, deliberately sought input from civil society groups in shaping the plan. Thanal was one among many other NGOs invited to help draft and revise the Biodiversity Strategy and Action Plan, which Vijayan had already begun to write.

"So both me and Usha went [to the Biodiversity Board office]. And we sat there, and then we looked to the Biodiversity Strategy Action Plan, we found that lot of things needed to come in there."

I nodded my head.

"And Dr. Vijayan was an extremely open person. This was the time when we were fighting genetically modified crops, we were starting to fight, you know, issues like that. So, we thought, that should come into the Biodiversity Action Plan. So we gave a huge number of, you know, inputs into the plan."

One of those inputs was the recommendation that the state should create an organic farming policy.[17] This suggestion piqued Vijayan's interest.

"Vijayan said that we should sit [in] on organic farming policy discussions," said Sridhar frankly. After the Biodiversity Board finalized the Biodiversity Strategy and Action Plan, Vijayan turned his focus, in 2007, to developing a separate organic policy. As Sridhar recounted, Vijayan reached out again to Usha and to him for their agricultural expertise. Together Vijayan and Thanal, along with Dr. J. Nair, a professor of agriculture in the state extension service and an informal expert member of the Biodiversity Board, formulated the first draft of the organic policy.[18] This proposed policy envisioned Kerala's conversion to organic farming happening within five years.

AFTER WRITING a draft of the organic farming policy, the next step was to obtain feedback from others. Vijayan and Thanal organized several workshops throughout the state so that farmers and communities would have the opportunity to provide input on the priorities and direction of agriculture in Kerala. At the first workshop, a two-day event at KAU-Vellayani, a branch of agricultural extension near the state capital, farmers and farmers' groups, university extension scientists, activists, officials from the Agriculture Department, and ministers from other government agencies discussed the early version of the policy. The LDF Chief Minister, V. S. Achuthanandan, presided.

Workshop discussions were intensely heated. Several attendees did not want to pursue a statewide strategy of organic farming. According to many I interviewed, the participants separated into three groups: farmers, media, and agricultural scientists and bureaucrats. The majority of the last group had been trained at agricultural extension agencies and worked in various branches of Kerala's Agriculture Department (including the department's local-level "agriculture houses" [*krishi bhavans*]).

Sridhar explained one heated exchange that occurred between the farmers and the scientists based at both KAU and the Agriculture Department: "At one point, one of these persons [a scientist] . . . got up and said that it is impossible to convert Kerala into organic." This scientist's opinion infuriated Sridhar and several organic farmers, who became confrontational. "So then I got up . . . and said, 'Tell us the crop, and we will give the answer now. . . . You tell us a crop, tell us, tell us your problem, and . . . our farmers are here who can tell you the solutions.'"

K. V. Dayal, an organic farmer, stood up next, to defend organic farming and to challenge the Agriculture Department. "We have been doing this for so many years!" he shouted back at the scientists, agreeing with Sridhar. "We've been experimenting. We know how to trap our pests. . . . And all of the experiments have been in the farmer's field!" He added: "When farmers are suicidal, when they're not getting enough income, when their land is spoiled, when their crops are becoming destroyed, when the climate [is] impacting them, if nothing is bothering you, then why should we have you?"

Why should we have you? Dayal's question was a common one among farmers, who were beginning to wonder whether they should continue to embrace information coming from the Agriculture Department and KAU about agriculture, given the terrible situation they found themselves in. This exchange and the many later debates pivoted around issues of expertise—whether farmers knew enough about farming practices to farm without the scientific and technical aid of agricultural bureaucrats and scientists, the majority of whom were trained at KAU in Green Revolution methodologies.

Many of the Agriculture Department officials and agricultural extension scientists who attended the two-day workshop did not favor organic agriculture. They did not believe that Kerala's farmers could successfully cultivate their crops without chemical inputs, and certainly not without the expertise of the agricultural scientists and bureaucrats. For example, Dr. George Thomas, a professor and extension researcher who attended the workshop, had many reservations. I met him in his office one day to learn more about this workshop, and he defended the position of the bureaucrats and scientists: "I am seeing this organic farming in a different perspective," he said. "If more and more people come forward to do organic farming . . . that may decrease the whole yield. That is our concern. For a developing nation like India, our population is going to double. . . . So that means in the next forty years, we have to double food production." His argument echoed that of advocates of conventional agriculture elsewhere, that organic farming cannot produce enough to feed the world's growing population.

Thomas then explained that experiments in laboratories and agricultural extension were important for the advancement of science and a scientific analysis of agriculture. "We conduct experiments, then only we will believe. If you want to prove that an organic product is nutritionally better, you have to conduct an experiment. We are for scientific methods, scientific thinking, scientific temper. . . . " He pulled out and showed me several studies he had printed that questioned the merits and yield potential of organic farming. His perspective, he assured me, was based in sound science and the mission of agricultural extension.

For opponents like Thomas, organic farming presented a threat to their livelihoods, science, and the status quo in which agricultural research prioritized yields—yields that required the use of chemical inputs. This program was precisely what the Government of India had aggressively promoted during the Green Revolution. Additionally, many officials from the Agriculture Department were displeased that the Biodiversity Board was trespassing on their turf and proposing changes to the state's agricultural priorities.

Led by Thomas, the Teachers' Association of KAU, a coalition of scientists and professors within Kerala's agricultural extension offices, wrote a rebuttal to the organic farming policy that summarizes the opposition to organic farming in the state. Entitled *Can Organic Agriculture Replace Conventional Agriculture? Reflections on the Organic Agricultural Policy Proposed by the Bio Diversity Board of Kerala* (2008), the report captures the allure the Green Revolution has had within Kerala's agricultural bureaucracy. It states, for example: "[The green revolution's] brilliant success depended on using scientific advances, which had already been made elsewhere in breeding and agronomy of wheat and rice and then adapting them to conditions in Central America and Asia.... In fact, [the] green revolution has solved the immediate problem of feeding the ever-increasing population."[19]

Throughout the report, Kerala's proponents of chemical agriculture argue that "modern" farming is necessary to protect the environment from the increasing food needs of a growing population. Later, the authors do acknowledge that chemical inputs and modern forms of farming have caused environmental destruction; they therefore call for an "evergreen revolution" that will better protect the environment but that is similarly rooted in Kerala's agricultural bureaucracy and technical science. As the document states: "It is hoped that we can have an evergreen revolution through the adoption of sustainable agricultural strategies focusing on the food crops grown by millions of people who lack food security."[20]

When reflecting on the report from the Teacher's Association of KAU, Vijayan, the former chair of the Biodiversity Board, recalled: "The agricultural scientists were quite clear that the [organic farming] policy will not be successful." However, discussions of the draft policy did not stall due to the support of a key ally within the bureaucracy: the Agriculture Minister. Mullakkara Ratnakaran (CPI) favored organic farming, so many officials, scientists, and staff in the Agriculture Department bowed to his judgment. Therefore, discussions surrounding the organic farming policy continued despite powerful opposition, in large part because of support from the governing coalition, the LDF, and bureaucrats' deference to their elected bosses. Sympathizers and supporters of the policy within KAU and the agricultural bureaucracy facilitated this progress.

To appease the reservations of those involved with agricultural extension and research, as well as officials in the Agriculture Department, the Biodiversity Board revised the policy for the next round of discussions. Nair, one of the original authors of the organic farming policy and a professor at KAU, called these revisions—including one lengthening the conversion period to ten years—a "dilution." He was disappointed that the Biodiversity Board did not succeed in persuading people that the conversion to organic farming needed to happen more quickly, within five years, as the original document specified.

But then Nair pointed out the long-term goals of the policy to me: "We decided—because there were a lot of differences in opinion from the scientists' side—we decided that, let us not bulldoze . . . let us bring them also together, [because] if the policy is formulated, [we'll] require their help also in implementation." As he noted, the board compromised on several points because its eventual goal was that the Agriculture Department, the official body regulating agriculture in the state, would manage the conversion to organic farming.

Implementation "is their domain," as Varma, the chair of the Biodiversity Board at the time, reminded me about the Agriculture Department in interviews. The board had no regulatory authority and did not wish to alienate necessary allies. Those like Nair, with direct ties to both the board and agricultural extension, assisted with negotiations and revisions to move forward with finalizing the policy.[21]

The Biodiversity Board then took its revised policy out for another set of consultations with farmers and local communities around the state, relying primarily upon channels and relationships it had already built while creating the Biodiversity Registers, as well as on Thanal's network of farmers and farmers' organizations. Discussions even occurred at the opposite geographic end of the state, in rural areas in the Western Ghats. As a result of these local-level stakeholder meetings, the policy came to highlight best practices in organic agriculture occurring throughout the state. For example, the policy now mentions that thousands of Kerala's farmers have been certified organic for export for some time, and that a locally based certification agency, which I will describe in chapter 5, has been facilitating these efforts. Adding this material demonstrated the broad support for organic farming already in existence across Kerala.

FINALLY, in early 2008, the Biodiversity Board submitted the policy for review and approval by the state's Cabinet and top officials in the Agriculture Department. In the fall, the Cabinet approved the policy. This made headlines. One newspaper explained in detail: "The Chief Minister, Mr. V. S. Achuthanandan, told newspersons after the Cabinet meeting on

Wednesday that a general council with the Chief Minister as Chairman and an executive council headed by the State Agriculture Minister would be formed to work out the modalities for implementing the policy."[22]

Vijayan was excited by the detailed news. He ran over to Ratnakaran's office to obtain a copy of the final document that had been approved and reported in the media. "I wanted to send it to the Prime Minister, saying that this is the model which should be followed in the country," he recalled. When he reached the office, an assistant handed over the policy to him. "[The] minister's personal assistant told me 'we have made some changes here and there, but not much . . . in the introduction some points . . . otherwise everything is fine, as it was.'"

Vijayan took the copy eagerly, only to have his excitement immediately crushed. "When I read it," he said, "I thought, my God, what they had done, they had completely changed it. That was a shock to me. Most of the clauses were completely changed or altered. I was so upset." The policy had been modified to suggest that intensive chemical agriculture was the best and most reliable type of agriculture available to farmers, while organic farming was just an optional alternative. This message contradicted the Biodiversity Board's vision of making organic farming the only acceptable agricultural practice within the state.

Vijayan went directly to Ratnakaran to complain. "Who has done this?" he asked, trying to pinpoint when the policy had changed and who had changed it. Apparently the minister was blindsided as well. "I told him what had happened, so he had the shock of his life. He could not answer me." The Biodiversity Board and Thanal, as well as their allies, protested against this version and petitioned for revisions. As a result, over another year and a half the Biodiversity Board and the Agriculture Department continued to deliberate and debate the policy, arbitrated by Minister Ratnakaran. Staff at Thanal described this time as a period of multiple levels of prevarication and delay. While neither members of Thanal nor the people on the Biodiversity Board felt comfortable publically elaborating on the details (so as to not alienate potential allies, they claimed), they did emphasize that certain officials and bureaucrats in the Agriculture Department and agricultural extension disliked the organic farming policy passionately and were intent on obstructing its approval for as long as possible.

Part of the tension between the two institutions stemmed from the Agriculture Department's continuing sentiment that the Biodiversity Board was overstepping its authority by telling the department how to advise farmers, plan agriculture, and perform its duties. One high-ranking official (who asked me not to use his name) said: "The Agriculture Department [has] the definitive manpower to provide the correct advice to farmers.... It is actually the department [that] is taking care of the welfare of the farmers of the state. They are the people who are giving technical support to farmers to raise crops and all this."

He continued: "I'm an agriculture man who has studied agriculture. Our intention, our main mandate, is to increase production, food production, and [the] agriculture welfare of farmers without harming the environment.... In [the] Agriculture Department, Agriculture University... you can get people who have studied agriculture, scientific agriculture. And the biodiversity man—the chairman—is not an agriculture man. He is a bird watcher."

Many employees of the Agriculture Department and other agricultural institutions shared this official's opinion—that the Biodiversity Board was imposing its unfounded and unreasonable ideals upon a department with a longer history and deeper knowledge of agriculture in the state.

When I asked K. Jayakumar, the Agricultural Production Commissioner and the second highest official in Kerala's agricultural bureaucracy, why the Agriculture Department demonstrated such opposition to the organic farming policy, he answered: "[The] policy is a bundle of pious wishes ... it is aspirational in nature ... but when it comes to practical reality, how do we encourage farmers to opt for organic farming?" He went on to explain that the market push around nonorganic inputs posed a strong competition to organic farming methods.

"Do you mean the price is cheap for those inputs?" I asked, to clarify.

"They are highly subsidized," Jayakumar said matter-of-factly. "Fertilizers are extremely subsidized by the Government of India. Then all your agricultural practices, encouraged by the universities, are all centered around this kind of interventions, where you have to use . . . fertilizers, pesticides, insecticides, everything. And the market, which pushes these things—products—is also extremely strong.

"And farmers are also used to it," Jayakumar added. "They know the results. They know, and also they are aware of the immediate benefits . . . they know the immediate benefits, and they know the ill effects of not using these things. . . . Therefore the farmer, and the scientist, and the administrator are already convinced about the short-term returns of continuing with the existing practices."

The Agricultural Production Commissioner stated one more thing: "Organic comes in as an uninvited guest, if I may say so."

In reflecting on the relationship between the farmer, the scientist, and the administrator, Jayakumar's words ignored the grassroots environmental activism behind the policy, as well as the top-down authority that decentralization was attempting to break. His words also confirmed the Agriculture Department's displeasure with the Biodiversity Board's meddling with the status quo and its disrupting the trend toward more and more chemical application in agricultural production. Data from 2001 to 2002 show that Kerala was the second highest consumer of fertilizers per hectare in India. Between 2008–2009 and 2009–2010 the application of chemical insecticides and fungicides increased in the state as well.[23] The Biodiversity Board's organic farming policy and initiatives threatened to upset this system. In other words, the Biodiversity Board was proposing changes not only in the relationship between farmers and agricultural scientists in Kerala but also between people and the government more broadly.

LDF politicians—Agriculture Minister Ratnakaran and the Chief Minister—were left to mediate between the Biodiversity Board and the Agriculture Department. According to Nair, the professor at KAU who had helped draft an early version of the policy, "The agricultural minister, you know, was caught between his office and the Biodiversity Board and his commitment to organic farming."

The high-ranking official in the Agriculture Department who had asked me not to use his name, and who had previously expressed his displeasure with the organic farming policy and the Biodiversity Board in our interview, even joked: "Actually, the Agriculture Minister is the only man who is giving support to this biodiversity." According to this official, the Agriculture Minister championed the policy throughout the department and, given his position, succeeded in reverting it to a document promoting 100 percent organic farming throughout the state within ten years. This official then explained that, despite his reservations about organic farming, as a civil servant he had no choice but to comply with what the top representatives mandated.

Finally, after Vijayan's considerable shock in October 2008, the policy was eventually finalized in early 2010 and allotted 100 *lakh* rupees that year under the newly created Organic Farming Programme.[24] The Biodiversity Board and Thanal were victorious: not only did the ruling government favor the policy, but the policy had also become an officially sanctioned and funded Agriculture Department program. Moreover, this version of the policy steadfastly championed organic farming as the best method of agriculture for Kerala.

Chief Minister Achuthanandan introduced the policy to the world in a media blitz in Kozhikode District on May 17, 2010, and in the following days the policy was featured by several national newspapers. Subsequently, Achuthanandan and Ratnakaran commenced an informal publicity tour throughout the state, broadcasting the policy's existence at various events and inaugurations for the remainder of the year.[25]

THIS PROTRACTED struggle between the Biodiversity Board and the Agriculture Department over the organic farming policy is part of a larger struggle within Kerala's civil society and government over environmental governance. Put another way, the Biodiversity Board sought to change agricultural standards, rules, and norms to extend the decentralization of civic engagement into sustainable agriculture and agricultural policy. The board gained momentum for these goals by tapping into the existing LDF campaign for decentralization and by relying on its political alliances with LDF leadership. The extensive network of farmers and environmentalists developed through the process of creating Biodiversity Registers and formulating the Kerala State Biodiversity Strategy and Action Plan supported the board's aims.

To elaborate, the organic farming policy promotes organic agriculture, but it also supports both further decentralization of agricultural decision-making and changing relationships within Kerala's agricultural sector, giving farmers more autonomy from the state government and the free market with their purchasing decisions, the making of fertilizers, and marketing. As such, the policy advocates that farmers exchange and save traditional varieties of seeds instead of HYV seeds, create organic inputs together as opposed to purchasing them from markets, and collectively find opportunities for selling organic goods. Its recommendations align with principles of Kerala's political reforms, by prioritizing the "seed sovereignty of the farmers and the State" and creating "a state-wide intensive campaign on organic farming in the form of a popular movement."[26]

The policy also advocates production for domestic consumption and supports the creation of domestic marketing channels, to break ties that farmers have to international commodity markets, a strategy not all farmers agree with, as I show in chapter 6. However, the policy does not require that producers farm for specific purposes, and it also remains unspecific about how to practice organic agriculture, giving local governments flexibility in making decisions. Hence, the policy is not imposing established and international organic standards on farmers but is offering opportunities for farming communities to create and agree upon their own organic farming norms. Additionally, Usha explained to me that one objective of the policy is to reform the Agriculture Department's Centralized Purchasing Policy, which requires farmers to buy inputs from accredited state agencies in order to qualify for government subsidies. The organic farming policy instead promotes and subsidizes the communal creation and organization of inputs at the panchayat level, such as shared vermicompost tanks, panchagavayya, and local manure production and distribution.[27] As a result, as framers of the policy hope, farmers will no longer have to rely on buying external inputs, and possibly go into debt to make such purchases, to grow food.

Organizers behind the policy see such reforms as the epitome of *swaraj*, Gandhian and local self-rule. Indeed, the revolutionary potential of the policy rests in the fact that it promotes self-sufficiency in food production and local-level decision making—severing farmers' dependence on external markets while increasing civic engagement and control in agriculture. The policy also disrupts the long-standing but dysfunctional relationship between "the farmer, and the scientist, and the administrator" in India. The organic farming policy weakens the power that the Agriculture Department has over farming activities in the state. The Biodiversity Board asserted itself in the department's jurisdiction by making agricultural policy, attempting to reshape the rules and norms around agriculture to promote organic farming exclusively as a solution to Kerala's agrarian problems, and incorporating farmers' input to make these changes.

THIS STRUGGLE between the Biodiversity Board and the Agriculture Department was also shaped by competing visions for agriculture and the environment in Kerala and the role of science in each vision.

The technological and scientific optimism behind the Green Revolution's increases in productivity have become entrenched in Kerala's agricultural bureaucracy, rendering alternative conceptions of agricultural production unthinkable. This optimism has had significant traction here because of the state's agricultural history and the priorities of its coalition governments.

A consistent theme in Kerala's state politics is the notion that the agricultural sector is stagnant and could be more productive in terms of yields per acre. The historical food shortages that the state has faced and the desire to earn more foreign exchange have influenced this perspective. The state's Five Year and Annual Plans, for example, regularly refer to increasing the productivity of agriculture in Kerala and have been doing so since the formation of the state in the 1950s.[28] The government—under both LDF and UDF (United Democratic Front) coalitions—has therefore promoted the use of chemical inputs to increase agricultural output. And, most important, the state has encouraged the increased production of cash crops to revitalize the agrarian economy. Maximizing yields and supporting commercial crops with chemical inputs have historically been key strategies for Kerala's existing agricultural institutions, such as KAU.

The Teacher's Association of KAU issued a rebuttal to the organic farming policy that regurgitates this line about productivity and therefore characterizes the policy as unscientific and the opposite of "modern" in its motives. The report even accuses Kerala's organic farming movement of pandering to the West's desire to control the Third World because, in the association's view, organic agriculture would undermine the nation's economic autonomy. This sentiment is in reference to the American PL-480 program of food aid, which was tied to economic and political conditions before the Indian government decided to pursue the Green Revolution. As such, the report implies that rational, scientific agriculture, such as that involved in the Green Revolution, can reduce India's reliance on the West for food aid. In sum, challengers to the organic farming policy characterize organic agriculture and modern, scientific agriculture as opposites—one is backward, unscientific, and could weaken India, whereas the other is modern, is scientific, and could strengthen the country.

This "modern" versus "tradition" divide in science and agriculture is stark and glaring in Kerala's government institutions. Not only have many members of the Assembly and Agriculture Department bought into the technological optimism of the Green Revolution as an answer to Kerala's agricultural troubles, but the Biodiversity Board itself has attached particular ideals around modernity and tradition to its organic farming policy, broadening this divide. As the policy itself states toward the beginning: "The Green Revolution, with a single slogan of 'grow more food', was only a natural outcome of a national challenge to meet the growing food requirements." The policy's analysis of the Green Revolution turns fully negative, however: "This development—unmindful of the ecosystem principles so revered and practiced for centuries—led to seemingly irrevocable ecological and environmental catastrophes in the country."[29]

In arguing that the Green Revolution did not achieve what it was supposed to, the policy reasons that these cataclysms came in part because of the substitution of the old ways and crops with new ones: "The green revolution essentially replaced the traditional varieties with high-yielding ones. These high yielding varieties now recognized as 'high input varieties' needed tonnes of fertilizers, to achieve the target growth. The crops and varieties alien to the soil attracted new pests and diseases and also outbreaks of existing pests." To deal with the pests, Kerala's farmers turned to pesticides, putting them on the treadmill: "[The] input of these 'exotic' elements into the traditional farming led to multitude of environ-mental issues."[30]

In short, argues the policy, modernity was not the panacea that Green Revolution advocates thought it would be: "As a result of all these 'mod-ern' techniques, the air, water and the soil were polluted; most food grains and farm products were contaminated by pesticides." Moreover, the Green Revolution did not reduce hunger, because "food crops became non-attractive, while cash crops became more remunerative." According to the board, "many farmers have realized that they are fighting a loos-ing [sic] battle with the 'high yield variety—fertilizer-pesticide pack' of Green Revolution. They have also realized that the degradation and disruption of the fragile ecosystems of the 'God's own country' are the chief culprits for the water scarcity, nutritional insecurity, loss of primary productivity and agrarian crisis being faced by the State."[31]

The solution, as identified by the board in the policy, was to reject the new system of doing agriculture: "The farmers in Kerala are convinced that the only way is to return to the traditional sustainable ways of cultiva-tion without harming the ecosystem."[32] Thus, within the organic farming policy itself, the Biodiversity Board explicitly positions organic farming as "traditional," in contrast to "modern" farming, and rejects the Green Revolution as a strategy for achieving Indian autonomy and food security.

The Biodiversity Board is not averse to innovations and technology, nor is it opposed to research. For example, the board partnered with sev-eral university scientists in Kerala to pilot an organic farming project in Palakkad District in 2008, and to evaluate and monitor the success of the project. Part of the board's positioning as the advocate of tradition, there-fore, is a strategic response to farmers' claims that contemporary agricul-tural research in Kerala occurs without them and is not to their benefit. After all, it was Dayal, an organic farmer representing many other farmers in the state, who publicly asked a scientist opposed to the organic farming policy at the first workshop: "Why should we have you?"

Thanal has toed this line about science and agricultural bureaucracy as well, and Usha and Sridhar constantly play down their own scientific training in laboratories and universities. Both Sridhar and Usha view mainstream science and research as disconnected from farmers and ordinary people, and they prefer politically to be associated with the latter group. For example, for a televised debate about GMOs in the state, Sridhar deliberately dressed in traditional formal attire—a white *lunghi* (a long garment wrapped around the waist in lieu of pants) with a button-down shirt—and refused to be addressed as "doctor." He hoped to be perceived publicly as sympathetic to farmers and agricultural concerns in the state and less as a disengaged expert. Hence, in contrast to many of the scientists at the Agriculture Department, staff at Thanal believe that good agricultural policy and practice cannot just be based on the scientific method alone, divorced from social and environmental realities, but should include input from farmers and communities. Therefore, the organization has prioritized its mission to mobilize farmers and communities throughout the state about environmental issues and to broadcast their voices as often as possible to the government, the media, and now in agricultural institutions.[33]

Overall, the Government of India has taken a different stance, and has championed the use of a detached science in agricultural extension and other government institutions. Scholars have posited that the government's preoccupation with science (for example, in nuclear research) is the result of India's condition as a postcolonial nation with a strong motive to assert its independence and its desire to claim its place in international relations as a modern, developed nation. With science comes legitimacy is the thought.[34] Yet it has been well documented that particular forms and uses of science, especially in relation to agriculture and the environment, lead to disastrous environmental and political outcomes for communities, delegitimize farmers' agricultural knowledge, and overlook the fact that knowledge about nature is socially constructed—that is, the experts who get to generate a more authorized yet removed knowledge also get to shape the content of that knowledge, as well as its use in sectors such as policy, even though their analyses of the environment may be incomplete.[35]

In the Indian context, activists such as Vandana Shiva claim that the Indian government's apolitical use of science to dictate natural resource management has undermined the livelihoods of groups like women, who now have little say in the use of common resources that they once relied upon for food and fuel. Shiva argues that thanks to the Green Revolution, previous forms of resource use have been devalued.[36] Science had functioned to exclude common Indian people, such as small farmers, from the process of making decisions about the management of natural resources. In casual conversations with me, Kerala's farmers would dismiss the work of agricultural extension scientists in the state as being shortsighted and frequently flawed, certainly not beneficial to the agrarian community.

ULTIMATELY, even though Green Revolution technologies and ideals were deeply ensconced in Kerala's government institutions, the Biodiversity Board prevailed in changing the links between "the farmer, and the scientist, and the administrator." The struggle between the Agriculture Department and the board shows that organic farming stimulated a meaningful transformation in farming standards and relationships within Kerala—a process that had commenced with the LDF's decentralization reforms of the 1990s and was galvanized to focus on environmental issues by the state's agrarian crisis.[37] The outcome of this struggle, a more inclusive agricultural system that incorporates greater input from farmers concerning the state's agricultural priorities, illustrates that radical politics continue to have an impact on Kerala's government institutions and their mandates. The organic farming policy is therefore far from just a pronouncement but is rather an exemplar of an alternative form of development—one that involves the input of communities and farmers and promotes local-level planning.[38] Kerala's organic farming policy also represents a noteworthy experiment that may provide answers to the country's agrarian problems.

Kerala's contemporary organic farming movement has taken this shape due to the state's particular history, which facilitated a bottom-up, people-oriented approach. Farmers and NGOs, with support from the Biodiversity Board, assisted in making organic farming a state priority. This circumstance suggests that organic agriculture is likely to develop differently in other places, contingent on local conditions, cultural specificities, global political economy, and history. For comparison's sake, consider organic farming in California: here, the movement has been dominated by large-scale, corporate farms because the high price of land, financial speculation, and other economic forces in the state. In other words, the existing characteristics of California agriculture drove the rise of large-scale, corporate organic farming in the state, leading many academics to warn that organic farming is becoming "conventionalized," like industrial agriculture. [39]

What are the implications of what is happening in Kerala for the organic movement in the United States and consumers who buy organic? The contrast between California and Kerala demonstrates that the global organic farming movement is not homogenous. Nor is the movement's future predetermined, because in various places local, cultural, and political forces are exerting influence on the direction of organic production. Despite globalization, agricultural systems continue to vary from place to place.[40] As such, in Kerala, organic farming has become an alternative to the chemical-laden agriculture of the Green Revolution and is creating avenues for transparency and political participation in the state's agricultural politics. It is currently the opposite of "elitist," "corporatized," or even "top down"—all terms critics of organic agriculture have used. Kerala's organic countermovement illustrates the kind of change that is possible, when and if activists, farmers, and policy makers collaborate and mobilize around alternative solutions to societal problems.

The Social and Ecological Benefits
of Organic Farming

IT WAS GOING TO BE a hot day. It was only 8:00 A.M., yet the temperature was already around eighty degrees Fahrenheit. I was en route again to Palakkad District, Kerala's rice bowl, to spend more time with Thanal. This time I was heading straight for the Palghat Gap, a valley in the Western Ghats mountain range. Buses filled with pilgrims bustled by the car, taking advantage of the national highway built between the mountain pass and the rural countryside, to go to worship in the Sabarimala temple in the south and also intent on beating the heat of the day. It was only November, a few months before India's hot summer season begins.

Farmers in the region have blamed Palakkad's heat on the Palghat Gap, saying it allows hotter and drier air from the neighboring state of Tamil Nadu to blow into Kerala. The well-documented *Palakkadan kattu* (Palakkad wind) has indeed been a major influence on the climate of the region. Farmers historically coped with the high temperatures by building rainwater harvesting wells, such as *kokkarni* (ponds) and *kulam* (tanks), and using this water to irrigate their paddy fields. These water collection methods have become rarer since the Green Revolution, when many were replaced by contemporary and more centralized irrigation techniques, including large-scale dams.

While the intense heat of Palakkad made me uncomfortable, the flatness of much of the district made it a suitable location for rice paddy cultivation, and also for the Biodiversity Board's hundred-acre organic farming pilot project from 2008 to 2011. The CPI's historic strength among the district's farm laborers also rendered the region a welcoming place for LDF experimentation in agriculture. And indeed, the roads out to the pilot farming area were arrayed with multitudes of posters, banners, and signs for Kerala's Communist parties.[1]

While Kerala's Agriculture Department and extension were laggardly scrutinizing drafts of the organic farming policy, the Biodiversity Board proceeded to fund an "agro-biodiversity enhancement programme" in the village of Padayetti in central Palakkad District, in the Palghat Gap. Through subsidies and training sessions, this three-year pilot project converted a large area to organic agriculture, a test of what the entirety of Kerala could become within a few years. To build legitimacy for the project, the board, in partnership with local universities and researchers, monitored and evaluated the agricultural biodiversity and soil structure of the fields. Thanal provided field support and even housed in the village a staff member, whose purpose was to attend local-level governmental meetings and organize farmers and their families around sustainable agriculture.[2]

The board's experiment at Padayetti significantly influenced the early years of the organic farming policy. After the policy's finalization, the Agriculture Department created the Organic Farming Programme to implement it statewide. In 2011, the state government allotted 10 million rupees (around $200,000) to the newly minted program. The majority of the funds were dispersed to twenty local-level units of government, called "block panchayats," for training and inputs such as organic fertilizer.[3] Bureaucrats and Thanal staff held up the board's pilot project as an example of how the conversion to organic agriculture could occur and be scaled up in these twenty pioneer block panchayats. Immediately after the Organic Farming Programme was created, agriculture officers from the block panchayats visited Padayetti's pilot farming area during state-sponsored training sessions.[4] One such officer, who visited from the northern Kerala district of Wayanad, felt so inspired by the trip that he became convinced that organic agriculture was one of the best methods for agriculture for his block panchayat.

From districts as far north as Wayanad to Kerala's central Palakkad District, such changes in individual perceptions of organic agriculture, as well as state priorities themselves, can be documented. Wayanad is, in fact, where Kerala's organic export movement and organic certification institutions have their roots. With the aid of the Indian Farmers Movement (INFAM), hundreds of farmers in this district started growing organic spices and crops before the finalization of the 2010 organic farming policy. These farmers are certified organic for export by a third-party certifier, Indocert, an India-based certification agency. Third-party certification has allowed these farmers to meet organic standards in the European Union and the United States and to market their foodstuffs at premium prices in foreign markets. Over fifteen thousand farmers are now either already certified or in the process of becoming so throughout the state.[5] Organic agriculture has therefore not been an alien concept in Kerala or among its farmers, a circumstance that facilitated the adoption of the new policy.

Together, Kerala's organic farming policy, along with its certified organic export movement, represent transformations occurring in the state's agricultural system. The new policy has been a catalyst for shifts in Kerala's agricultural governance to further engage organic farmers, local and state officials, and NGOs in local-level decision making. This policy has also stimulated significant conversations about the norms of an agricultural system that has historically prioritized yields and chemicals. The state's Agriculture Department now has several staff, materials, and programs dedicated to organic farming—novel developments.

Furthermore, Indian farmers are now participating in globalized organic markets on favorable terms, thanks to the advent of India-based certification. Working with Indian certifiers that charge less money for inspections and share farmers' cultural background has facilitated the greater involvement of Indian agriculturalists in organic food chains. Organic certification has also enabled farmers to earn greater income from their crops, money they are investing in scholarships and farm improvements. These and other outcomes of organic farming are the result of a political and social culture in Kerala that has supported development

innovations and local-level empowerment, both built up through years
of mobilization and fostered through government reforms, educational
programs, and government agencies.

WHEN I FINALLY reached Padayetti after the long, hot drive, I was
greeted by Suresh, a staff member at Thanal who had been living in the
village for several months to assist with monitoring and implementing
the Biodiversity Board's organic farming pilot. An activist by training, he
had settled contentedly into village life . He said that he was active within
the community of sixty-six families who were participating in the pilot.
His community outreach on behalf of Thanal had included organizing
a regular book swap among young adults in the pilot area to encourage
reading, leading field trips for children to the park nearby to teach them
about biodiversity and natural history, and giving families lessons on how
to easily cultivate vegetable gardens for personal consumption in their
yards, maintain organic paddy fields, and produce organic farm inputs.
As a result of Suresh's and Thanal's activities, the majority of the farmers
now had kitchen gardens filled with organic vegetables in their backyards,
and they had become familiar with organic input production methods.
According to the Biodiversity Board's interim report on the pilot project:
"A marked change in the skills and knowledge of the farmers regarding
farming, especially organic farming is seen. . . . Farmers also reported
better understanding of paddy cultivation, especially the importance of
looking at it from an ecosystem basis."[6]

Acquainted with every participating farmer, Suresh took me on a tour
of the plots—a hundred acres of flat paddy fields surrounded by rocky
hills. Most of our stops involved the inputs that participating farmers
were applying to their fields. We first visited two vermicompost tanks
in a farmer's yard, filled with composting worms digesting food scraps
(fig. 3). In 2009, the Biodiversity Board subsidized twenty such tanks for
the pilot project, thirteen of which produced eleven tons of compost in
2010. To supplement the early stages of vermicompost output, the board
had also shipped in additional organic compost for the pilot area, about
one ton per acre.[7]

3. The Kerala State Biodiversity Board's subsidized
vermicompost tanks at Padayetti. Photo by the author.

Our next stop included panchagavayya drums, the contents of which
were being applied to the rice fields as well. Thanal staff, familiar in creating these mixtures, had assisted in training farmers how to make the dual
fertilizer-pesticide concoction. Vermicompost and panchagavayya were
the main agricultural inputs in the fields and gardens of this pilot project.

To combat heat and drought, the Biodiversity Board had also assisted
in the construction of a few traditional rainwater-harvesting kokkarni,
which dotted the landscape. The Biodiversity Board had decided to subsidize kokkarni construction after drought conditions destroyed six acres
of paddy fields in 2009. Staff found that paddy fields near existing sources
of water and kokkarni fared better during the drought.[8] One newspaper

4. Rice paddy plots in Padayetti. A flier for a CPI(M)candidate
for the 2011 election is pasted to the tree in the foreground.
Photo by the author.

reporter extolled these new ponds as part of Padayetti's "second independence," referring to the fact that the ponds diminished area farmers' reliance on Green Revolution technologies, such as irrigation from water
sources farther afield. Locally based water sources provided the rice farmers with more latitude in determining their cropping patterns and seed
choices each growing season.[9]

We then toured the rice paddy fields that had just been planted with
seeds a few weeks earlier (fig. 4). The Biodiversity Board had supplied
several of these farmers with seeds, including *navara,* a medicinal red rice
traditionally grown throughout Kerala. As we walked along the raised
footpaths between the plots of rice, Suresh marveled at the changes he

had witnessed over the months since the board had launched its pilot project. According to him, many of the fields had previously been left fallow or had been filled with various cash crops. In contrast, after just the first year of the pilot, the hundred acres produced enough organic rice to feed the village's sixty-six families, with excess that was sold to local markets and in Thanal's organic bazaar in Thiruvananthapuram.[10] In 2010, Padayetti's residents had also cultivated around nine metric tons of organic vegetables in their home gardens and around the margins of the paddy fields in 2010. They sold about 30 percent of these vegetables in local markets as surplus, a new source of income for these families, for a total profit of 85,000 rupees. Suresh noted that this amount was extra cash for the families, who had not grown their own vegetables before the start of the Biodiversity Board's project but had purchased the majority of their food from markets.[11]

Between 2008 and 2011, the board also commissioned several scientists from local universities to monitor the biodiversity and soil conditions in the area. The initial results suggested that organic farming methods and the application of vermicompost and panchagavayya enhanced the soil ecology of the paddy fields and protected the biodiversity of the area. For example, in preliminary research on soil chemistry and wetland fauna, Dr. S. Bijoy Nandan at Cochin University of Science and Technology in Kochi, Kerala, found the organic soils of the pilot area to be healthier than nearby soils receiving chemical fertilizers.[12] The soils of the pilot paddy fields contained more organic carbon, for example, as well as more bacteria, microorganisms important for soil metabolism and decomposition.[13] Another preliminary study by Dr. Sabu K. Thomas from St. Joseph's College in Calicut, Kerala, discovered that the soil biodiversity of arthropods (basically, insects, spiders, and crustaceans) was higher in Padayetti compared to a nearby area cultivated with chemical inputs, an important fact given that many of these are natural predators of crop-eating insects.[14] Additionally, Biodiversity Board researchers recorded an increased numbers of bird species in the organic area and hypothesized that their abundance was the result of the larger number of insects likely present in organic fields.[15] Similarly, farmers reported anecdotally that local fish species had reappeared in their paddy fields.[16]

For advocates such as Thanal and the Biodiversity Board, these early outcomes reinforced the ecological and social viability of organic farming. To them, the organic farming project at Padayetti, despite a few setbacks, exemplified their ideal of what agriculture could and should look like in Kerala.[17] Not only was the pilot producing several tons of food but initial research was proving that organic farming was improving the biogeochemical and ecological conditions of the area. Organic agriculture was protecting Padayetti's agrobiodiversity. The two organizations also used Padayetti as an example to illustrate concretely that organic farming could make individual farmers and communities self-sufficient, especially in making their own fertilizers, pesticides, and food. Usha and others at Thanal argued that the pilot project demonstrated how farmers could break their reliance on external markets for their basic nutritional needs—a stark contrast to the existing, Green Revolution–based agrofood system in Kerala.

Additionally, during ongoing policy discussions with the Agriculture Department and its new Organic Farming Programme, Thanal and the Biodiversity Board held up Padayetti as a model of successful local self-government planning based on organic farming principles.[18] Much of this assessment was based on their interaction with the local *padakshera samithi*, an existing farmers' group created by the LDF government in the late 1980s to encourage effective joint management of financial, natural, and human resources. During decentralization, the LDF relied on these groups throughout Kerala to foster local self-government, in collaboration with the Agriculture Department. Thanal and the Biodiversity Board worked with and through Padayetti's padakshera samithi to make decisions about the entire organic farming process—from what seeds to plant to how to market their surpluses, from plow to plate. Both Thanal and the board believed that their efforts upheld the values embodied in the People's Plan, an LDF priority.

PADAYETTI'S SUCCESS had a ripple effect in the state. Under the new Organic Farming Programme, the Agriculture Department initially selected twenty block panchayats, dispersed throughout each of Kerala's fourteen districts, to follow Padayetti's example. The northern district of Wayanad, for example, received about $30,000 for organic farming in three block panchayats: Kanyambetta, Nenmeni, and Edavaka. Each area was expected to convert forty-five contiguous acres of rice and/or vegetables to organic agriculture by the end of 2011, in collaboration and discussion with local farmers' groups. In alignment with principles of decentralization, the local agriculture officers and farmers' groups could use the funds as they saw fit within these areas.[19]

For instance, the Kanyambetta block panchayat dispersed its funds to subsidize organic paddy cultivation alone, by providing organic inputs to 135 farmers. These inputs included neem (the byproduct of neem trees) and pseudomonas (a naturally occurring soil bacteria that is regularly used for biological pest control). According to the panchayat's agriculture officer, when the Organic Farming Programme's funds became available, officials from the Agriculture Department's local office facilitated meetings of the padakshera samithis; at the gatherings, farmers decided what inputs were necessary for organic rice farming. The department then supplied these inputs to a nearby warehouse. The department also selected a farmer to preside over and monitor the other farmers participating in the scheme. In contrast, after holding five meetings in the Nenmeni block panchayat, the local agriculture office and the padakshera samithi decided to use their funds from the Organic Farming Programme in another manner. They gave both cash (about 6,000 rupees per hectare) and inputs to about 250 farmers, to support organic rice and vegetable cultivation. Nenmeni also held organic farming training sessions, so that farmers could learn to create their own inputs with cow manure and vermicompost.[20]

For ongoing training and advice, agricultural officials in each block panchayat are relying upon two manuals from the Agriculture Department and KAU: *Jaiva Krishi Sahai* (2010), which translates into "organic farming help," and *Ad-Hoc Package of Practices, Recommendations for Organic Farming* (2009). These advisory materials, which detail best practices for organic farming production in Kerala, are completely new resources coming from the historically pesticide-friendly agricultural bureaucracy, the result of changing norms within KAU and the Agriculture Department, initiated by the debate and discussions around the organic farming policy.[21]

Each local agriculture office is also assisting farmers in selling their surplus rice to nearby markets—some of it at a price premium and some of which is being claimed by interested consumers before harvest even occurs. At meetings of padakshera samithis and gatherings of farmers in their panchayats, local people now regularly discuss these issues of the supply chain, production, and consumption. At one of the meetings I attended in Wayanad, farmers debated ways in which they could promote direct and local procurement and marketing under the Organic Farming Programme, without any middlemen. The local agriculture officer also brainstormed techniques and means by which farmers could obtain (and then preserve) quality organic seeds that season, without having to buy them from the market. The Organic Farming Programme has therefore been critical in promoting the active engagement of farmers in organic agro-food chains and governance, as they make decentralized decisions about how to utilize Agriculture Department funds and scale up organic production.

AS THE Organic Farming Programme grows in scope, it encounters farmers and communities in Kerala who have already been farming organically for years—many of whom are certified organic for export. Hundreds of farmers in Wayanad District, for example, have chosen to focus their agricultural efforts not solely on rice for domestic consumption, as the Biodiversity Board has envisioned with its policy, but organic cash crops for export. Kerala's certified organic farming movement has its origins here, and the debate about whether organic agriculture serves locals or wealthy foreigners re-emerges, bringing globalization back into the picture.

Geographically, Wayanad seems very unlike Palakkad, where the Biodiversity Board's initial efforts were based. It is located farther north, in Kerala's highlands in the Western Ghats and on the boundary of India's Deccan Plateau. Only one major highway crosses the district, a steep climb that has nine hairpin turns from the south and often just one lane for traffic. At the top of the ascent, the air temperature is significantly cooler.

Wayanad's agrarian sector revolves mostly around cash crops, much of them for export. Its climate, remote setting in the highlands of Kerala, and plantations made it "the scene of the 'wildest, maddest, and grossest speculation'" under British colonialism, especially as the region faced competition from the commercialization of raw materials from around the world.[22] In the nineteenth century, British investors and planters created large-scale teak, coffee, tea, and rubber plantations in the area, contributing to Britain's economic power, trade, and infrastructure.[23]

After Indian independence, the newly formed Kerala state government continued to promote the extensive cultivation of cash crops in Wayanad by exempting many of the existing plantations from the ceilings imposed by the land reforms and by promoting Green Revolution chemical inputs. For example, Kerala's legislators exempt coffee from land reforms to placate the several, large-scale coffee plantation owners who were bringing foreign exchange into the state.[24] Thanks to the creation of a real estate market by the land reform laws, the cheap price of land in isolated areas of Wayanad, and food shortages after World War II, the district also experienced several waves of immigration.[25] Many of these settlers were Indian-born Christians (who refer to themselves as Syrian Christians, demarcating their Eastern Christian religious roots) from southern Kerala, who previously had little access to land ownership as a result of historical caste discrimination and political economic relations.[26]

With its extraordinary dependence on cash crops and chemicals compared to other districts, Wayanad experienced Kerala's agrarian crisis acutely. It had the highest number of farmer suicides of any district in the state in the first few years of the century: 534 between 2001 and 2006, largely as a result of agrarian distress.[27] Of Wayanad's current residents, 90 percent depend on agriculture for sustenance, and they aren't growing rice: 80 percent of Kerala's coffee comes from the district, and it is the largest producer of ginger in the state. Wayanad is also the second largest producer of spices such as black pepper and cardamom.[28] As the state's Department of Economics and Statistics says, "The back bone of the economy of this district is plantation crops."[29]

Despite—or because of—this dependence on cash crops, Wayanad has been at the forefront of Kerala's *certified* organic farming movement for over ten years. Several leading organizations dedicated to certified organic agriculture are now based in the district.

The first historically significant certified organic entity is INFAM, the Indian Farmers' Movement. In response to the suicides and agricultural hardships in the district, many of which were affecting the recently settled Syrian Christian groups, several religious leaders and activists of the Catholic Church came together in 2000 to form INFAM.[30] INFAM was originally a Wayanad-based movement populated by mostly Syrian Christian producers concerned about crop die-offs, declining prices for their commodities, suicides, and pesticide poisonings. The organization purports to "[enable] the farmers to improve their agricultural methods, to demand reasonable prices for their products, and to fight together against injustice, bribery and exploitation. It promotes also communal harmony and understanding among the people."[31] Led by Catholic priests, the organization is comprised of committees of elected officers at the diocesan, district, and panchayat levels. INFAM meetings are regularly held on church grounds or after Catholic Mass on Sundays.

On behalf of farmers and the agrarian sector, INFAM regularly protests government leaders and banks, fields candidates for political offices, organizes seminars and training sessions, sets up self-help and support groups for communities, and develops crisis hotlines—common activities among political groups in Kerala.[32] Several Catholic priests involved in organic farming in the state also confided to me their admiration for its history of radical labor politics. Hence, while not officially affiliated with a political party, INFAM's membership and organizational aims have built on the momentum generated by previous social movements and reforms within Kerala.[33] INFAM claims to now be the largest farmers' organization in Kerala.[34]

One of INFAM's priority project areas is organic farming and moving farmers away from chemical-intensive agriculture. As its website states: "INFAM promotes eco-friendly farming habits, bio-diversity and diffusion of folk wisdom related to farming.... We also provide the farmers with region-specific advice regarding seeds, manure, and crops and about the marketing of agricultural produce."[35] This has translated into INFAM encouraging farmers "to adopt the best farming techniques from various parts of the world and popularize natural food and medicine."[36]

One organic farmer and INFAM member divulged to me that the emphasis on sustainable agriculture was so strong in the organization at its inception that leaders told the members they *must* convert to organic farming because chemical farming had contaminated the land, water, and soil. According to this farmer, Catholic priests also insisted that farmers in Wayanad—already tied into international markets through cash crop agriculture—could earn more money from European and American markets if *certified* organic. These leaders believed that certified organic production, as opposed to organic production without any certification, could provide a competitive edge for Indian farmers in foreign markets. Although INFAM shared many of the goals and values expressed in the state's 2010 organic farming policy, it did not emphasize growing staple crops for domestic production as strongly as the Biodiversity Board.

Certified organic farming, full of established national and international rules, was a completely new venture for INFAM. Organic certification— a system of standards, legally agreed-upon claims and labels, and inspections conducted by a third party—guarantees that crops are grown without harmful chemicals. In India, organic standards are set by the Agriculture and Food Products Export Development Authority (APEDA) of the Ministry of Commerce, under India's National Programme for Organic Production (NPOP). In 2006, both the United States and the European Union approved these Indian standards as sufficient to meet their import requirements for organic food. Certified organic and Fair Trade farmers in Kerala have received up to five hundred times the price for their products compared to conventionally grown foodstuffs.

Father Joseph Varghese Peringarapillil, a leader in INFAM, explained to me how the organization came to be involved in certified organic agriculture. He himself had grown up in a farming family in Kerala and was therefore familiar with the trials of an agrarian livelihood. "The social . . . conditions, and the conditions of farmers, impressed me," Peringarapillil began. "And [the] social teaching of the Church inspired me; the last few Popes inspired me. So I took to agriculture, went to Milan University, [and] took to the agriculture faculty." While he was a student in Italy, the Church held the Second Vatican Council, a convocation of

Church leaders that unrolled modernizing reforms in the institution, to encourage greater lay participation. Peringarapillil elaborated on how the Second Vatican Council moved him: "I consider myself a real product of Vatican II, change in the Church. . . . That has influenced my social outlook, my theological outlook, and all that formation."

Yet it was not just the reforms within the Church that inspired Peringarapillil to work for change. The writings of Japanese farmer Masanobu Fukuoka, which had also influenced Usha's thinking at Thanal, clinched his decision to focus on farming in ways different from those that had been promoted under the Green Revolution. "He was a scientist—university scientist—and a professor, who gave up everything and came back to be a farmer, yes," Peringarapillil said of Fukuoka. "So that inspired many groups in the South. He was an inspiration, especially . . . through one of his books, *One Straw Revolution*. . . . And I . . . got the confidence I can work, I can go, anybody can go the organic way."

Certified organic agriculture, according to Peringarapillil, held the key to "going the organic way" in South India. For him, organic certification represented "ample opportunity for growing and marketing, and farmers' condition [would] become better." When I asked him how he had learned about the certification process, he credited his time in Europe for his discovery that there were growing consumer markets for organic foodstuffs. Around the same time, in the late 1990s, the Indian government had also started to consider national organic farming standards. Several farmers had even begun experimenting with certification in Wayanad; however, funding for their efforts was limited.[37]

P. J. Chackochan, a Syrian Christian farmer from Wayanad involved in INFAM and a friend of Peringarapillil's, was one such farmer encouraged early on by INFAM to pursue certification. He had been growing medicinal plants, vegetables, and cash crops organically since 1991, after being haunted by the memory of an event that had occurred several years earlier: His young cousin accidentally mixed a bag of the pesticide ecalex into a pond of pet fish, leading to the sudden death of the fish. Chackochan had vowed to promote organic agriculture ever since. On one occasion, he explained to me his initial inquiry into third-party certification, through an inspection and certification agency based in Europe. He recollected the certification and inspection fees he was quoted in the year 2000: over 200,000 rupees per year as an individual farmer. A fee equaling nearly $4,000, just to be able to export organic foodstuffs abroad, was too high for him to pay on an annual basis.

Other international agencies had similar pricing schemes; according to staff at the India-based certification agency, Indocert, some international entities would charge more than the annual income of an Indian farmer just for one day of inspection. Peringarapillil argued vehemently that such fees were unscrupulous: "Some of the clever Western . . . certification bodies were exploiting . . . farmers. And the corporates, in a big way, like, like, they used to get a remuneration of five hundred dollars per day, and a posh star hotel . . . for certification. . . . And the corporates could afford [it]." In other words, the majority of Indian farmers—unlike larger farmers or those connected to corporate bodies—could not manage the cost of having a third party guaranteeing that their farms were authentically organic.

To circumvent these hefty certification fees, Peringarapillil and others began investigating other options for any farmer interested in organic crops in Kerala, not just in Wayanad. In 2000, with financial assistance from the Catholic Church, Peringarapillil attended an IFOAM meeting in Switzerland. He took along a congregant in his church, Mathew Sebastian, who had a business background and had approached the priest earlier to express his interest in certification. During this trip, Peringarapillil recalled that they encountered members of Organic Agriculture Certification Thailand (ACT), an organic certification agency based in that country. The existence of ACT, an organization outside of Europe and America, fueled their desire to set up a similar entity in India.

Serendipitously, Peringarapillil and Sebastian also met with a German staff member of IFOAM who had previously traveled to Kerala. He so fondly recalled his experiences that he introduced the two Keralites to the Swiss State Secretariat for Economic Affairs (SECO), a government agency under the Swiss Ministry of Commerce. This agency had been investing in development initiatives in countries like India, and the idea of India-based certification piqued its interest.[38] After several rounds of discussions, SECO eventually funded two organizations to set up an Indian pilot certification body: the Research Institute of Organic Agriculture (FiBL) and Bio.Inspecta, a Swiss certifier. Together with Peringarapillil and Sebastian, FiBL and Bio.Inspecta formed an experimental body: the Indian Organic Certification Agency, now colloquially known as Indocert.

Indian certification proceeded to take off rapidly after this watershed event. The Indian Ministry of Commerce immediately took to Indocert, holding it up as a model for new and future Indian certification bodies.[39] In 2002, Indocert received accreditation from APEDA. Indocert then certified its first organic farmer under the requirements of India's new NPOP: Wayanad's own Chackochan. As for FiBL, it continued to fund Indocert and train staff in organic certification, inspection, quality control, and accreditation until 2008. Today, Indocert is an independent entity. Peringarapillil is currently the president of Indocert, and Mathew Sebastian is its executive director.[40]

Peringarapillil believes that India-based certification empowers farmers in Kerala, by providing them access to foreign markets without having to rely on European certifiers who require "posh hotels" when visiting India. According to him, certification based in India is "revolutionary" and "something popular, for the people, for the ordinary [farmer]."

Indocert now works like this: It has sliding fees, depending on the size of a farm, the hours involved to inspect it, and travel time. Costs are calculated on an hourly basis. One large-scale farmer reported paying around 14,500 rupees, about $270, for certification in one year.

These fees are even less for individuals participating in group certification through an internal control system (ICS) or an official certified organic farming group.[41] IFOAM defines an ICS as "a documented quality assurance system that allows an external certification body to delegate the annual inspection of individual group members to an identified body/unit within the certified operator. This means in practice that a growers group basically controls all farmers for compliance with organic production rules according to defined procedures."[42] A third-party certifier like Indocert audits an ICS for compliance by reviewing the group's documentation and inspecting some (but not all) farmers on its own.[43] Because many Indian farmers have struggled to pay Indocert's annual fee—despite how much cheaper it is than those of foreign certifying bodies—INFAM advises groups of farmers to form ICSs.

The recognition of ICSs is relatively novel. In 2000, IFOAM had vigorously explored systemizing certified organic group farming because of the high number of small farmers who were unable to participate in certified organic farming as individuals, mostly due to certification costs. The history of ICS recognition is detailed on IFOAM's website: "In 2000, IFOAM . . . brought together certifiers, producers and certifying authorities during 3 workshops (2001–2003) and led to the production of the document on 'Smallholder Group Certification: Compilation of Results.'" After this process, the EU began recognizing ICSs as reputable organic farming entities—this recognition encompassed 150,000 small farmers, organized under 350 ICSs.[44]

One of those three workshops was held in Bangalore, India, less than a day's drive from Wayanad. Several farmers with connections to INFAM attended. The resulting smallholder ICS manual—IFOAM *Training Manual for Organic Agriculture in the Tropics* (2004)—is based on the experiences of group farming in Wayanad. Kerala's organic farmers therefore played a pivotal role in shaping global organic group-farming standards.

In 2003, INFAM created an ICS of its own, Organic Wayanad, to assist small landowners with organic group certification.[45] Farmers earn profits individually (depending on how much they grow and sell) but are certified together as Organic Wayanad. Farmers who join this organization pay 300 rupees (less than $6) per acre on an annual basis for organic certification. Half of that cost is currently subsidized by a national scheme through the Ministry of Agriculture's National Horticultural Mission, at a rate of 150 rupees per acre for each farmer during each year of the three-year period needed for converting land to organic agriculture.[46]

Organic Wayanad was the first ICS that Indocert certified. As an ICS, it pays annual inspection and certification fees to Indocert, at a rate of 750 rupees an hour for no more than 6,000 rupees in a day, the equivalent of $100. Because Organic Wayanad is an ICS, only a few farms are actually the subject of on-site visits every year, which cuts costs for the organization. Currently, Organic Wayanad includes around four hundred households with a total of twelve hundred acres of certified land. About 80 percent of farmers involved in this ICS have connections to INFAM, and the majority of them are from Syrian Christian communities. Chacko-chan, Indocert's first certified organic farmer, is also a member of Organic Wayanad.[47] Organic Wayanad is split into several smaller groups that are anchored in geographic areas, such as panchayats. These groups meet regularly, from once a month to once every two months, to share information about government subsidies for agricultural production, communicate difficulties, pass on advice, and debate how profits from organic production should be allotted and used. At one Organic Wayanad meeting, Chackochan informed attending members about a new organic banana subsidy from the local agriculture office. At several additional meetings I attended, I witnessed farmers making arrangements to share traditional seed varieties by picking them up from the houses of their colleagues and inviting others over to observe new methods of cultivation. These ICS meetings, therefore, serve as crucial seed-sharing, networking, and knowledge-transfer opportunities for like-minded farmers that did not previously exist in an organized form.

After forming Organic Wayanad, INFAM was also fundamental in setting up one more organization: the Indian Organic Farmers Producer Company Limited (IOFPCL), bringing the number of seminal third-party organic certification institutions in Kerala to four:

- INFAM: Indian Farmers Movement
- Indocert: Indian Organic Certification Agency
- IOFPCL: Indian Organic Farmers Producer Company Limited (marketing company)
- Organic Wayanad (ICS in Wayanad, Kerala)

Registered in 2004 under the Indian Companies Act of 1956, IOFPCL is a marketing and procurement entity for organic products that acts as a liaison between its organic shareholders and buyers. It facilitates the pooling of agricultural commodities for export by small farmers and shareholders so that they can avoid middlemen. Rather, the farmers are now their own middlemen: IOFPCL does the work, but on their behalf, not its own profits. IOFPCL has over six hundred organic farming shareholders from South

India, and it is headquartered in Kerala. All of its members are certified by Indocert. Shares cost a one time fee of 1,000 rupees but can be purchased by an ICS, making it affordable for small farmers; the minimum membership requirement is ten shares. Organic Wayanad is a shareholder. Peringarapillil and Chackochan are board members.

With financial assistance from Indian government agencies, IOFPCL staff attend international and national trade fairs to negotiate directly with buyers. Since 2007, they have been attending Biofach, a global exhibition of organic products, organized by IFOAM and other partners and held annually in Germany.[48] Chackochan usually attends Biofach on behalf of IOFPCL and Organic Wayanad. At these gatherings, literate and able to speak English, he meets directly with various buyers interested in organic products from Kerala. Chackochan has subsequently conversed with several of these buyers via phone and email. A few interested buyers have even come to visit him in Kerala, and he has been to Europe to meet with these buyers, one on one, as well. Because of the connections made at Biofach, IOFPCL has been exporting several organic commodities to European and American buyers through the port of Kochi, Kerala, since 2007.[49]

Between 2010 and 2011, IOFPCL exported several organic products, all at premiums between 5.77 to 500 percent above the market price for nonorganic foodstuffs (table 1). Shareholders in the organization have therefore obtained better financial returns by changing their production practices to qualify for organic certification, a value addition to their commodities. This revenue has allowed farmers to expand and improve their businesses. Chackochan, for one, built a testing and processing facility for his organic medicinal plants business called Vanamoolika. IOFPCL now shares this facility to test several of the commodities it has procured from farmers for chemical residues, moisture, and microbial content.[50]

In 2010, IOFPCL connected with a German coffee buyer at Biofach, and since then it has been shipping around eighteen tons of certified organic coffee to Germany each year.[51] Organic Wayanad has been filling most of this order, marking a significant change in Kerala's history of selling coffee.[52] Prior to joining Organic Wayanad, farmers had been selling the entirety of their coffee crops to local and regional agents and shops. Most

TABLE 1. Average Price Premium Received for Certified Organic
Commodities for IOFPCL Farmers from 2010 to 2011*

Product	Conventional price (rs./kg)	Organic price (rs./kg)	% difference in price	Quantity sold (kg)
Black pepper	150	180	20	1,300
White pepper	200	350	75	101
Cardamom	1,000	1,300	30	135
Coffee	52	55	5.77	57,555
Vanilla	1,000	2,000	100	329
Coconut (fresh)	14	18	28.57	8,573
Turmeric (fresh)	20	25	25	2,500
Ginger (fresh)	20	40	100	500
Chili (fresh)	50	300	500	500

*As reported by IOFPCL.

of this coffee, typically of the robusta variety, would end up in blends marketed by national and multinational corporations such as Nestlé India, Tata Coffee, and Hindustan Lever.[53] Therefore, before the introduction of organic certification, Kerala was not known for high-value coffee and did not trade directly with international buyers, despite being one of the largest producers of coffee in India. Organic certification changed this landscape.

Since many farmers had complained about the time lag between harvesting their coffee and then receiving compensation, IOFPCL negotiated an advance payment from the German coffee buyer before its second shipment of coffee the following year. Typically, buyers agree upon an advance purchase price with the marketing agency, and they only pay it in full after they receive their products. The period between the harvesting of a commodity like coffee (which happens in January and February) and the arrival of foodstuffs in Europe or America is several months. During these months the coffee is dried, hulled, and graded, then shipped via boat.

In November 2010, the coffee buyer agreed to pay Organic Wayanad's farmers 51 rupees per kilogram for dried coffee, with an advance to provide for processing costs and to pay a portion to farmers at the time of procurement.[54] The market rate for nonorganic coffee at the time the agreement was drafted was 38 rupees per kilogram. Farmers in Organic Wayanad therefore considered the buyer's offer of 51 rupees a fair price and were glad to be receiving payment for their work more quickly than usual.

However, the global price of coffee increased between November and January, due to widespread disease in Brazil's coffee crops.[55] In January 2011, at the time of harvesting and processing in Wayanad, the price of nonorganic, dried conventional coffee rose to over 52 rupees per kilogram in the area—one rupee above the agreed-upon price for Organic Wayanad. Buyers and traders quickly moved in to procure organic and nonorganic coffee from farmers throughout Wayanad at a price higher than what Organic Wayanad had agreed to in advance with its buyer in Germany.

K. M. George, the coordinator of the ICS, explained how the organization coped with the situation: "When the price was thirty-eight [rupees per kilogram], we made an agreement to sell at fifty-one. In January, the price of coffee went to fifty-two here. Now, can we change an agreement?" he asked me. "We made an agreement and they gave us an advance. So, can we change the agreement?" He emphasized again that Organic Wayanad and IOFPCL had already negotiated the contract, and well in advance to accommodate farmers' requests. George had worried that farmers would renege on their end of the arrangement, but he was also anxious about how the buyer would respond. "Anyway, we mailed a request," he explained.

"Okay, so you wrote a letter?" I asked.

"Yeah, we wrote saying that a problem happened, the price went up ... so think about it," said George. "So, they made calculations ... they reversed and gave us fifty-five."

"So, you wrote the letter, and the buyer said 'it'll do fifty-five?'"

"Yeah," George answered. The buyer had been willing to renegotiate the contract. "We asked sixty rupees. We need sixty rupees. But they increased to fifty-five."

"Do you know, when you wrote the letter, did the buyer get angry? Did the buyer understand?"

George replied that his opinion was that they understood: "I think they understood, because we sent the letter along with [news]paper cuttings. So they must have understood." The newspaper stories that he mailed with the letter included information about the rise in coffee prices in South India.

To gauge the receptiveness of the buyer, I questioned him further. "Then how many weeks, months, did it take for the buyer to respond?"

He answered, "We wrote in January, and in February—"

I interrupted him. "Oh, in one month?"

He nodded and confirmed it. "In one month, they decided."

Organic Wayanad, with IOFPCL's help, not only bargained to get an advance from its coffee buyer in 2010 but successfully and quickly persuaded the buyer to increase its payment to farmers to 55 rupees per kilogram for coffee (table 2). This type of bargaining is uncommon, particularly in conventional coffee markets. Organic Wayanad's organic certification and IOFPCL's assistance with marketing created this opportunity for direct negotiation, with real benefits for farmers. During a monthly meeting of Organic Wayanad, farmers agreed to utilize the profits from this and previous orders toward school scholarships for the children of group members.

To understand the role certification is playing in Kerala's organic farming scene, and to find out how farmers are feeling about certification processes, I asked Chackochan, as a pioneer certified organic farmer in Kerala, for his thoughts about IOFPCL's and Organic Wayanad's relationship to this particular coffee buyer. George, for instance, had admitted that some of the ICS's farmers were disappointed that the buyer would not give them more money per kilogram of coffee, given the current market rate of 52 rupees per kilogram for conventional coffee. Chackochan, on the other hand, remained convinced that IOFPCL and Organic Wayanad had established a long-term and dependable relationship with this buyer. This relationship would likely provide income security and stability for farmers in years to come, especially through the inevitable boom-and-bust cycles of agriculture. He admitted that relationship building with

TABLE 2. Market Rate vs. Negotiated Price for Organic Wayanad's 2011 Organic Coffee Order

	Market rate for nonorganic coffee (rs./kg)	Negotiated price for Organic Wayanad's coffee (rs./kg)
November 2010	38	51
January 2011	52	55
Percent increase	36.84	7.84

buyers at conferences like Biofach was time consuming and stressful, but he stated proudly that IOFPCL now had a reputation for being trustworthy in European organic circles; this had been, after all, the second order of coffee from this particular buyer. And indeed, Organic Wayanad and IOFPCL have been shipping around the same quantity of coffee to the same buyer on an annual basis ever since.[56]

"Doesn't this mean that Europeans and Americans are still the ones setting standards and controlling trade?" I asked Chackochan candidly one evening, after learning about the certified coffee order and the small price differential between organic and nonorganic coffee.

Chackochan repudiated my statement. "Organic standards say 'no chemicals,'" he responded, "and we don't use chemicals." He pointed out that he had already been farming organically before receiving certification. Certification merely enabled him to access competitive markets while he engaged in the same production practices he had long been doing.

"But," I continued, "isn't it difficult to learn all the rules and read about all the standards in the NPOP?"

Chackochan responded that to help farmers learn about national standards, Organic Wayanad hosted frequent training sessions, with assistance from the Malayalam speakers at Indocert. Indeed, a two-week training session sponsored by the ICS that I had attended laboriously defined the key organic institutions, how inspections worked, and how to fill out necessary forms. Peringarapillil had also pointed out that most farmers in Kerala already knew how to read and write, thanks to the state government's investment in education; and with the advent of Indocert and the hiring of Keralite inspectors to explain guidelines and the inspection process to local farmers, certification did not involve cumbersome standards that were difficult to decipher.[57] And Chackochan, Peringarapillil, and George all insisted that compared with farmers' previous encounters with certification programs run by foreign entities, Indocert's certification process was friendly to the culture and language of Kerala.,[58]

Several other farmers I spoke with informally during regular Organic Wayanad meetings and training sessions also told me that prior to certification they were farming organically—that is, without pesticides. Certification merely rewarded these existing practices.[59] Chackochan and other farmers regularly compared their organic farming practices to what their fathers and forefathers used to do, with older Indian technologies and traditions that predated the Green Revolution. At one of the ICS's organic farming training programs, leaders emphasized this point—that organic farming was the farming of previous generations—again and again. Furthermore, George, who led the training, pointed out that today's *certified* organic farming scheme was fortunately more flexible and technologically savvy compared to the agricultural practices of the previous generations. Unlike earlier farming practices, certified organic farming encompassed zero-budget, natural, Vedic, and biodynamic farming, as well as other technologies and methods, such as no-till agriculture.[60] His point was that farmers could pick from any one of those production methods, whichever they saw as suitable for their lifestyles, and still be certified organic for export. They all fostered sustainability and biodiversity by prescribing practices such as crop rotation, companion planting, and the utilization of organic inputs.

Chackochan also emphasized that IOFPCL and Organic Wayanad had now earned the reputation domestically of being a group of veritable organic farmers in northern Kerala—something that certification guaranteed and was a necessity for concerned Indian consumers. At a monthly meeting of Organic Wayanad's farmers that I observed, Chackochan announced that several consumer groups and outlets in nearby cities had heard about their organic farming activities and had approached him and

George to develop the equivalent of a Community Supported Agriculture (CSA) program, where farmers would directly provide weekly boxes filled with local, organic produce to interested consumer households. "We can now decide which crops to grow," Chackochan had declared, because of the financial flexibility these increased marketing opportunities would bring, and because many of these consumers were looking for a variety of seasonal vegetables and fruits from their local farmers. He encouraged members to help him develop these local consumer-farmer connections.

Chackochan used such examples to prove that he and others in Organic Wayanad were not farming just for external markets, or according to European and American standards. Instead, certified organic farming is creating opportunities for like-minded groups of farmers to discuss how they can better their own farming practices and livelihoods through organic farming. These efforts are paying off at home as well as abroad by expanding markets and benefiting farming communities that had been hard hit by the agrarian crisis.[61]

NOT SURPRISINGLY, Kerala's 2010 organic farming policy has been the subject of much discussion among certified farmers in districts like Wayanad who had already been farming organically. One afternoon, for instance, I was eating lunch with trainees in Organic Wayanad's two-week workshop for new organic farmers. We had been together for eight days already, learning about panchagavayya, vermicompost, IOFPCL, the benefits of organic farming for human health and the environment, and how to fill out forms for Indocert. As we chatted casually over our meal of organic rice and vegetables and became better acquainted with each other, George launched into a discussion of the organic farming policy. "Because it's there," he told the trainees, "funding for organic farming projects is likely to increase." He encouraged them to take advantage of the current favorable policy climate, especially since several farmers in the neighboring Kanyambetta, Nenmeni, and Edavaka block panchayats of Wayanad were initial beneficiaries under the Organic Farming Programme. George used the existence of the policy to argue that the attendees were not venturing into unknown territory with their newfound interest in certified organic agriculture, where they would be peculiar or alone in farming circles. Organic farming was a growing movement in Kerala, he emphasized, and increasingly supported at the state level.

George then turned to one of the attendees, Nina, who had announced earlier that she was involved in Kudumbashree, the LDF's local political engagement initiative for women. He suggested that she broach the issue of organic farming in that organization, and put bottom-up pressure on the state government and political parties to further increase organic farming projects in the state. "You can influence politics," he said to her, hoping to take advantage of the decentralized local political channels in Wayanad. Nina had nodded. She was a new organic farmer herself, hoping to make her land more productive and earn more income for her family.

George's request to Nina stemmed partially from Organic Wayanad's existing and growing political work. Several organic farmers in the ICS were beginning to feel politically confident enough to lobby for their interests at the state capital. In 2010, they prepared and delivered a memorandum of understanding to the Chief Minister, requesting remuneration for losses endured by farmers who were engaged in organic agriculture. One of the farmers told me that he had not considered himself active politically before becoming engaged in organic farming, which had empowered him and his community.

George's comments also illustrate the fact that existing organic farmers have been observing the progress of Kerala's organic farming policy with interest. His discussion with Nina in reference to Kudumbashree, the local-level institution, also exemplifies how farmers in the state are taking advantage of the momentum from decentralization to put greater and ongoing pressure on the state government to continue its experimentation with organic agriculture.

ORGANIC AGRICULTURE is reembedding market-driven agriculture into social and ecological relations in Kerala, as farmers become more empowered to participate in globalized commodity chains on favorable terms *and* in the state's decentralized planning processes.[62] Both the organic farming policy and organic certification have also been crucial in transforming agriculture in the state to become more self-sufficient and

ecologically viable—for example, through certification with a more affordable, India-based certifier, and through the production of less poisonous farm inputs by farmers themselves on their land. Kerala's particular
political and cultural history facilitated these developments and experiments. Its educated and organized populace, for instance, was in a position to take advantage of certification, perhaps unlike other communities
in the global South.[63]

Organic farming in Kerala is empowering farmers. The state's Organic
Farming Programme is now promoting and increasing small farmers' engagement in decentralized governance. The organic farming policy is the
latest, most far-reaching instance of an ongoing shift in state agricultural
governance to better engage farmers and local communities in an agricultural system that once prioritized yields and chemicals. Similarly, organic certification is providing opportunities for farmers to work with
distant buyers in globalized commodity chains and to negotiate the terms
of trade (such as purchasing prices) through direct marketing relationships. Certified organic farming is also boosting the political presence of
farmers regionally by facilitating the formation of local farmers groups
(for example, the ICS Organic Wayanad). These groups now collaborate
on and determine which production processes will best benefit them.

In light of these political and economic benefits, it is not surprising that
the momentum for organic agriculture in Kerala is growing. The year
after the government finalized the organic farming policy, India's national courts ordered a ban on the manufacture, sale, and use of endosulfan in the country.[64] Kerala's Agriculture Department went further a few
months later: in 2011 it issued an immediate order banning all red- ("extremely toxic") and yellow- ("highly toxic") labeled chemical pesticides in
the state—totaling fourteen chemicals.[65] This ban was upheld even after
the LDF lost power in the state parliamentary elections and a coalition
led by the more moderate Congress party took over the Assembly in May
2011, a testament to broad support for organic farming across party lines.
The successive political coalitions have channeled more funds to the Organic Farming Programme, so that its annual budget is now close to $2
million, to continue growing organic farming in the state.[66]

Other Indian states are following in Kerala's footsteps. Twelve are currently either discussing or have organic farming policies in place, some of which were inspired by organic farming within Kerala. Many visitors, including Vandana Shiva, have repeatedly come to the state to learn about and laud its organic farming efforts. India is now one of the fastest growing areas for organic production, and over half a million organic farmers are located in the nation.[67] And in India, more than twenty other organic certification organizations have been established since the formation of Indocert.[68]

The diversity of Kerala's organic farming movement—from policy to certification, from Palakkad to Wayanad—illuminates that a broad spectrum of farmers and communities are yearning to break from India's Green Revolution. Even as the state's organic agricultural movements evolve in many different directions, they remain united in their mission to revolutionize an agro-food system reliant on chemicals, monocrops, and fickle markets. Farmers are reclaiming more of their agricultural processes and practices, to ensure that pesticide poisonings, suicides, and plant disease epidemics become phenomena of the past.

Local versus Organic Markets

STORIES OF FOOD contamination and poisoning are not uncommon these days, from outbreaks of multidrug-resistant salmonella in American chicken supplies to milk laced with melamine from China. It often seems as if the food produced in our globalized food system cannot be trusted.

A particularly horrific story of food contamination broke recently in India: In the summer of 2013, twenty-three elementary school children in the North Indian state of Bihar died after eating free school lunches that had traces of a pesticide called monocrotophos. Like endosulfan and DDT, monocrotophos is a persistent organic pollutant, banned in the United States and the European Union. However, it is still used in Indian agriculture to control pest outbreaks in crops like rice. Authorities speculate that the school lunches came into direct contact with monocrotophos because the cooking oil used to prepare the food may have been stored in an old drum that once contained the pesticide. Monocrotophos is extremely toxic.[1]

What happened in Bihar is not an isolated incident. Traces of pesticides continue to be found on vegetables sold in Kerala's markets. One recent study by KAU discovered "dangerous levels" of the pesticide profenofos on several vegetables.[2]

P. J. Chackochan, Indocert's first certified organic farmer, did not express surprise when I shared such stories with him. "Wayanad's own bananas have been the object of such scares," he told me. Consumers and stores had unofficially boycotted bananas from his home district of

Wayanad for several years, due to fears of excessive residues of the pesticide furadan in and on the fruits. I had heard similar information from K. M. George, the organic farmer who had warned his fellow farmers at a training session about the dangers of eating the popular banana chips and buying them for children.

Chackochan also disclosed that while he was representing Kerala's organic farmers and IOFPCL at Biofach, the annual global organic trade fair in Germany, European buyers had approached him and expressed their reluctance to purchase Indian organic products due to worries about chemical contamination. Given this encounter and the adulteration-prone fruits and vegetables of India, he believed that there was only one solution for honest Indian farmers wanting to make a living in agriculture: to obtain third-party certification of their organic products. Certification could ameliorate such concerns about the safety of food both within and outside the country. He also insisted that third-party organic certification was the key to gaining the trust of consumers and buyers and building a dependable reputation in international markets.[3]

By contrast, another organic farmer and vocal proponent of the state's 2010 organic farming policy, K. V. Dayal, regards organic certification as another form of unsustainable agriculture. "If organic farming is [done] for export purposes," he told me during an interview, "it will be polluted. It will be destroyed."

Dayal is not certified organic for export, but he is an organic farmer who does not use chemicals, synthetic inputs, or GMOs, and he is considered a champion of organic farming in many environmental circles in Kerala. He was also present at several of the discussions leading up to the enactment of the 2010 organic farming policy, where he publicly confronted several agricultural scientists when they dismissed the knowledge of Kerala's organic farmers.[4] "Why should we have you?" he had asked the Agriculture Department. Thanal features Dayal at many of its events and demonstrations and describes him as one of the first organic farmers in the state.

"A certificate—a mere paper—cannot declare that it is an organic product," Dayal said of a crop. "The human being who is involved in that farming must be having the mentality that [farming] should not affect the earth."

Throughout my interview with Dayal, he insisted that a statewide conversion to organic farming would only come about through a change in farmers' mindsets, which was unlikely if farmers cultivated for export. "So there has to be a mental change?" I asked, hoping he would expand on these thoughts.

He answered, "I have . . . declared that . . . organic farming can be implemented if you can put [an] idea in the mind first."

"Do you think it is in the mind of those doing farming for export?" I prompted.

"No, no, no," he said. "They, those who are in the organic farming movement for export, . . . their mind has not changed. Whenever they get the chance, they will put chemical pesticides or chemicals, whenever they can, whenever they are in a problem."

Dayal then provided an anecdote to elucidate his position. "There is an organic farmer in Idukki [District]—he's doing organic farming in cardamom. But when the price [for conventionally grown cardamom] has gone up, he has introduced pesticides—because of that money, that money he gets." He paused, and then explained, "He didn't care about organic farming . . . [just] money from that product, which is not a change. The human being has to be changed. The thinking has to be changed . . . the 'export variable thinking,' that by exporting so much, money will come." In other words, as soon as global prices made it possible, the farmer in Dayal's story had abandoned organic farming practices to obtain higher yields and a nicer-looking product, free of damage from pests. As Dayal explained further, it was easier to export foodstuffs that were blemish free, to better appeal to the aesthetic tastes of foreign consumers.

He concluded his anecdote: "He cannot be considered as an organic farmer. [Only] an organic man can do organic farming."

Dayal's comments suggested that an organic farmer's practices on a farm reflect his character—and a real organic farmer conducts agriculture in a particular way.[5] That way is not for export, and it does not include certification. As he specifically said, one who farms *certified* organic foodstuffs does not have the essential and inherent qualities of a true organic farmer, because his farming practices revolve entirely around price and market signals.

As an organization, Thanal agrees with Dayal. The organization's staff would frequently assert that they did not favor third-party organic certification for the purposes of export. By extension, they also believed that the government should not prioritize it, either. As Usha would say time and time again, the role of the Agriculture Department should instead be to augment the domestic consumption of organic staples, like traditional varieties of rice, to enhance domestic food security and improve the livelihoods of farmers. Since Thanal has been one of the main advisers to the Biodiversity Board on organic farming, this vision of agriculture was explicitly written into Kerala's 2010 policy, and was equated with "traditional" agricultural practices in the state.

Yet farmers certified organic for export in districts like Wayanad dismissed the opinions of Thanal and Dayal with a shrug. "Certification is important," said one to me, "[Our] crops are mainly pepper, coffee, cardamom. They don't have a big market here." He echoed Chackochan's opinion that certification helped—not hindered—farmers.

The contrast between Dayal's and Chackochan's perspectives represents a cleavage in Kerala's organic farming movement. It is currently divided between those who advocate growing staple crops (like rice) for Indian consumption and those who support the cultivation of cash crops (like coffee) for the global market, to achieve better price premiums that can improve their livelihoods. Each side encourages different practices and methods of organic farming, and each also defines organic farming differently.

While the majority of Kerala's organic farming proponents rail against the Green Revolution and hail the important benefits of organic agriculture for the environment and farmers, they disagree about what role organic farming should have in the national and international economies. Should Kerala's farmers be growing food for people in India or for those in Europe and the United States? Can organic exports be environmentally sustainable? Is a reliance on localized food production the ideal goal for Kerala's agrarian economy?

Debates addressing these questions can be distilled into a theme common in sustainable food circles worldwide: local versus global food. The rise of the alternative food movement and concerns about food miles have brought into favor the notion that local food is more sustainable and equitable. While many divisions exist in India's organic sector, this particular issue has a distinctive flavor in Kerala.[6] As a state that instigated redistributive land reform in the 1960s and 1970s, the "local versus global food" discussion participates in a long-standing debate about what an ideal farm should look like—big or small? Cultivated by its owner or by tenants? Growing food for domestic consumption or cash crops for export? What is the most productive and best use of Kerala's cropland? These are questions that Kerala's early leaders grappled with when it came to either justifying or fighting against land reforms. However, consensus was difficult to obtain, even within circles of the intellectual Left and the Communist Party.[7] As the implementation of land reforms went into effect, most political leaders eventually agreed that it was necessary to bolster the productivity of the state's cash crop sector so that the nascent economy could grow.

The debate surrounding local versus global is made even more complicated by the increasing attention paid to Kerala's biodiversity, as well as complex issues around food security and yields, free trade agreements, food miles, market prices, caste, culture, definitions of nature, and a slew of other factors. Hence, neither the pro-certification or anti-certification advocates can claim that their position is "traditional" to agriculture in the state. Instead, as an analysis of districts like Wayanad and its Christian communities illustrates, the tensions in the state organic farming movement reflect a complex intersection of its cultural, political, environmental, and economic histories.

WHEN KERALA'S LDF government finalized the organic farming policy in 2010, some estimates claimed that around nine thousand farmers throughout Kerala were already certified organic for export at the time.[8] Yet, relying on older figures, the policy does not encourage farmers to pursue third-party certification. Instead, the policy simply states the existence of organic certification in the state:

Currently there are a number of certified organic farmers in the state, those cultivating cash crops such as spices, tea, and coffee, mainly targeting [the] export market and also noncertified organic farmers who focus on food crops and biodiversity. All of them, whether certified or not, focus clearly on soil health improvement. Kerala also has an accredited organic certifying agency catering to the needs of the farmers.

. . . Currently, about 7,000 farmers practice organic farming in the State as per NPOP standards, covering a total area of 5750 ha. But non-certified organic cultivation area, assessments of which have not been done, is expected to be much more than this.[9]

These sentences are the only ones that mention certified organic farming for export in the twenty-one-page organic farming policy. What is note-worthy is the fact that the policy states that certified organic agriculture for export is focused on cash crops, like spices, coffee, tea, and bananas. Organic farming that is not certified for export, on the other hand, pro-tects biodiversity and cultivates food crops—which people within India can eat for daily sustenance.

While the state's organic farming policy claims that both of these forms of organic farming "focus clearly on soil health improvement," it explicitly heralds the superiority of growing for specific markets (domes-tic over export) and specific types of crops (vegetables, fruits, and staples such as rice). The funding under the policy even reflects this preference: the Agriculture Department's Organic Farming Programme only cov-ered the cultivation of rice, tubers, and vegetables in 2011 and 2012. The Biodiversity Board's pilot project and model cultivation area in Padayetti also only included paddy fields and vegetables. The board helped in mar-keting these goods to local businesses, fostering a local food economy. Certification, on the other hand, has not been funded under the state's organic farming policy. Nor has organic farming for export.[10]

As a major consultant to the state's organic farming policy, Thanal was able to incorporate its interests in promoting a system of organic farm-ing for domestic consumption and staple crops into the priorities of the Organic Farming Programme. Yet, in personal conversations with me,

other organizers who had participated in making the policy shared similar views. They, too, strongly admonished against certified organic agriculture for export. Thanal's position, therefore, was not unique. Many
proponents, including farmers such as Dayal, argued that certified organic farming practices fixated on generating money, promoted cash crop
agriculture over necessary staple food items like rice, and did not benefit
Kerala, historically short of food.

A prominent figure in Kerala's LDF government reiterated this perspective in an interview: "Some people in Kerala, even some farmers, their
interest is to make money, in the sense if it is organic, they will get more
money." This angered him. "Let us not bother about people in America
or Europe," he asserted. "Let us be concerned about our own people in
Kerala. Let us produce and give it to our own people so that the health of
our people is not affected [by pesticide poisoning]." This official did not
believe that certified organic agriculture for export benefited the Kerala
populace as a whole. He, too, held the belief that farmers growing crops
for export were concerned about individual profit, as opposed to the
greater good. He considered these farmers not to be authentic organic
farmers, because, in his opinion, they most likely would not maintain sustainable agricultural practices in the long run.

One young laborer and CPI(M) party member with whom I spent time
repeated these opinions. He justified his views by pointing out that the
number of certified organic farmers in Wayanad District and throughout
India were decreasing.[11] According to him, some farmers left organic agriculture once the prices of certain commodities on conventional markets
skyrocketed. Like Dayal, he argued that to make money quickly, these
farmers abandoned organic practices so that they could sell their products
on nonorganic markets. He also alleged that certification agencies were
competing with each other in districts like Wayanad and would lower
standards of soil conservation and biodiversity protection to collect annual fees from farmers more easily. Certified organic farming for export
was a corrupt system in India, he believed.

Given these setbacks to certification, Thanal and the Biodiversity
Board have proposed another solution to ensure the reliability and trust-
worthiness of organic food supplies: the Participatory Guarantee System

(PGS). As defined by IFOAM, "Participatory Guarantee Systems (PGS) are verification systems alternative and complementary to ISO-type independent third-party certification."[12] PGSs are similar to the microloan projects for small groups that have become popular in development circles in the past few years. Members of a PGS police and guide one another to fulfill mutually agreed-upon practices. Such group monitoring is what guarantees that crops from these farmers are of a certain quality and devoid of chemical residues. PGS groups are not certified, like ICSs, and currently there are no official or regulated PGS standards in India.[13] Thanal and the Biodiversity Board agree that PGSs are compatible with Kerala's larger project of decentralization, local political mobilization, and economic self-sufficiency.

To guide implementation, the state organic farming policy lists twenty-four "strategies." The sixteenth one specifically prescribes the PGS and advises that the state "develop diverse channels for [the] marketing of organic produce" by setting up "separate markets/facilities for organic produce certified by the PGS process."[14] This strategy is described in further detail in the policy and suggests that the government establish several organic retail outlets throughout Kerala to sell organic food, and work with existing retailers in the state to source and provide organic food. It also recommends the creation of farm-to-institution linkages, so that farmers can sell their food directly to hotels, schools, and government entities. Notably, this strategy does not refer to export at all. Certification is referred to at the very beginning of the section (in section 16.1), but by the "PGS process" only.[15] Groups that participate in a PGS would be unable to export crops as organic, however, without additional third-party verification by an accredited agency.

When I brought up this possible limitation of PGS processes with Usha, she emphasized that export and meeting the expectations of foreign consumers were not the end goals of the organic farming policy. Instead, the goals were to produce safe and poison-free food without introducing additional middlemen. She believed that no outside party should be involved in the relationship between a grower and consumer, and that they could build a trusting relationship without certification but with guidance from the government alone. "The government, along with the village system can produce the guarantee system [on its own]," Usha explained simply, continuing to argue against the need for a third-party certifier to enter into the equation. "Basically, it should be based on a faith, the system. People should not cheat. Farmers should not cheat the consumers, and also consumers should not exploit farmers. That should be the system."

In light of the language in the organic farming policy itself, as well as the widespread support for it, the organic farming practices advocated by the 2010 organic farming policy can be distilled into the following formula: agricultural production of vegetables and rice for domestic consumption, not cash crop agriculture. The policy casts certified organic agriculture for export as unreliable, unsustainable, and unnecessary, the pursuit of those motivated by individual gain and not the greater good of Kerala's population and the environment.

IN DECEMBER 2010, Kerala's State Horticultural Mission, a branch of the Agriculture Department, hosted an event, the International Horticultural Expo, in Thiruvananthapuram. The governing Chief Minister delivered an inaugural speech that extoled the virtues of organic farming. In attendance were several organic vendors and farmers, selling and advertising their products and activities. I ran into Chackochan, who had come down to the city to showcase IOFPCL's and Organic Wayanad's exportable and organic (and Fair Trade) black pepper, coffee beans, and medicinal products. I had just finished an interview with an official behind the organic farming policy who, in his statements, had decried organic agriculture for export, so I brought up this topic in conversation with Chackochan. I was curious to see how he would reply.

"There seems to be a division among organic farmers here," I mentioned casually. "A division between those who think it's okay to export organic products, like you, and those who believe farmers should only do agriculture for domestic consumption."

Chackochan agreed that there was truth to my observation. He knew of people who advocated organic farming in Kerala for domestic consumption only, and he disapproved. "We need to think about the world as a whole," he said. "We should import stuff from America, and vice versa. No one in Kerala wants to eat all this pepper that we're growing, so what are farmers to do? Whereas if they export, at least they get a premium."

His comments echoed other opinions I heard justifying export: that Kerala's farmers should think of the world holistically, especially given the state's extended history of maritime and Silk Road trading. Chacko-chan expounded on that point: local farmers had been cultivating several of these spices, like pepper, for centuries, and had been trading them for centuries as well, since one could only sell and eat so much black pep-per within Kerala itself. For certified organic producers like him, export represented a method for sustaining the livelihoods of farmers who had grown various spices and cash crops for generations.

Furthermore, Chackochan and other certified organic farmers repudi-ated the claim that organic farmers fixated only on cash and on making a profit. To demonstrate otherwise, they often took me on tours of their farms to showcase their vegetable and tuber plots—some of which were being intercropped with the cash crops. Indeed, many certified organic farmers are currently cultivating both cash crops for export and staple crops such as vegetables (fig. 5). And many are keen on becoming con-nected with local markets in addition to ones abroad. Chackochan him-self was investigating the possibility of starting a CSA with urban consum-ers in the city of Kozhikode. Another farmer with whom I spent time in Kollam District had utilized the extra revenue from his certified organic cash crops to invest in a marketing van, which he is currently using to transport and sell organic vegetables and fruits directly to urban consum-ers in southern Kerala.

Additionally, although Chackochan and other certified organic farm-ers have welcomed government support and subsidies for organic farm-ing, they claimed not to appreciate being told what and how to farm—especially by the LDF government. Many preferred policy makers to take a laissez-faire approach to agriculture. I asked several certified organic farmers why they had such disdain for the state government. Said one, ac-rimoniously: "Agriculture officers often want bribes from me. I'm not part of a party because the government is all the same, like cobras, even [LDF Chief Minister] Achuthanandan." This farmer deemed the government

5. Organic vegetables (a type of cucumber), to be sold
in local markets, growing in a certified organic plot in
Kollam District of Kerala. Photo by the author.

corrupt and inefficient, and he insisted that the organic farming policy
would likely lose steam. Meanwhile, efforts to develop relationships with
buyers abroad were gaining momentum.

Kerala's certified organic farmers do not have a united vision of an ideal
organic farm and instead believe that "organic agriculture" simply means
farming without chemicals. The organic farming practices that proponents of certified organic farming for export generally advocate are more
general than those of Dayal and organizations like Thanal: good farming practices can be compatible with cash crop agriculture for export,

keeping the welfare of the whole world in mind, not just that of people in Kerala. The government should be supportive, they believe, but it should not dictate what and how to grow, particularly given allegations of officials' dishonesty and ineptitude.

THIS DIVISION IN Kerala's organic farming movement is a typical environmental conflict—a disagreement between two groups of people over how to manage natural resources. For years, many environmentalists blamed such conflicts on population pressures or some peoples' supposed inherent qualities. For example, utilizing Malthusian logic, much mainstream environmental sentiment contended that overpopulation led to battles over limited natural resources, resulting in environmental destruction. Another line of analysis, called "environmental determinism," located the source of environmental struggles in the climatic and geographic characteristics of a place. This kind of thinking suggested that people in hot places like the tropics were "lazy" or "dirty" for climatic reasons, leading to inefficient resource use.

In the 1980s, activists and scholars began to criticize these traditional analyses of environmental conflicts, arguing for greater attention to historical, social, and political factors.[16] For instance, in his analysis of environmental struggles over conservation and national parkland in Zimbabwe, Donald Moore found that "differing cultural understandings of the meanings of land were central to these resource conflicts."[17] Contemporary disputes over land use in eastern Zimbabwe did not demonstrate a lack of concern by native communities toward the environment, as some environmentalists had argued. Instead, skirmishes over parks and conservation were just one front in decades of antagonistic land relations between white settlers (who arrived during the period when Britain controlled the country) and native communities, many of which were dispossessed from their ancestral land under colonialism.[18]

In the Indian context, scholars have used this kind of analysis to (1) question notions that certain groups of people have "essential" qualities that predispose them to waste natural resources or abuse the environment and (2) illuminate the importance of the cultural politics at work in

India's environmental movements.[19] The relationship certain groups have with the environment is shaped by complex factors, from environmental histories of their regions to their historical and contemporary interactions with other communities. Human beings and environmental movements are situated within social relations, from the local to global scales. As I have shown in this book, the statewide adoption of organic farming in Kerala resulted from its very particular history of radical economic and political reform, and for this reason its emerging organic agriculture industry looks very different from organic movements elsewhere.

Analyzing Kerala's organic farming movement in this way helps shed light on why it is bifurcating, notwithstanding its proponents' common goal of eliminating chemical use in agriculture. Despite claims by both sides that the other is corrupt and unsustainable, an analysis of the state's political economic and environmental history illustrates that the relationship between development and land use for agriculture in Kerala is far more complex than the political rhetoric admits.

Fundamentally, Kerala's organic countermovement is situated within a broad, global movement to reform industrial agriculture, by making it both less chemical intensive and localized. From the United States to India, there has been an observable trend toward favoring local food production. This trend represents a major shift in thinking for the contemporary globalized agro-food system.

Our contemporary food system took shape just a few centuries earlier. While human populations have been trading spices and other foodstuffs for a long period of time, Columbus's first encounter with the Americas in 1492 accelerated the movement of people, plants, animals, and other organisms around the world in unprecedented ways. Pioneers and explorers introduced large domesticated animals into the Americas, for example, and brought back to Europe American crops such as corn.[20] Colonialism and postcolonial arrangements further rearranged the distribution of biological organisms globally. Products formerly known only in specific regions, from sugar to bananas, became commonplace in households and markets around the world.[21]

In the past fifty to one hundred years, another set of major transformations occurred in our global food system. In the twentieth century, agricultural systems became more homogenous and subject to more corporate control and long chains of production that stretch from country to country. Food now travels farther than ever before. Countries like England currently import the vast majority of their fruit and vegetables, often from places thousands of miles away. Farming is now less than 1 percent of Britain's GDP, and local farmers are continuing to lose their market share.[22] In the United States, the number of farms and the percentage of people employed on them have both decreased, as a result of mechanization and the ongoing consolidation of farmland.[23] Farming is no longer a lucrative profession for many Europeans or Americans, who are leaving rural areas. This story is being repeated elsewhere in countries like India, where farmers are moving away from agriculture and migrating to cities for better economic opportunities. My own parents are one such example, having left behind their agrarian roots in India for other professions in the United States. Furthermore, fueled by programs such as the Green Revolution, contemporary agricultural production has become increasingly dependent on inputs of fertilizers, pesticides, and fossil fuels, leading to environmental degradation and food safety problems. Agriculture has become a significant source of environmental degradation and health risks, from *E. coli* outbreaks to groundwater contamination, often from unknown and faraway sources.[24]

The confluence of these factors—from the invisibility and complexity of contemporary food chains to economic hardships faced by farmers—has helped to spur a movement in several places to support local farmers and their produce.[25] In Kerala, the issue of local food is also intimately related to broader discussions about the future of agriculture in the state. Farmers and government officials increasingly accept that the status quo of chemical agriculture and the Green Revolution have distressed the state's agrarian sector so much that a change is needed. Despite any agreement, these discussions are influenced by the intersection of several factors, including ever-evolving definitions of nature and questions about how to best conserve it, the historical relationships particular cultural groups have had with nature and land in Kerala, and the state government's own changing environmental priorities.

HOW AND WHERE these numerous global and local factors collide can be best illustrated by Wayanad District, where the state's third-party certification institutions have roots. People in Wayanad have been fighting with each other over the ownership of land for centuries. The district has also been the site of state agricultural experimentation and, more recently, large-scale biodiversity conservation. Given its geography and history, it exemplifies the tensions over proper organic agricultural practices in the state's organic farming countermovement.

Early in my time in India, when I notified neighbors and friends in Thiruvananthapuram that I was planning to spend many months in Wayanad, I got an assortment of reactions. One woman with whom I had grown close while I lived in the city, which is at the opposite end of Kerala from Wayanad, gasped when I told her I planned to live in this northern district. She commented that while it was beautiful, it was still just a jungle. Several organic farming activists, like George, lamented that Wayanad was historically Vaillenad, the "land of paddy fields." Now, however, due to the destructive behavior of the recent settlers, it had become Vazhanad, the "land of bananas." Environmental organizations like the Thiruvananthapuram-based Thanal have become so concerned with Wayanad's agricultural transformation that it has acquired land in the district to set aside for conservation. Historical documents, on the other hand, translate the name "Wayanad" into *Vananad*, the "land of forests."[26]

So, was Wayanad a jungle now, or entirely a banana plantation? Did it used to be a jungle, or full of paddy fields? What was it supposed to be? A jungle or an agrarian landscape?

Implicit in these debates about what Wayanad is and should be are questions about what "real" nature is, what the right form of land use is, and what relationship humans should have with the environment. For some people and groups, Wayanad is merely a jungle. For others it should be the land of paddy fields; and for still others its biodiversity needs to be protected against the expansion of agriculture. These differences of opinion are seeping into Kerala's organic farming movement, affecting judgments about the type of agriculture farmers should be engaged in.

The contemporary debates about land use in Kerala and Wayanad build on a long history. Neighboring kingdoms and the British colonial

settlers considered Wayanad a wild jungle, but also a place with potential for extensive cultivation and profit, due to its expansive forests and
plethora of natural resources. Before British rule, several Adivasi (tribal)
communities populated the area today known as Wayanad, and local
kingdoms battled over its forest resources and spices. During the colonial era, however, many colonialists came to view Wayanad's peoples as
"profligate natives," lazy and ignorant of how best to capitalize on the
natural resources of the region.[27] To turn the unproductive "wastelands"
of the region into plantations and farms, the British forced local people
out of their homes and into new settlements.[28] Colonial officers and policies also promoted heavy use of the forests for economic and recreational
purposes, from logging to hunting.[29] Wayanad's vast forests and newly
created plantations contributed greatly to British economic power, trade,
and infrastructure.[30] The district, therefore, came to be regarded as an
area rich with agrarian bounty.

Wayanad's history after India became independent is in many ways a
microcosm of Kerala's history. After the formation of the state of Kerala
in 1956, the new government promoted cash crop agriculture throughout Wayanad, to continue developing the area economically, to boost
foreign exchange, and to minimize food insecurity in the state. During
the era of land reform, the government broke up and parceled out several
plantations in Wayanad to former tenants and laborers, encouraged the
migration of new settlers to the area, and promoted cash crop agriculture.[31] Then, in 1984, KAU set up Krishi Vigyan Kendra (KVK), an agricultural research station, in Ambalavayal, Wayanad. This organization has
received funding from various sources, including the Indian Council of
Agricultural Research (ICAR). ICAR, a national institution, played a pivotal role in disseminating Green Revolution knowledge and technologies
throughout India.[32]

Wayanad has therefore served, and is serving, as a place of agricultural
experimentation, which Kerala's Agriculture Department and Assembly
have encouraged in the past few decades. Today, KVK is a place where
farmers can purchase hybrid seeds for commercial crops, pesticides, and
other farming technologies. KVK also provides subsidies for growing various crops, and it has several experimental plots on its campus. These

agricultural experiments continue on today: in 2010 the LDF government rolled out a "pepper revival package" for the district through agricultural extension and the KVK, to boost pepper production and the competitiveness of Wayanad's crops in international markets.[33]

Many of the beneficiaries of these programs are new settlers in the region. Promised land from the nascent Kerala government in return for converting Wayanad's "wastelands" into productive fields (the same rhetoric British colonialists had used), hundreds of settlers migrated to the area from southern Kerala. As I noted in chapter 5, many migrants were from the state's Syrian Christian communities in the Travancore region, who were historically denied land ownership and government jobs because of strict caste hierarchies. However, they had accumulated some wealth in other occupations, such as banking and trading, and their capital accumulation facilitated their purchase of cheap land in rural areas such as Wayanad, especially after the state's land reforms made more land available and eliminated caste discrimination.[34] As traders, these Syrian Christian communities chose to grow cash crops such as pepper and other spices.[35] Hence these new farmers came to specialize in non-rice agriculture and to dominate export agriculture in Kerala, particularly in newly settled areas such as Wayanad.[36] Today about a quarter of the district's population is comprised of Syrian Christians.[37] The majority of farmers who are certified organic for export in the district are also from these Syrian Christian groups.[38]

In the late twentieth century, Wayanad entered into the international environmental spotlight after the World Wildlife Fund (WWF) and Conservation International demarcated the district and nearby areas as the Western Ghats Biodiversity Hotspot, because of its numerous varieties of endemic species. In response, the state and national governments created thirteen wildlife sanctuaries and five national parks in Kerala, to protect and showcase this flora and fauna. The state government enthusiastically absorbed this imaginary of Kerala as fecund and Edenic by launching a tourism campaign that calls the state "God's Own Country."

International environmental organizations have argued that the Western Ghats are in dire need of additional, immediate intervention, because human activities—especially agriculture—threaten its biodiversity.

Nearly 70 percent of the species found in these areas are critically endangered or almost extinct.[39] On its website, WWF claims that agriculture is one of the biggest threats: "The Western Ghats were once covered in dense forests. Today, a large part of the range has been logged or converted to agricultural land for tea, coffee, rubber and oil palm, or cleared for livestock grazing, reservoirs and roads."[40]

Thanal and the state's Biodiversity Board endorse a similar logic, although they are more nuanced in recognizing the importance of agricultural biodiversity, or agrobiodiversity, in the Western Ghats. Agrobiodiversity is a recent derivative of the concept biodiversity, defined as local and traditional knowledge and practices about crops, as well as the diversity of these crops.[41] Agrobiodiversity emphasizes that the diversity of plants in lived landscapes are just as important to protect as what some environmentalists might consider "wild" biodiversity.[42] According to the Biodiversity Board, growing organic rice is compatible with maintaining biodiversity in the Western Ghats, since paddy cultivation preserves wetlands, natural geographic features of the tropical ecosystem. Moreover, human populations have been cultivating rice in the region for centuries, and rice paddy fields are important habitats for birds like the baya weaver.

The Biodiversity Board attributes biodiversity decline in the Western Ghats to another type of agriculture: that which is cash crop.[43] The board's former chair, V. S. Vijayan, expressed to me his concern that GMOs were making their way into the Western Ghats, as a result of agricultural experiments by institutions like the Agriculture Department and improper farming by those interested in quick profits and Green Revolution technologies. Vijayan considered cash crops to embody this agricultural intensification, thereby being a threat to the biodiversity of the region.[44] As the board's Kerala State Environment Policy states: "[The] conversion of paddy fields for cash crops, construction and other development activities has made serious erosion in food production in the State. As much as 5 lakh ha have been reclaimed in 30 years since 1971.... [The] highest priority must, therefore, be given to the protection of paddy fields and revival of paddy cultivation."[45] Cash crop agriculture has been compromising the landscape of Kerala, argues the board. As a result, it has been advocating different forms of agriculture, like rice paddy cultivation, in districts like Wayanad.

Organic agriculture has therefore become the state's latest project for improving land use in Wayanad. But as the preceding quotation demonstrates, the board and Thanal have been promoting organic agriculture in a particular way: away from cash crop agriculture to farming rice (and vegetables) for local consumption. The Biodiversity Board's efforts led one state official to announce at the 2010 International Horticultural Exposition that Kerala could now not just be called "God's Own Country" but "Food's Own Country" as well.

"COMMUNISTS ARE hypocrites because they first wanted to promote migration to Wayanad, and now they're against it because of biodiversity," Chackochan told me vehemently one evening, as we conversed about the organic farming policy and the Biodiversity Board. His own parents—from a Syrian Christian background—had migrated to Wayanad decades earlier, and his family had been farming various cash crops for generations both in Wayanad and in southern Kerala. He steadfastly defended his position that third-party certification of organic agriculture for export benefited Kerala's farmers. He also argued that certification was just as good for biodiversity, because certified organic farmers did not use poisonous chemicals that killed off beneficial insects and wildlife. Further, many of these farmers were growing a variety of crops, not just monocultures. Organic Wayanad's coffee farmers, for example, continue to intercrop coffee and pepper vines, meaning that their coffee is shade grown. Growing coffee under a canopy of trees fosters the biodiversity of bird species.[46] Additionally, coffee farmers tend to cultivate several other crops on their farms, including bananas, mangos, coconuts, and even rice paddy fields in the flatter areas. Chackochan admitted to being frustrated with receiving mixed signals about agriculture and land use from the government.

Other certified organic farmers in Wayanad also directed their dislike of government at the Communist parties. Over dinner one evening, a self-identified Syrian Christian, organic farmer, and member of the Congress party (the more conservative party of Kerala) expressed to me why he would never vote for a candidate from one of Kerala's Communist parties: In 1959 he had been recruited by a Catholic priest to protest the reforms the Communists (who then held power in the state) were proposing to the educational system. These reforms included giving the state more authority to appoint and pay teachers, which disgruntled many in the Syrian Christian private-school sector. Conflicts over school reform were part of the unrest that led to the dissolution of the state government and the imposition of presidential rule, as I outlined in chapter 3. During one violent protest, this farmer was jailed for ten days, a time during which his father passed away. Since then, he has never forgiven the Communist parties of India, which he also claimed made fun of the Pope, the leader of the Catholic Church.[47]

Many members of Kerala's Syrian Christian community share such feelings.[48] Although many studies confirm that several Communist-led reforms played a significant role in the high literacy rates and standard of living in Kerala, several Christian leaders repudiate this information. Father Peringarapillil, for example, the priest active in INFAM and Indocert, explicitly attributes the high educational achievements of Kerala's communities to Jesus Christ and the early missionary activities of the Church in Southern Kerala.[49] "I only follow Jesus," he insisted, and he grumbled that many organizations in Kerala committed to education, including the KSSP, had become co-opted by members of the Communist parties.

Peringarapillil's impassioned feelings reflect both the influence the Syrian Catholic Church has had in many rural farming areas and the deep commitment of these communities to their religious institutions. Scholars have documented that those who identify as Syrian Christian tend not to vote for Communist candidates in Kerala's elections because of the latter's stance on various policy matters, including mandating that private Catholic schools accept state-regulated appointments of teachers and the cap on the size of landholdings after land reforms.[50]

The combination of their religious commitments and their familial histories in rural Wayanad has made many in these communities indifferent and even antagonistic toward the organic farming policy, which was originally spearheaded by the LDF government. Adding to their antipathy has been that their own involvement in organic agriculture has been geared toward export markets, because of the types of crops they have chosen to specialize in—a decision influenced by a variety of economic, cultural, and historic factors. Farmers have grown these cash crops in the area for hundreds of years; colonialism and then later the postcolonial Kerala government encouraged their expansion. Ironically, the Left's successful campaigns to demolish feudalism, open up land markets, and promote cash crops created the conditions in which specialized agriculture for export could continue to flourish. Organic certification has represented a way of maintaining this way of farming, while also bolstering the competitiveness of Kerala's spices and other foodstuffs in a globalized and liberalizing marketplace.

The organic farming policy, however, disapproves of the trend toward cash crops and exports that has benefited many Syrian Christian farmers in districts like Wayanad. This condemnation relies in part upon the image of Kerala as biodiverse—as a place that should be kept *as is*, protected from certain forms of human agricultural activity. The imaginary helps to make the organic farming policy conservative in some respects, and it shapes the policy's vision of an ideal and static human-environment relationship in Kerala—one that pivots around a localized food shed as the ultimate solution for protecting the animal and plant biodiversity of the Western Ghats. This localized vision of agriculture is widely shared around the world by advocates of an alternative to the industrial food system.

Yet local does not always mean sustainable, just, and appropriate. The organic farming policy asserts that "modern" practices (such as the Green Revolution), supported by the newly independent nation state of India, fueled Kerala's land use change. The emphasis on "tradition" in the policy encourages a sort of "defensive localism" in Kerala's environmental circles—a reactive insistence that the local sourcing of foodstuffs is the ultimate solution to the negative economic changes that are affecting farming and rural countrysides.[51]

As persuasive and attractive as such arguments can be, they also raise serious problems. As many scholars have pointed out, romanticizing "local" as a bounded, static, and homogenous place is "a recrudescence of some very problematical senses of place, from reactionary nationalisms, to competitive localism, to introverted obsessions with 'heritage.'"[52] An emphasis on "local" has been used to justify xenophobia, elitism, and cultural exclusivity.

Furthermore, the elevation of "local" as the ideal space for food production neglects many complex issues that affect the politics and social life of local communities, such as national politics and environmental history.[53] In the case of Kerala, the obsession with local food production glosses over the multifaceted history of places like Wayanad, which has experienced waves of migration, land use changes, and various forms of political rule and government oversight. These factors have led to the establishment of particular agrarian communities that have been connected with export markets for decades, if not centuries, since the time of Marco Polo. Growing spices for foreign trade is as traditional in Kerala as is growing rice for local consumption.

A HUNGER STRIKE dominated the national news and captivated those in Kerala soon after the passing of the state's organic farming policy. On April 5, 2011, Anna Hazare, an elderly social activist and self-described Gandhian, launched a hunger strike in the capital of India, New Delhi. His protest was stimulated by a series of corruption scandals that had recently befallen the Congress-led national government, ranging from the Telecommunications Minister's illegal sale of mobile phone frequency licenses, to the disorganization surrounding the 2010 Commonwealth Games and horrid reports of landgrabbing by government leaders for personal use and business gain. Hazare insisted that he would not end his fast until the government enacted stringent anticorruption legislation, including the appointment of an ombudsman who would investigate allegations of fraud and perversion. Hazare's fast mobilized students and protesters across the country and made headlines in most papers. A few days later, the Indian government acquiesced to his demands and created a committee to look into such legislation.

Hazare's cause frequently came up in discussions I had with organic farmers, especially because Kerala's own parliamentary elections took place around the same time, in April 2011, almost a year after the finalization of the organic farming policy.[54] Dayal jokingly told me during an

interview that "[the] government system is not properly working because
... government staff are only salary-taking machines—salary-taking
machines, ATMs." Dayal's comments are similar to Chackochan's claim
that the Communist parties of Kerala are hypocrites. Their comments,
and several others about official corruption, signaled that proponents of
organic farming in Kerala are constantly ruminating about the place (and
morality) of their government in society. Many organic farmers and advocates are cautious about the role of government, and are unsure what
relationship civil society should and can have with it, especially in light of
Anna Hazare's very visible hunger strike.

What role (if any) government should play in regulating organic markets is not a question unique to Kerala or India. However, in the state
this discussion is informed by years of debate within the Left on how to
dismantle the feudal economic system. Part of the solution the Communist Parties initially came up with was to pursue both land reform and
the Green Revolution, to increase agricultural production and therefore
revenue for the state. As I showed in chapter 4, the Green Revolution became enmeshed in Kerala's agricultural bureaucracy, rendering alternative methods of agriculture difficult to fathom and pursue, even given
the state's decades of progressive reforms. "Modern" agriculture, after all,
was promoted by leftist coalitions in Kerala's parliament. Syrian Christians, ironically, have been among the major beneficiaries of agricultural
reforms in districts like Wayanad. To further complicate matters, these
Green Revolution reforms led to the high rates of suicide in Wayanad's
Syrian Christian community, which, supporters behind the organic farming policy argue, organic rice cultivation for local consumption could help
avoid in the future.

The result of the various policies and political economic changes
in Wayanad was the increased cultivation of cash crops with chemical
inputs—and then, also, a turn toward certified organic agriculture for
export. In other regions of the state, particularly in lowlands suitable for
rice cultivation, where farmers like the activist Dayal is from and where
the Biodiversity Board's organic farming pilot is located, the government
maintained strong subsidies for growing rice. In these regions where
rice cultivation remains more popular, the organic farming policy has

received a lot of support. Therefore, the bifurcation of Kerala's organic farming countermovement is far from a natural outcome representing innate interests of communities like Syrian Christians; it is, rather, a reflection of Kerala's multifaceted society and complicated political economic history. These complexities of Kerala's agrarian and environmental politics render it difficult to find answers to several fundamental questions: For whom should Indian farmers produce? Moreover, who should decide, and how? And what should be taken into account in this decision? Historical trade with foreign countries? Contemporary free trade agreements that may depress this trade?

As organic agriculture becomes increasingly tied to biodiversity conservation around the world, important questions arise for environmentalists as well: What forms of organic agriculture are best for biodiversity, and who decides? Are all cash crops created equal, like organic shade-grown coffee versus organic natural rubber? Should agrobiodiversity and how communities interact with the land be allowed to evolve, given that ecological systems are naturally and always in a state of flux? While the exact effects of organic agriculture on biodiversity are debated within the field of ecology, it is clear that the agrarian practices of different cultural groups may foster agrobiodiversity in unexpected ways.[55]

There are several other practical questions bearing down on Kerala's organic farming movement: What is the best way for Kerala to move ahead with verifying the authenticity of its organic foodstuffs? Through ICS or PGS schemes? Or different forms of government intervention? Should the organic farming policy make overtures to certified organic agriculture for export? How should each side of Kerala's organic farming movement address claims of corruption? And more broadly, what does it mean for alternative agriculture movements in general if sustainable farming practices affect cultural groups differently?

How Kerala's Communist and other parties ought to tackle these environmental and political challenges going forward—such as by promoting sustainable agriculture—is further complicated by the state's place in a larger nation that is grappling with free trade policies and corruption scandals related to the increasing commercialization of Indian society. In an era of ongoing economic liberalization and privatization, where commodity prices continue to fluctuate unpredictably, protecting the state's economy and environment will remain a challenge for all of Kerala's parties.[56] The example of Syrian Christian organic farmers in Wayanad also illustrates the fact that the development of alternative agricultural production in India is and will be an uneven process, full of challenges and contestation between diverse communities.

The complexities that the people of Kerala face in trying to figure out the future of agriculture aren't unique. Agriculture occupies a complex position in our globalized society, and future changes in this realm will require cooperation and collaboration between various stakeholders. These complexities and disagreements do not have to paralyze advocates interested in reforming industrial agriculture, though. The heterogeneity of Kerala's organic farming movement and the debates in the state confirm that organic agriculture can take on many forms, and that the trajectory of alternative agriculture movements is not necessarily already written in stone. I find this to be hopeful.

Organic—a Good Option for Dinner in Our Globalized World

WRAPPED IN A SLEEVE of gold-colored foil, with an early European trade ship on the front, the "Incredible India" extra-dark chocolate bar made its debut at the International Sweets and Biscuits Fair in Cologne, Germany in 2011. Containing over 70 percent cocoa, it was the first candy bar of its kind to be made wholly with Indian cocoa. And the certified organic cocoa was sourced entirely from Kerala.

Chocolat Stella-Bernrain, a Swiss-based chocolate manufacturer, had been working with IOFPCL and Organic Wayanad since 2007 to create this line of organic chocolate. At a meeting of Organic Wayanad's farmers in May 2011, I had the opportunity to meet a representative from the chocolate company, Anthony Panakal, originally born and raised in Kerala but now living in Switzerland with his wife and three children. In May, he had returned to Kerala to meet directly with Organic Wayanad's farmers. At the meeting, he announced his company's advance offer to pay 3,600 rupees (over $60) per metric ton for Fair Trade and organic cocoa. The figure was a thousand rupees above the current market rate. It was also a return offer from Chocolat Stella, which had previously sourced cocoa from Organic Wayanad.

Speaking entirely in Malayalam, Kerala's official language, Panakal also revealed that the unveiling of the chocolate at the international candy fair had been a success. He proclaimed that although tasters and buyers were astonished to learn about the existence of Indian cocoa, they were just as surprised with the good quality of the chocolate. As a result, Chocolat Stella wanted to continue the Incredible India line and sell the chocolate at major European outlets such as Marks and Spencer. Panakal also mentioned that Chocolat Stella was currently the only manufacturer marketing single-origin Indian chocolate in Europe.

As promised, by 2013 Kerala's chocolate was being sold at major urban outlets in European and Indian cities. Certified organic producers in districts like Wayanad were also receiving more per kilogram of cocoa—50 rupees more than the 36 rupees per kilogram they earned in 2011. Additional organic farmers groups in Kerala have been recruited for this venture with Chocolat Stella, including Hops Adimaly and Organic Malabar. Together they exported sixty tons of cocoa to Europe in 2012.[1]

The debut of the organic chocolate bar was not the only promising development during my time in Kerala. KAU faculty were also developing and rolling out organic farming curricula and modules. In October 2010, a professor from KAU, Dr. A. K. Sherief, invited me to participate in one such training module he had developed for his undergraduates. He and I had met over a year earlier, during my first research visit to Kerala in 2009. He had been extremely excited about my interest as an American in India's organic farming research and development.

Over the course of three days, Sherief's students and I visited with an organic farmer in neighboring Kollam District, observing and learning about his organic farming methods. The students took diligent notes on how to make organic fertilizer mixtures, including versions of panchagavayya. The farmer also imparted information about growing seasons, marketing opportunities, pest control, and other aspects of organic production. He confided that he was worried about the erratic seasonal rains, high labor costs, and yield output. "I'm telling you all of this," he said to the students at the end of the session, "because you're probably going to become agriculture officers one day, and you need to know what farmers are thinking and doing."[2]

This sort of training and interaction between organic farmers and students is relatively new in Kerala and at KAU, and the idea for it came from Sherief, an original commenter on and supporter of the 2010 organic farming policy. He believes that it is important to train students coming

through KAU—those who are likely to go into professional and governmental agricultural positions—in organic methods and practices. In our
conversations, he told me that change was coming to KAU and state agricultural offices in general; students and professors increasingly considered organic farming a viable method of agriculture and were interested
in researching it in depth and with vigor.[3]

Sherief himself continues to develop KAU's organic farming curriculum. He plans to use the *Adhoc Package of Practices: Recommendations
for Organic Farming* (2009)—which had come out of discussions and
debates around the state's organic farming policy—as a manual for the
new courses. Having previously conducted research on organic farming
in the United Kingdom, he also intends to draw from these experiences
and to invite guest lecturers from around the world to participate in the
new organic farming program at the university.

These two small examples from Kerala illustrate the fact that although
we live in a globalized world, meaningful environmental and social
changes in our industrial food system are occurring around us—and
many of these local changes are happening through global relationships.
Sherief's international experiences and IOFPCL's connections to Chocolat Stella through Panakal are just two elements in the shifts toward sustainability in Kerala's agriculture. Notably, they are also examples of the
shift toward sustainability in Europe—in the growth of organic and Fair
Trade options for consumers. More significantly, through the development of the 2010 organic farming policy and Kerala-based certification
institutions, Kerala's state government and civil society are now promoting the growth of organic farming as a response to the environmental and
social destruction resulting from the Green Revolution. The state's farmers are actively involved in agricultural governance and are taking a more
active role in long, globalized commodity chains. As the conversations
I had with Sherief and colleagues who share his enthusiasm for organic
agriculture also confirm, there are substantive changes taking place in
Kerala's agricultural institutions. Organic farming has created political
openings for farmers and activists to better regulate agriculture in Kerala.

Decades of political struggle between leftists, feudal interests, and market forces laid the groundwork for creating a society in Kerala whose elected government prioritizes redistributive reforms and decentralized planning and whose educated populace is readily mobilized politically. Therefore, when the agrarian crisis hit in the 1990s, the legacies of these struggles, institutions, and cultural and ecological circumstances combined to generate a diverse and statewide organic farming movement. In short, the situation in Kerala illustrates that alternative agriculture movements are complex phenomena, shaped by conjunctures of local histories, geographies, and politics.

KERALA'S EXPERIENCES with organic farming can offer significant insight into the three broad critiques of organic food systems that I detailed in the first chapter. The state's experimentation with organic farming troubles arguments that claim organic food is not nutritious and healthy, that it cannot feed a growing world population, and that it is coming to emulate industrial farming.

On the health and nutrition front, one of the biggest and healthiest advantages of organic agriculture lies in the realm of *production*, before the crops even arrive on consumers' plates. Shunning pesticides like endosulfan and furadan, organic agriculture relies on fewer toxic chemicals that can damage human health when released into the environment. This way of viewing human well-being encompasses a more complete and holistic definition of health, beyond nutrition, and connects individual health to the environment.[4]

It's not just farmers and farmworkers who suffer from the negative effects of pesticides. Many agricultural chemicals, such as endosulfan, can be found far away from the fields on which they were applied. Scientists have detected them in homes, waterways, and even in the air, long after they have been spread over croplands. Exposure to these residues increases the risks of developing many diseases, from certain forms of cancer to neurological disorders. Health researchers have shown that young children are particularly at risk, given their physical immaturity and the fact that they crawl and play around outside, rendering them susceptible to toxins in the dirt and air. Pesticides have even been detected in the umbilical cords of infants, as well as in other bodily fluids.[5] In Kerala, communities exposed to chemicals like endosulfan have been overwhelmed with cases of developmental disabilities and birth defects.

The shift to organic agriculture limits the amount of chemicals running off into watersheds and being released into the air, thereby reducing everyone's exposure to toxic chemicals, from producers to consumers.[6] Evaluating the health benefits of "organic" purely from a nutritional standpoint ignores these realities and benefits. Chemical-free farming—very much in contrast to the status quo of the Green Revolution and industrial farming—is healthier for the environment and human populations before anyone has even taken a bite.

Dismissing organic agriculture on the grounds that it can't feed the world's population is problematic as well. As I noted in chapter 4, the Teachers' Association of KAU asserted in its rebuttal to the draft organic farming policy that because yields *could* decline under organic production methods, organic farming *could* increase the state's food *in*security. Likewise, many Indian politicians and bureaucrats argue that organic farming threatens the nation's food security—that is, if farmers don't use chemical fertilizers and pesticides, yields will fall, increasing the number of Indians suffering from hunger and making the nation more vulnerable in international affairs, as it was during the PL-480 era. These fears are compounded by research indicating that India's food demand will outpace its food supply by 2026.[7] Adding fuel to these concerns is that organic farmers themselves in places like Padayetti, Kerala, reported drops in their yields immediately after converting to organic farming.

Such Malthusian logic assumes that if there are either fewer people on our planet or more food available (through higher agricultural output), food insecurity would disappear. Unfortunately, this assumption is ill conceived, because it doesn't take into account whether or not communities can afford to buy food. In an era when the prices of vegetables, grains, and meat continue to rise, poor people will continue to struggle to get enough food, regardless of the world's population levels or the amount of food harvested.[8]

But what about the declining yields in Padayetti? Because the village farmers no longer had to purchase inputs like artificial fertilizers, they had more flexibility around how to use their incomes, even though their yields had fallen. Additionally, by growing their own food, Padayetti's farmers did not have to purchase rice and vegetables at market prices in shops, increasing their community's food security. Organic farming, therefore, can offer one pathway to decreasing the dependence of farmers on external markets and debt. Furthermore, researchers working for the Biodiversity Board predict that yields are likely to go back up once soil health is restored.

Decades of fear about overpopulation and resource scarcity served as a major motive for introducing Green Revolution technologies in India, which ultimately and dramatically altered social and ecological relations in several destructive ways. The resulting agrarian crisis in this and the previous century led to thousands of farmer suicides. Ironically, chemicals have only stripped soils of nutrients, rendering them incapable of producing large yields in the long-term. Kerala has already experienced declines in pepper and coffee output, for example.

Ultimately, food security is tied to economic and political decisions, not solely to population numbers or agricultural output. For example, during the India-Africa Forum Summit in 2010, the Government of India for the first time pledged over $5 billion in food aid to Africa; much of this was in the form of infrastructure development, financing, and training. This decision to provide food aid stemmed from the government's desire to secure greater market opportunities on the continent, stimulate India's economy, and increase opportunities for Indian investors. Unfortunately, millions of people in India were estimated to be malnourished in 2010. Several million metric tons of food grains also rotted in government reserve silos that year.[9] A fixation on yields does not address this type of disconnect in India's trade and domestic policies.

To date, few studies that examine yields from organically farmed plots in comparison to those grown under conventional and industrial methods have come out of India.[10] The small number of existing studies have suggested, though, that organic production and yields could be improved with better training and more efficient disbursement of government subsidies to farmers.[11] And still others have argued that because many Indian producers already farm without chemicals, yields are unlikely to decline for them if they pursue organic farming in a more systematic manner; production output is instead likely to increase, after farmers receive formal training on organic methods, and after farmers apply greater and more targeted organic inputs to their fields.[12]

Furthermore, studies of organic farms in countries like the United States have actually documented similar or increased yields from organically farmed fields over time, which has brought in substantive revenue for farmers.[13] Phasing out chemical-intensive industrial agriculture in favor of organic production could therefore benefit producers economically. Critics have argued, however, that the increased supply of organic products could erode the price premiums organic farmers now receive, threatening the growth potential of organic agriculture.[14] This may turn out to be the case. Yet, as I have shown, producers receive myriad other benefits from organic production—more self-sufficiency in input making, increased opportunities for directly negotiating relationships with buyers and consumers, the potential to revitalize soils (and possibly increase yields), as well as improved human and environmental health. These factors provide important economic flexibility for farmers and their families.

Undeniably, given the multitude of factors that play a role in our agricultural production, from soil type to climate, we can't predict exactly how each farm will take to organic farming.[15] A strong argument can be made that no general conclusions about the scaling-up of organic farming can or should be drawn for the entire food system, based on one plot in a particular locale. However, it can definitively be said that agriculture's reliance on artificial inputs is tenuous, shortsighted, and both ecologically and socially destructive.[16]

As for the third and last claim, that organic farming is getting to look a lot like industrial agriculture—I hope my portrait of Kerala's unfolding transition has shown the limits of this argument. Several scholars have argued that organic agriculture does not transform the economic system but instead represents another frontier in the commodification of nature, leading to ecological destruction.

Evidence from Kerala complicates this simplistic analysis of social change. Neither nature nor our economic system are static and monolithic. As contemporary ecological thinking posits, change is the norm, "without any determinable direction and goes on forever, never reaching a point of stability."[17] As with natural systems, there is no predestined or linear way for economic systems to evolve. This evolution does not happen in a vacuum but is actively shaped by people, governments, social movements, and nature itself. Paying attention to the everyday material conditions in the lives of people—material realities that inform social action—should give us cause for hope that things can be different.

Specifically in Kerala, its markets and emerging organic farming movement operate with a legacy of radical politics built into state institutions and civil society by decades of political struggles. Because of the existing long-standing commitment to land redistribution and agricultural experimentation, organic agriculture has become embedded in Kerala's institutions and communities. State agencies like the Biodiversity Board and local farming groups are now using organic farming to resist a liberal economic system dependent on chemicals to maximize output and profits, which has led to severe environmental degradation and social distress.

The implementation of a statewide organic farming policy represents the decision by Keralites to prioritize human health and the environment, not the expansion of the industrial farming model to encompass organic as a niche product. The empirical evidence from Kerala demonstrates that organic farming movements do not have predestined outcomes but can take a variety of paths, including ones that are valid critiques of chemical-dependent, capitalist agriculture. To put it more simply, organic farming in Kerala counters notions that all organic agriculture—even that which is third-party certified—has become corporate led and top down, or that it is destined to become so.[18] The geographies of alternative agriculture movements are diverse and dynamic—and are strongly influenced by local factors.

Several other examples from around the world, from Poland to California to Cuba, validate my argument that globalizing pressures do not have uniform and predictable effects everywhere. In Poland, for instance, pork producers have responded in heterogeneous ways to mandatory European Union sanitary and phytosanitary standards—contrary to predictions by food activists. While large-scale pork producers had more capital to easily conform to these regulations, small producers found they did not have to sell out to the larger enterprises. Instead, they tapped into a network of informal markets and personal ties—legacies from the country's socialist era—to create informal, unregulated pork markets inside Poland and remain afloat.[19] On another continent, in the San Francisco Bay region of California, a "food industrial district" emerged as a result of the area's agrarian history, progressive politics, and the state's regulatory history around parks and planning. Although large-scale agribusiness dominates the state, because of San Francisco's particular urban and cultural history, it is today one of the hubs of the alternative agricultural movement in the United States.[20] Farther south and east, the nation of Cuba turned to organic agriculture in the 1990s out of necessity. After the collapse of trade with the Soviet Socialist block in the 1990s and the American trade embargo, the country found itself facing shortages of fertilizer and other inputs. The government and farmers soon turned to organic agriculture, ensuring the food security of the region as well as economic and environmental benefits to rural communities.[21] These three distinct examples illustrate that responses to globalization and industrial agriculture are taking different courses and timelines, depending on cultural and creative differences, as well as local and global histories.

THE DIVERSITY OF responses to globalized industrial agriculture, as well as the bifurcation of Kerala's own organic farming movement, trouble the narrow geographic focus of the buy-local movement. From the United States to India, the local food movement has grown in popularity in recent years, heralding the environmental superiority of commodities grown from within a small geographic radius. I saw this in my research in England as consumers and the government exalted local food because it was lower in food miles. In Kerala, the state's organic farming policy upholds a similar idea: that local production for local markets will make the state self-sufficient. As I have shown, however, the state's agrarian economy has been tied to international markets for centuries. This connection was solidified under colonialism, as Indian markets as a whole became enmeshed in international trade. As a result, generations of farming families and cultural groups have produced foodstuffs for world markets. Calls by groups from both within Kerala and outside of the Indian subcontinent to purchase food only produced in a small nearby area would sever these relationships.

When producers and consumers are integrally connected because of historical and contemporary political economic dynamics, can ethical and environmentally sustainable consumption and production be confined only to "local"?[22] The cultural politics of Kerala's organic farming movement suggest otherwise. Tensions within the state's agricultural sector suggest that the buy-local movement everywhere would be well served if it integrated social, cultural, and historical factors in its political analysis of the food system. Truly reforming our industrial food system to become more equitable and ecological will require us to rethink the politics of "local." After all, and as others have pointed out, it is still possible to exploit workers and harm the environment while buying only local goods.[23] To rethink "local," however, is not meant to efface its place in our globalizing world but to better see how its politics are intimately connected to global politics.

The twentieth anniversary of La Via Campesina, a global agrarian peasant movement comprised of over 150 member organizations in 70 countries, underscores a more sagacious and radical way of thinking about "local." Since 1993, La Via Campensina has been advocating for "food sovereignty," a concept that goes beyond self-sufficiency and localism.[24] This more comprehensive concept has been gaining momentum among social movements, farmers, agrarian communities, and alternative agricultural organizations worldwide.

Food sovereignty refers to the ability of local farmers and agrarian communities to democratically make decisions about their production practices, marketing strategies, and livelihoods, with local and global consumers in mind. As food activist Raj Patel recently stated in an interview, food sovereignty does not trump swaraj or self-sufficiency: "It is just that in practice in the world that we live in at the moment, it is hard to imagine a country or a territory or a city being self-sufficient, but it is easier to imagine that people can carry on exchanging but exchanging in terms where there is actually a democratic discussion first about the terms of that exchange."[25]

Unlike self-sufficiency or more narrow conceptions of "local," food sovereignty recognizes the interconnectedness of local communities with other local communities across the world. By empowering people to engage with these connections, food sovereignty can be a powerful force that pushes back against the harmful effects of industrial agriculture. Given Kerala's history of radical politics, a more concentrated focus on food sovereignty by the state and its organic farming advocates is possible—and may present a way to mediate the divisions in its organic movement.

UNFORTUNATELY, in spite of Kerala's progressive politics and strides in its agricultural sector, several challenges still remain for the successful implementation of its organic farming policy and its certified organic farmers. Within the first few years of implementation of the state policy, several farmers reported yield declines in their rice paddy fields. During the first year of the Padayetti pilot, many organic farmers also lost their first rice crops to destructive weeds that sprouted up after an intense rainstorm and then to an outbreak of mites; this led some farmers to resort to herbicides and other chemical inputs during the pilot period. A few others decided to grow ginger and cash crops. As a result, after 2009 the Biodiversity Board gave direct cash subsidies to pilot participants to incentivize organic agricultural practices in rice production. With forces such as climate change altering rain patterns and temperatures in Palakkad, causing unpredictable seasons and affecting the lifecycles of pests, such outbreaks might be a trend. Farmers may only continue to grow uneasy with existing organic practices, rendering current government involvement and subsidies insufficient for supporting organic agriculture.

Pesticide use also continues in the state, despite the Agriculture Department's ban. Farmers have reported that endosulfan and other prohibited red- and yellow-labeled pesticides are being smuggled into the state from neighboring Tamil Nadu and Karnataka and are still being applied in fields, facilitated by the department's failure to enforce the ban. Moreover, key and vocal industry and lobbying groups, including one representing pineapple growers, have claimed that the state's organic farming efforts will depress their yields and export profits. They have threatened to take various organic farming supporters to court as a result.[26]

IOFPCL bore a large amount of debt in 2010, and it failed to sell enough of its members' organic products at a price premium to buyers both in and outside of India. The organization's difficulties with marketing disgruntled many farmers who hoped certification would provide them with immediate competitive access to foreign markets. Chackochan himself has taken out several loans to support fledgling certification projects in Kerala. This situation indicates that voluntary certification alone cannot be the only solution for alleviating poverty, encouraging sustainable farming, and ending Kerala's agrarian crisis.[27]

THE FUTURE and long-term impact of Kerala's organic farming movement has yet to be determined, given these challenges. How well the state's organic farming policy will be enforced, how well it will succeed in mitigating the effects of the agrarian crisis, and what relationship there will be between the policy and certified organic farming, remain to be seen. However, despite a change in the state government leadership in 2011, the new UDF-led state Assembly is maintaining a commitment to organic farming. UDF leaders, including the new Agriculture Minister, K. P. Mohanan, frequently herald the merits of organic agriculture at various public events.[28]

Additionally, while originally opposed to the organic farming policy, Kerala's Agriculture Department and extension now publish promotional materials on sustainable agriculture. Funds for organic farming also continue to increase. Moreover, the policy has initiated and regularized discussions of organic farming among local farmers, interlocking with processes of decentralization already in place and further empowering farmers in agricultural governance. At present, therefore, Kerala's government remains committed to alternative agriculture and the 2010 organic farming policy.

Despite their disagreements, both sides of Kerala's organic farming movement share many long-term goals. To an extent, both sides advocate for greater—albeit very particular forms of—government involvement in developing and promoting organic farming in the state.[29] For example, P. A. Jose from the ICS Wayanad Social Services Society, which assists farmers with third-party certification for export, told me that "government agencies are needed." While, like most farmers involved in the certification area, Jose preferred minimal government intervention, he conceded that farmers needed financial and technical help from state agencies during the transition to organic farming. And once they began producing their organic items, they needed assistance in finding markets and buyers interested in consuming organic food. Usha and the NGO Thanal agree. Through marketing, Usha argued, "we can motivate more farmers—especially small and marginal farmers—to change to organic farming." These comments illustrate the fact that shifting to a sustainable agro-food system cannot be a task that falls only on farmers.[30]

In fact, consumers, buyers, governments, and activists are much-needed partners in the world's organic farming movement—very consistent with the idea of food sovereignty. IOFPCL's relationship with its 2011 coffee buyer and its partnership with Chocolat Stella, mediated by a person with cultural roots in Kerala who now lives in Switzerland, affirm the necessity for ongoing negotiation between buyers and consumers to establish long-term commitments and flexibility for commodity procurement and prices. Such guaranteed markets and assurances from buyers can ease the economic burden for farmers who might see their yields drop as they transition to organic farming, while they are also shouldering potential cost increases for inputs such as higher labor requirements. Kerala's organic farming policy has great potential to create such linkages.

One reliable buyer of Kerala's organic products could be the state government itself, as a part of its Public Distribution System (PDS). The PDS is a social safety net formed during the early years of Indian nation-building to combat food insecurity. It rations and guarantees commodities such as rice to low-income families. Incorporating organic procurement into an expanded PDS would not only guarantee an income to organic farmers but would also subsidize the cost of organic produce and grains for consumers, some of whom complain about the higher price of organic goods. Additionally, the state government's promise to procure organic foods could mitigate risks that organic producers currently face, including the potential fall in prices as the supply of organic products increases and declines in yields during the conversion to organic production methods.

Partnering with producers in Kerala may also ensure that the state can readily supply the needed goods for ration shops.[31]

Currently, Kerala and South India in general need more retail outlets so that farmers can sell a variety of commodities to a variety of markets of different scales, and so that consumers can buy the farmers' products. In 2011, Kerala's capital city of Thiruvananthapuram only had one regular organic bazaar, hosted by Thanal. Only a handful of other shops in the city sold a limited amount of organic goods, and currently very few ration shops (under the PDS) supply organic foods. Since then, several additional organic shops have opened in Thiruvananthapuram and throughout Kerala, signaling increasing support for organic farming in the state.

Despite the many challenges it faces, Kerala's organic farming movement remains one example of the growing pockets of alternatives and resistance to industrial agriculture that merit attention. These initiatives have taken different shapes and forms and are a mixture of public and private partnerships. From Cuba to California, farmers are actively engaging in setting organic farming standards and governance. They are steadfastly committed to farming without chemicals to protect human health and the environment.

Ultimately, organic food is *still* a good option for dinner for those of us living far from Kerala, because there, and in places like it, organic farming has become a sustainable alternative to industrial agriculture. Kerala's 2010 organic farming policy and its certification-based entities are part of a strong countermovement against chemical-dependent, debt-ridden agriculture in India. The next few years are likely to produce even more transformation in the state's agricultural sector. The looming question now is, Can its policy completely solve its agrarian crisis by 2020? While early explorers like Marco Polo and Christopher Columbus sought out this region just for spices, the world today has the opportunity to learn a lot about organic farming's global and local possibilities by watching Kerala's latest sustainable development initiative unfold.

AFTERWORD

The Ongoing Work

I CAUGHT UP WITH Usha over the phone after Kerala's government released its 2013–2014 budget. Funding for organic agriculture under the new budget looked promising: the UDF government had increased funds for the organic farming policy to over 100 million rupees, close to $2 million for the year. The government had also earmarked separate funds for organic farming under other programs, including a cashew improvement project.[1] The channeling of specific funds to organic cashew cultivation is indicative of how the state's endosulfan tragedy involving cashew plantations in Kasaragod District is still haunting Kerala's political climate.

Usha happily reported that support for organic farming was continuing to increase in parts of the state. "The pesticide ban and the policy [are] still in place," she said incredulously. Kudumbashree, the women's neighborhood groups that had been created under the People's Plan had also taken up organic farming as an official project. She reported that women participating in Kudumbashree brought twenty-four thousand hectares in their communities under organic farming methods in the past few months. Usha believed they were influenced by the Biodiversity Board's pilot project in Padayetti, which received considerable media coverage.

Usha had expected the more conservative UDF government to backtrack on the work that Thanal and Varma and Vijayan, the former Chairs of the Kerala State Biodiversity Board, had done on organic farming in the state under the LDF, before the latter was voted out of power in 2011. Thus far this has not been the case, and the UDF has even appointed officials to cabinet-level positions who are proponents of organic agriculture.

When I spoke with K. M. George of Organic Wayanad, he had good news to share as well. Organic Wayanad was continuing to maintain the relationships it had developed with overseas buyers. In early 2013, for in-stance, it exported 19.2 tons of certified organic coffee to the same buyer in Germany at a price of 75 rupees per kilogram. This was an increase of 5 rupees per kilogram from the previous year, 2012.

Usha's optimism, however, was tempered by other developments—or, more precisely, the lack of developments in the realm of implementation. Despite Kerala's ban on pesticides, she reported, they were still being sold in the state. "There's no enforcement, no action," Usha complained. Her comment aligned with recent testing done by KAU that found pesticide residue on vegetables in Kerala's markets.[2] Furthermore, funding for the Biodiversity Board's pilot in Padayetti had ceased. "The new Planning Board says [this project] is not in the board's jurisdiction," she lamented, suggesting that the Biodiversity Board's efforts to change power relations in agriculture were far from over. The government instead chose to chan-nel its limited funds in 2013 and 2014 elsewhere, such as the district of Kasaragod, still reeling from the effects of endosulfan. Usha admitted she was worried that several families in Padayetti might abandon organic rice-paddy farming without the continued support of the government in finding marketing venues and supplying quality inputs such as seeds and manure. After all, signals for such moves by some farmers had already been present while the pilot was being implemented.

George's good news was similarly dampened by other events. Later in 2013, the price of robusta coffee rose to 120 rupees per kilogram in some conventional markets, a difference of 45 rupees per kilogram above what his organic farmers received. Such a large gap between conventional and organic coffee prices could slow or reverse the trends in Kerala's organic production. Farmers could switch back to other agricultural methods to take advantage of higher prices in the conventional coffee market, partic-ularly if consumer confidence in organic markets wavers.

Meanwhile, Kerala's organic farming policy is making national news. Debates about the role of organic farming and the appropriateness of human activity in ecologically sensitive places remain ongoing across sev-eral South Indian states. A current case in point has been the fallout from the Gadgil report by notable ecologist Madhav Gadgil, containing con-servation and sustainable agriculture recommendations for South India.

The *Report of the Western Ghats Ecology Expert Panel*, as it is formally known, was submitted to India's Ministry of Environment and Forests in 2011 by a panel of scientists, including former Kerala State Biodiversity Board chairs Vijayan and Varma. It contains a blueprint for protecting the biodiversity of the Western Ghats, advises a ban on several forms of industrial and agricultural activities in the region, and recommends a complete conversion to organic farming as a form of sustainable development. It also suggests the adoption of Kerala's organic farming policy across state lines: "The Organic Farming Policy of Kerala . . . could be adopted as a model not only for the Western Ghats, but also for all the six States benefitted by the mountain system."[3] The Gadgil report, therefore, gave the proponents of Kerala's organic farming policy a vehicle for protesting the Green Revolution and scaling up organic agriculture nationally, using Kerala as an exemplar.

The release of the report, however, incited uproar among many individuals from rural areas such as Wayanad. Echoing misgivings similar to those dividing Kerala's organic farming movement, several rural farmers and laborers claimed that carrying out the recommendations of the report would threaten their livelihoods. They were joined by mining industry interests and even political and religious leaders from several states.

In response, the Ministry of Environment and Forests created another panel, led by Dr. K. Kasturirangan, to study the Gadgil report. Kerala's current Chief Minister welcomed the resulting "Kasturirangan report" of 2013 and was quoted in a national paper as saying, "we are now relieved . . . the Gadgil report had impractical recommendations like adhering to organic farming."[4] His surprising words confirmed some of Usha's fears: while Kerala's new UDF government will continue to fund organic farming, proponents of Kerala's growing organic farming countermovement cannot be guaranteed the same amount of support they received under the previous political front. Nor can they be guaranteed that the UDF will champion the organic farming policy both within and outside of Kerala, a situation that is causing Thanal much apprehension now that the state's organic farming policy has entered into political discussions at a national level.

The Kasturirangan report, like the original, Gadgil report, also en-

dorses organic agriculture in the Western Ghats, and still points to Kerala
as a leader in this regard. Yet it has been denounced by Kerala's environmental community, including Thanal, as not strong enough on sustainable agriculture or environmental conservation. Further complicating
matters, many farming communities are claiming that implementing the
organic agriculture and conservation measures within the Kasturirangan report would be just as detrimental to cash crop agriculture in the
region as the original report. Political leaders from multiple parties and
farmers in districts such as Wayanad have taken to protesting in the state
Assembly and cities throughout Kerala in disapproval of both reports and
of proposed changes to regulations governing the Western Ghats. Given
the ongoing turmoil, Kerala's UDF government has now asked Oommen
V. Oommen, the new, UDF-appointed chair of the Biodiversity Board, to
analyze both reports and their appropriateness for protecting the environment in the state. Keralites are currently awaiting Oommen's findings.

These battles and conflicting political signals over how land should be
used in the Western Ghats and what kinds of human activity are appropriate are illustrative of the enduring legacy of Kerala's cultural politics
and the Green Revolution. But they are also emblematic of the fact that
trajectories of alternative agriculture movements are not necessarily already determined—despite the passage of promising policies in receptive
regions. This does not have to be discouraging, but it shows that there
is much work still left to do to shape, sustain, and support the local and
global organic farming movement so that it is accepted, effective, ecologically sustainable, and socially just.

SINCE WRAPPING UP my fieldwork in India, I continue to be involved
in sustainable food advocacy in the United States, specifically in the consumer arena. It is encouraging to see consumer interest in organic foods
continue to grow; this heightened demand is good news for farmers both
in the country and elsewhere.

Ultimately, as the stories from Kerala have shown, appropriate government backing is needed for substantial change in agriculture to occur.
Yet given the impasse on major pieces of legislation and regulation from
within the United States Congress to Kerala's Assembly, consumer action

on sustainable food purchasing is evermore important. I'm not suggesting that the weight of reforming industrial agriculture fall on the shoulders of consumers alone, but I have come to see in political meetings that elected officials find more courage to act on and remain committed to passing sustainable food policy and regulating markets when consumer trends can support their actions. Legislators are reading consumer signals.

Creating a sustainable agricultural system is going to require ongoing work on multiple fronts, from the market to the policy sectors. It is promising that major development entities, such as the United Nations Conference on Trade and Development (UNCTAD), have declared strongly in recent influential reports that industrial agriculture is not sustainable. *WAKE UP BEFORE IT IS TOO LATE*, in all caps, is the title of the new UN report that warns us about our current model of producing food.[5] My time in India, England, and now the United States has shown me that many people are already waking up—questioning the industrial agriculture system and working to reform our food system in meaningful ways, one day at a time.

Some minor edits to spelling and grammar have been made to improve the readability of this legal document; these are unmarked. Where deletions have been made, ellipses appear; where words have been added, they appear in brackets.

2010 Kerala State Organic Farming Policy, Strategy and Action Plan

Vision

Make Kerala's farming sustainable, rewarding, and competitive, ensuring poison-free water, soil, and food to every citizen.

Background

India has a glorious history of farming, starting probably from the 6th millennium BC in the Indus Valley [with the] harnessing [of] annual floods and the subsequent alluvial deposits. The Indus Valley Civilization was founded on sustainable farming practices. Subsequently, our culture and ethos became reflections of the agricultural practices and it became mutually inseparable until recently. Harvest of the main crops is celebrated throughout the country.

[Farmers] in Kerala . . . went to the extent of identifying the farmland with Mother God or a female. Just as the female has to take rest after delivery, the farm land has also to be given rest for three months after the harvest; tilling is strictly prohibited during this period. Although [this practice] may look [merely] superstitious, the ecological reason behind this ritual is that tilling during monsoon leads to severe soil erosion, and thus is an unsustainable practice. Therefore, sustainability has been the hallmark of our farming system from time immemorial, growing the time-tested, weather-suited, traditional crops with or without additional organic input, but deeply interwoven with the ecological systems and climatic conditions.

The once flourishing *Pokkali* cultivation in the coastal districts and the *Kaipad* farming system in the Kannur district are testimonials to man's ingenuity in harnessing the natural events for farming [...] without affecting the natural ecological processes and without even any external input.

However, the so-called modern agriculture—unmindful of the ecosystem principles so revered and practiced for centuries—led to seemingly irrevocable ecological and environmental catastrophes in the country. The [so-called] Green Revolution essentially replaced the traditional [crop] varieties with high-yielding ones. These high-yielding varieties, now recognized as "high input varieties," needed tons of fertilizers to achieve the target growth. The crops and varieties alien to the soil attracted new pests and diseases and also outbreaks of existing pests. To combat them ... huge quantities of pesticides [were brought in]. Input of these "exotic" elements into the traditional farming led to [a] multitude of environmental issues.

The microorganisms declined; the soil lost its fertility and vitality; water demand increased and the time-tested traditional varieties disappeared. In short, the centuries-old practices came to a halt. The eternal relationship between the farmer and farmland was lost. More importantly, sustainability of the agriculture systems collapsed, the cost of cultivation soared, the income of farmers stagnated, and food security and food safety became daunting challenges.

Biodiversity in the agricultural fields has now become [only a memory]. The farmland became silent, devoid of the croak of frogs, chattering of warblers, whistling of Whistling Ducks. The long tubular straw ... nests of the Baya weaver bird hanging on the fronds of palm—a once spectacular sight—have disappeared from most localities. The insectivorous birds such as drongo, bee-eater, even the house sparrow became rare or locally extinct, indicating the collapse of the entire food webs of the farmland.

In the forestry sector, fortunately, the use of pesticides has been much less [frequent]. However, the aerial spraying of pesticides in India was first tried in Kerala in 1965 to control the teak defoliators in the Konni forest division. It was noted that within 48 hours nearly 162 non-target species of arthropods were knocked down.

The mentally and physically retarded and handicapped children in Padri village in Kasergod tell the world in unequivocal terms the tragedies and disasters that aerial spraying of pesticides could inflict on human life.

As a result of all these "modern" techniques, the air, water, and soil were polluted; most food grains and farm products were contaminated by pesticides. The run-off from the farmland contaminated the wetlands—rivers, tanks, ponds, reservoirs, lakes, and all water bodies—and the life in them. Fish carried high levels of pesticides and also heavy metals, the latter as a result of the many chemical industries that sprang up to provide chemical fertilizers.

Health hazards became unimaginably high. Incidence of fatal diseases rose. Hospitals with modern amenities came up in the cities as profitmaking industries. Pharmaceuticals flourished.

Food crops became non-attractive, while cash crops became more remunerative. Rice fields have been filled up for nonagricultural activities. The area [planted with] cash crops expanded during the last 20 years (16 percent in rubber alone), while that [planted with] food crops plummeted (to just 9 percent of the total cultivated area). The monoculture of such economically valuable crops led to soil erosion and loss of soil fertility to a great extent. The advent of chemical-intensive farming and its prevalence in Kerala for the past 50 years . . . resulted in the near stagnant levels of productivity of many . . . economically important crops such as coconut, cashew, pepper, coffee, tea, cardamom, and areca nut. Besides these, many regions in Kerala, [such as] Wayanad, started facing acute water scarcity. The State has taken note of it and given priority in the Eleventh Five-Year Plan.

[In addition], economic liberalization and WTO policies added to the woes of the farmers by bringing down the prices of agricultural commodities. [Farmers] are caught in a debt trap, owing [money on] the loans taken to meet the high cost of farming, as it demanded more external inputs such as fertilizers, pesticides, and water. These led to increasing instances of suicide by farmers. Investment in agriculture has essentially changed from the farmer to the industries supplying input to the farmer, and as a direct consequence, net income for farmers decreased while the industries supporting agriculture in the country flourished.

The national policies of opening a retail sector to national and multinational companies pose a great threat to our food sovereignty and right to safe food. The enhanced "food miles" led to increased carbon emission, further increasing the load of greenhouse gases. The potent danger of introducing Genetically Modified crops, the monopoly of seeds by national and multinational corporate bodies, could very well be the last straw on the camel's back for the farmers of Kerala.

Many farmers have realized that they are fighting a losing battle with the "high yield variety—fertilizer-pesticide pack" of the Green Revolution. They have also realized that the degradation and disruption of the fragile ecosystems of the "God's own country" are the chief culprits for the water scarcity, nutritional insecurity, loss of primary productivity, and agrarian crisis being faced by the State.

The farmers in Kerala are convinced that the only way [out] is to return to the traditional sustainable ways of cultivation without harming the ecosystem. Thus organic farming, a system with the broad principle of "live and let live," came up which was recognized nationally and internationally.

Organic agriculture is not limited to crop production alone, but encompasses animal husbandry, dairy, fisheries, poultry, piggery, forestry, beekeeping, and also uncultivated biodiversity . . .

By and large, there is an increasing awareness among consumers on the deleterious effects of pesticides and hence there has been a high demand for organically cultivated food products. Therefore it has become a solemn responsibility of the Government to encourage organic farming to ensure poison-free food at affordable prices to every citizen.

There have been . . . doubts on the practicability of organic farming on the grounds that [food] production would plummet and the country would [experience] yet another food crisis. This is quite unfounded. Success stories on the high productivity of organic farming are now abundant. The Food and Agriculture Organization reported at the International Conference on Organic Agriculture and Food Security in 2007 as follows: "Conversion of global agriculture to organic management, without converting wild lands to agriculture and using N-fertilizers, would result in a global agricultural supply of 2640 to 4380 kcal/person/day. Sustainable intensification in developing countries through organic practices would increase production by 56 percent. Organic yields on average are comparable to conventional yields; although yields do decline initially when converting from high-input systems and almost double when converting from low-input systems." It also has found that organic farms use 33 to 56 percent less energy . . . than conventional farms.

Worldwide, as of now, more than 22.81 million hectares of land area are managed organically and the market for organic food is around $30 billion. It may be noted that Cuba, a country with 42,402 square miles of land and with 11.3 million people, is completely organic.

A Brief History of Organic Farming

Pesticides have been in use in agriculture since the Second World War and from the very beginning there have been concerns about the commercialization of chemical pesticides. Rachel Carson's *Silent Spring*, published in 1964, brought out the scientific certainties of the impacts of pesticides on environment. Although DDT was banned in the developed world in the 1970s, and its use in the agriculture fields of developing countries later, [other] varieties of toxic pesticides found their way into the farms. The scientific predictions of Rachel Carson became true and the public, especially farmers and scientists, . . . realized the dangers of pesticides. This led to the beginning of nonchemical farming. Research and trials of traditional methods and also new models of soil and crop management began to appear.

For the last 4–5 decades scientists have been trying to find a sustainable agricultural system. One of the prominent personalities among them was Sir Albert Howard, the Advisor for Agriculture in India from 1905 to 1924. *An Agricultural Testament*, written by him, is considered to be the first authentic book on organic farming in India. The "indoor method" in organic composting was also worked out first by him.

The permaculture (permanent agriculture) experiments of Bill Mollison and [David] Holmgren in the 1970s gave hope to many farmers the world over. The permaculture wave had its impact in Kerala too and since then many farmers have started experimenting [with] this methodology and they found that this is one of the best practices for Kerala, with its topographical peculiarities and high rainfall, . . . to conserve soil and water and improve productivity of their farms.

In a report submitted in 1983 to the Department of Agriculture of the United States, Robert Papendick and James Parr, agriculture scientists of the same department, had emphasised the crucial need for focusing research on sustainable agriculture to replace the farming systems being followed using chemical pesticides and fertilizers.

The infamous Bhopal tragedy of 1984 was an eye-opener to a larger section of people in India and abroad [after which] discussion on alternatives began seriously. The publication of the *One Straw Revolution* in 1984 by Masanobu Fukuoka (a Japanese scientist turned farmer), on his success in natural farming for the last half a century, and translation of his book into Malayalam in 1985 were timely in channelizing such discussions in Kerala. Biodynamic farming was another method of organic farming which attracted many farmers.

The very sustainability of agriculture assumed serious concern in the discussions among the farmers and organizations in Andhra Pradesh, Karnataka, Tamil Nadu, Gujarat, Maharashtra, Punjab, and Kerala during the same period. The total external dependence of farmers for agriculture inputs had started affecting their economies, leading to desperation among farming communities and ultimately to an agrarian crisis. As an alternative, to make farming sustainable, Low External Input Sustainable Agriculture (LEISA) thus gained momentum in many places, especially . . . among small and marginal farmers. The agricultural crisis that began in the late 1990s further strengthened this movement. Many individuals and organizations started interacting with farmers to make them understand the problems of the modern agriculture.

Thus, from a simple beginning, organic farming later matured to such dimensions as women's empowerment, seed conservation, development of seed banks, value addition and, more importantly, food and nutritional security. It took only 10–15 years for this transition and the results are encouraging.

Currently there are a number of certified organic farmers in the state, those cultivating cash crops such as spices, tea, and coffee, mainly targeting export markets, and also noncertified organic farmers who focus on food crops and biodiversity. All of them, whether certified or not, focus clearly on soil health improvement. Kerala also has an accredited organic certifying agency catering to the needs of the farmers.

Some of the farming systems such as *Pokkali* and *Kaipad* cultivation, cultivation of *Jeerakasala* and *Gandhakasala* varieties of paddy in Wayanad, and homestead farming systems all over the state are default organic. Studies have established the economic viability and productivity of homestead farms in the State and elsewhere. Recently the Adat panchayath in Thrissur district has started organic cultivation of rice in an area of 2,500 acres, promoting an integrated farming system that is known as the Adat model. Similarly, Marappanmoola in Wayanad has another model organic farming system involving hundreds of farmers.

Marketing of organic produce is also being experimented with, in many places like the Organic Bazaar in Thiruvananthapuram, Eco-shops in Thrissur and Kozhikode, and Jaiva Krishi Sevana Kendram in Kannur. Self-help groups of women are encouraged to undertake the organic farming of vegetables in some panchayats.

There is a rich potential for promoting organic farming in Kerala, [given] that the intensity of inorganic agriculture here is not as severe compared to that in other States in the country. While the national average consumption of fertilizers and pesticides during 2002–2003 was 90kg/ha and 288g/ha respectively, it was only 60kg/ha and 224g/ha respectively in Kerala. This points to the positive side of agriculture in Kerala in terms of the already low levels of consumption of hazardous chemicals and, therefore, the chance of redeeming farmers to organic agriculture are quite high.

Realising the [stark] realities, the State Department of Agriculture commenced organic farming promotional activities in 2002-2003. In the following year, the Department set up a cell for Promotion of Sustainable Agriculture and Organic Farming. It has also launched two brands, namely "Kerala Organic" and "Kerala Naturals," to market organic farm produce. Currently, about 7,000 farmers practice organic farming in the State as per NPOP standards, covering a total area of 5,750 ha. But the noncertified organic cultivation area, assessments of which have not been done, is expected to be much more than this.

Benefits of Organic Farming

- Makes agriculture more rewarding, sustainable, and respectable
- Sustains soil fertility by preventing the loss of soil and leaching of minerals
- Protects and enriches biodiversity—micro-organisms, soil flora and fauna, plants and animals
- Requires less water and promotes water conservation
- Improves and maintains the agro ecosystem and natural landscape for sustainable production
- Depends mostly on renewable on-farm resources
- Encourages consumption of renewable energy resources—mechanical and other alternate sources of fuel
- Includes domestic animals as an essential part of the organic system, which helps maintaining soil fertility and also increases the income of farmers
- Ensures pollution-free air, water, soil, food, and natural ecosystems
- Improves agro-biodiversity (both varieties and crops)
- Protects and enhances traditional knowledge in farming, processing, and seed improvement, leading to its protection for the future generations
- Reduces the cost of production through locally suitable methods and inputs
- Produces an adequate quantity of nutritious, wholesome, and best-quality food and develops a healthy food culture
- Reduces food mileage and, thereby, carbon emission

The State Government has seized on the importance of organic farming and realized the health hazards and un-sustainability of chemical farming, as it clearly states in its Biodiversity Strategy and Action Plan that the state has to have an organic farming policy to protect its rich biodiversity and thus sustain various livelihoods dependent on this precious resource.

Organic Farming Policy, Strategy, and Action Plan

Objectives

1. Make farming sustainable, remunerative, and respectable
2. Enhance natural soil fertility and productivity
3. Ensure soil and water conservation
4. Ensure agricultural biosecurity and food and nutritional security
5. Create and ensure domestic markets for organic products, controlled by the farmers
6. Avoid the use of agrochemicals and other hazardous material and ensure chemical-free water, soil, air, and food

7. Ensure seed, food, and sovereignty
8. Promote biodiversity-based ecological farming
9. Ensure quality control in organic inputs and agricultural produce
10. Enable human health promotion by providing safe agricultural products and commodities
11. Conservation and extension of traditional knowledge related to agriculture

FAO put the objectives succinctly: "Organic agriculture improves food access by increasing productivity, diversity and conservation of natural resources, by raising incomes and by reducing risks for farmers. Improvement also results from sharing of knowledge among farmers. These benefits lead to poverty reduction and a reversal of rural outward migration. Policy requirements to improve food access include: increasing farmers' rights to seeds, local varieties, and biodiversity; expanding fair-trade systems along the full value chain; evaluating current emergency aid and procurement programs; and strengthening the rights of indigenous farmers."

Strategies and Action Plans

General approach: The mission to convert Kerala into an organic State is to be achieved focusing on potential crops and areas in a phased and compact manner, with the aim of converting a minimum of 10 percent of the cultivable land into entirely organic every year and thus achieving the target within five to ten years. On completion of the third year of implementation of the organic farming policy, a Committee of experts comprising representatives of farmers and scientists should make a comprehensive assessment of the farmer's well-being, economy, and environment, and only after rectifying the drawbacks, if any, can the policy be implemented in rest of the areas.

Definition of organic farmer: A farmer may be defined as an "Organic Farmer" provided he/she adheres to and practices the following three essentialities of organic farming.

1. A farmer who practices mixed farming including food crops.
2. A farmer who ensures the conservation of soil and water.
3. A farmer who conserves the biodiversity of the farmland.

Strategy 1: Ensure seed sovereignty of the farmers and the State.

ACTIONS

1.1 Establish seed villages exclusively for organic farming.

1.1 (a) Begin programs for the production of seeds, seedlings, planting materials, and traditional animal breeds at the Panchayat level, so as to become self-sufficient in the availability of good quality local seeds, both indigenous and breeder seeds developed by the KAU and other institutions of agricultural research.

1.1 (b) Begin at the farmers' group levels, seed banks, and seed cooperatives to produce, store, share, and supply good quality seeds, including those which are traditional and location specific.

1.1 (c) Promote farmers who can produce organically, good quality seeds and develop participatory seed production programs along with the KAU and other institutions of agricultural research.

1.1 (d) Develop storage facilities/protection measures using traditional methods.

1.2 Ensure maintenance of traceability chain mandatory at the Local Self Government Institution level by the Biodiversity Management Committees (BMC) with regard to seeds produced, sold, transferred, and shared in the Panchayat to protect the farmers from spurious low quality seeds, including hazardous genetically modified seeds.

1.3 Declare and ensure Genetically Modified(GM) free villages/panchayats and State.

1.4 Establish a mechanism to regulate the prices of seeds.

1.5 Ensure supply of locally suitable seeds in each agro-climatic zone.

Strategy 2: Implementation of organic farming policy in a phased manner.

ACTIONS

2.1 Conduct an initial assessment of the status of organic farming and farmers in the State including cultivated, certified, and non-cultivated wild organic areas in the State.

2.2 Develop an action plan with an objective of converting annual crops such as grains, fruits, and vegetables to organic within five years and the perennial crops with in 10 years.

2.3 Develop a clear plan of action with budgets for incorporation into the planning process of the Local Self Government Institutions for phasing in organic farming in the State.

2.4 Special thrust should be initially given to complex, diverse, and risk-prone areas such as rain-fed districts, drought-prone districts, food-crop producing districts and tribal districts.

2.5 All agricultural practices to be launched in the tribal belts of Kerala should compulsorily be organic.

Strategy 3: Compact Area Group approach in organic farming.

ACTIONS

3.1 Encourage the formation of Organic farmer groups, especially women organic farmer groups, clubs, SHGs, and cooperatives for the purpose of cultivation, input production, seed/seedlings/planting materials production, certification, and marketing.

3.2 Each group should be a minimum five members (as stipulated under the Participatory Guarantee System of Certification).

3.3 Models such as Vegetable and Fruit Promotion Council of Kerala (VFPCK), Maarappanmoola Cooperative Society, Adat Cooperative Society for paddy, GALASA, Compact Area Group approach of Kannore KVK, Harithasree may be adopted.

3.4 Encourage Kudumbasree, Vanasamrakshana Samithi, Theera SVS, Grama Haritha Samithi to develop organic farming enterprises.

Strategy 4: Strengthen soil and ensure water conservation measures.

ACTIONS

4.1 Declare the existing sacred groves, ponds, and mangroves as protected areas and ensure their conservation.

4.2 Ensure organic farming approach in all the watershed development areas and extend support, including capacity building and financial assistance for soil and water conservation measures, through ongoing watershed development programs.

4.3 Integrate the various institutions presently involved in watershed management and introduce organic farming as a key component.

4.4 Adopt appropriate agronomic practices suitable to the agro-ecological conditions as well as the topographical conditions at the micro watershed level and discourage/restrict inappropriate crops and cropping practices.

4.5 Kerala Agricultural University and other research institutions should develop suitable crop combinations and locally suitable technology, through participatory research with farmers.

4.6 Encourage landowners and part-time farmers by providing adequate financial support to utilize their lands for organic farming, if left un-utilized.

4.7 Formulate legislative measures to rejuvenate and protect traditional water resources including fresh-water lakes [and] *surangas,* and rain water conservation, restriction of bore wells, especially in dark zones, and recharging of existing bore wells, open wells, and ponds, and other conservation measures so as to improve ground water table and also conserve top soil.

4.8 Establish testing facilities for soil, water, micronutrients, and microorganisms . . . and introduce the system of providing Soil Health Cards.

4.9 Promote bio-fencing and thus help ensure soil and water conservation and availability of green manure and green leaf manure.

4.10 Conduct training programs for resource persons at the Local Self Government Institution level on soil and water conservation measures.

4.11 Avoid use of plastics in agricultural practices. Coir and other natural fibers should be encouraged to prepare shade for nurseries and flower farming.

Strategy 5: Promote a mixed farming approach for livelihood security and ecological sustainability.

ACTIONS

5.1 Make crop-livestock (including poultry) integrated farming a part of organic farming, with women-centered ownership and management in the farmer households and groups. Emphasis may be given to Kerala's traditional farming approach of integrated farming of dominantly coconut with cattle and poultry.

5.2 Develop beekeeping, fisheries, duckeries, and similar enterprises as part of the mixed farming program.

5.3 Promote decentralized production of livestock feed from locally available resources, but excluding spurious ingredients such as growth promoters and hormones.

5.4 Document and popularize traditional knowledge related to animal health care.

5.5 Develop linkages between organic farmers and livestock-growing farmers for exchange of manure for fodder.

5.6 Encourage mixed cropping of indigenous trees and medicinal plants through organic farming.

5.7 Promote proven and successful practices developed by farmers.

5.8 Tax relaxation shall be given to the landholding with maximum forest and wild trees.

Strategy 6: Conserve and improve agro-biodiversity and undomesticated biodiversity.

ACTIONS

6.1 Document agro-biodiversity and related traditional knowledge and practice, both cultivated and un-cultivated, in each Panchayat.

6.2 Encouragement in the form of financial support may be given for the establishment of model agro-biodiversity conservation farms.

6.3 Develop programs for farmers to collect, purify, and multiply traditional seeds.

6.4 Encourage protection of traditional agricultural systems such as *Kaipad, Pokkali, Kole,* and *Kuttanad* as the "agricultural heritage of Kerala."

6.5 Promote indigenous rice varieties such as navara, jeerakasala, and gandhakasala, and also other traditional indigenous varieties of crops.

Strategy 7: Launch a state-wide intensive campaign on organic farming in the form of a popular movement: "Jaiva Keralam."

ACTIONS

7.1 Organise Organic Melas in all districts.

7.2 Begin state-wide awareness programs for the promotion of organic farming focusing on the advantages of organic produce and harmful effects of chemical-based farming.

7.3 Produce handouts, publications of case-studies and best practices, video films, posters, and other awareness materials to reach out to all sections, especially women.

7.4 Organize workshops, seminars and exchange programs for consumers, teachers, traders, farmers, government, and semi-government officials in the related area.

7.5 Ensure the strict enforcement of the provisions of the Food Adulteration Act, 1954, and rules 1955, and bring suitable legislations to notify and enable Agriculture Officers, Veterinary Doctors, and similar professionals as Inspectors under the Act, and also establish quality and adulteration testing facilities at district level.

7.6 Encourage setting up of organic kitchen gardens [and] organic orchards in urban and rural households.

Strategy 8: Ensure availability of quality organic manure to the farmers.

ACTIONS

8.1 Encourage, with adequate support, the availability of biomass in the organic farm itself, through programs such as crop rotation, tree crops, cover crops, leguminous crops, green manure, and green leaf manure.

8.2 Provide support for cow, buffalo, duck, fish, poultry, and goat, preferably traditional breeds, to organic farmers/groups to ensure integrated farming and the availability of farmyard manure and urine.

8.3 Required changes in the existing Cattle Breeding Policy may be made to ensure availability of indigenous varieties of cow and buffalo to the organic farmers.

8.4 Encourage the production of various types of compost in the farm itself, including vermicomposting and bio-gas slurry.

8.5 Formulate special programs for increasing the biomass and organic manures, especially in rain-fed cultivation areas where soil depletion is high, so as to drought-proof the farm.

8.6 Encourage indigenous species of earthworms and effective microorganisms in composting.

8.7 Establish a decentralized system to produce organic manure from biodegradable organic waste segregated at source.

8.8 Ensure the quality of the organic manure and establish a centralized testing laboratory to monitor the same.

8.9 Discourage burning of all organic materials in the field, which could be utilized as manure.

8.10 Under the leadership of the "Padasekhara Samithi" and other farmer groups, draw the benefits of the provisions of the National Rural Employment Guarantee Program to ensure production of green leaves and extraction of silt from the rural ponds, tanks, reservoirs, streams, and rivulets, for augmenting the fertility of the farmlands.

Strategy 9: Ensure farm inputs for organic farming.

ACTIONS

9.1 Implement programs for the production of seeds, seedlings and other planting materials, manure [and other] plant protection materials at the farm with the help of the agriculture department, Agricultural university, at the local level.

9.2 Encourage Farmers Associations/Clubs/Cooperatives/Companies of farmers, SHG's/Youth groups at the local level to produce need-based farm inputs.

9.3 Link organic municipal solid waste segregated at source—especially from markets, hostels, densely populated areas, and other institutions—including night soils to farms through such means as simple and cost-effective decentralized composting, biogasification, and vermicomposting, and thus ensure organic matter recycling. Organic waste treatment plant should be made compulsory for the flats.

9.4 Conduct training programs for local resource persons for producing good quality input, quality testing, and for such related aspects at the Local Self Government Institution level.

9.5 Formulate legislative measures to empower the Local Self Government Institutions [and] reputed NGOs for ensuring quality of inputs, including necessary rules, guidelines, standards, monitoring, and testing procedures and establishment of laboratories.

9.6 Establish special financial assistance schemes, and/or link existing support schemes to groups, to start production facilities for farm inputs.

9.7 Develop local linkages for low-cost input materials to farmers and ensure markets for good quality input materials at reasonable prices.

9.8 Steps may be taken to formulate the organic farming packages developed by the Agricultural University in collaboration with organic farmers. Priority may be given for crops like banana, ginger, pineapple, vegetables, pepper, cardamom, paddy, etc.

9.9 Prepare a database on the organic content of the soil in different zones of Kerala.

9.10 Ensure the quality of fruits and vegetables coming from other states.

Strategy 10: Capacity-building for farmers, implementing officers, agencies, and local self-government members.

ACTIONS

10.1 Conduct orientation, training, and exposure-visit programs.

10.2 Group of 10–20 unemployed youth in each Panchayat (50 percent women) in the model of kudumbasree would be designated as "Karshaka Sevakar" [and] trained in all facets of organic farm management, supported through Local Self Government Institution programs to assist farmers in organic farming.

10.3 Develop the existing Agro-clinics of the Department of Agriculture into Organic Farming Resource Centers, and the staff should be given training on organic farming.

10.4 Create awareness on organic farming practices among the agriculture officers in the Agriculture Department.

Strategy 11: Develop Model Sustainable Organic Farms in the State

ACTIONS

11.1 Every Local Self Government Institution would develop model organic farms in select farmers' fields.

11.2 Research Stations in each agro-ecological zone under the KAU and other agricultural institutions should be converted to organic management systems, and thus become a field study center for students, farmers, and peoples' representatives.

11.3 Such farming areas could be made as part of the responsible tourism program.

Strategy 12: Ensure and improve the health and well-being of
the tribal through special tribal agriculture programs.

ACTIONS

12.1 Ensure adequate nutritional food availability for tribals, whose traditional agriculture has been degraded.

12.2 Develop specific programs for the rejuvenation of their traditional agriculture and knowledge protection.

12.3 Ensure sustainable collection of minor forest products and facilitate the fair marketing of these products through organic outlets.

12.4 Formulate specific schemes to provide tribal children with their traditional food at least once in a day.

12.5 Develop village (*ooru*) level seed banks of their traditional crops and medicinal plants.

12.6 Integrate watershed programs, NREG, etc., in the rejuvenation of tribal agriculture.

Strategy 13: Establish Producer Companies
promoted by organic farmers.

ACTION

13.1 Facilitate the establishment of organic farmer producer companies or similar concerns as an organic-farmers promoted enterprise, with shared investment by the organic farmers and the LSGs.

Strategy 14: Establish storage and transportation facilities.

ACTIONS

14.1 Establish separate and decentralized storage facilities for organic farm produce to ensure its organic integrity and help farmers in certification processes.

14.2 Provide separate local transportation facilities for organic produce to nearby domestic markets.

Strategy 15: Promote farm-level processing [and] value addition and encourage the use of organic farm produce in the food industry.

ACTIONS

15.1 Encourage farm processing by farmer groups, SHGs, and farmer/producer companies for value addition.

15.2 Ensure value addition does not compromise organic produce quality by facilitating testing and evaluation of processes with help from KAU and other research institutions.

15.3 Encourage organic food-based industry in Kerala to procure and use organic produce in their products.

15.4 Set up food industries at manageable decentralized levels in the State with special incentive packages.

Strategy 16: Develop diverse channels for the marketing of organic produce.

ACTIONS

16.1 Set up separate markets/facilities for organic produce certified by the PGS process through the existing channels of marketing of Agriculture products such as the Milma, Supplyco, Horti-corp, Haritha, and People's Market.

16.2 Encourage direct marketing/linkages by farmer groups with end-user institutions such as schools, hostels, hotels, hospitals, Ayurveda centers, SHGs making food products, and food-based industries in the State.

16.3 Encourage institutions such as schools, hostels, hospitals, and government institutions to procure local organic produce following rules and specific guidelines.

16.4 Disallow large private retail corporations through suitable legislations.

16.5 Encourage existing vegetable, fruit, and grocery vendors to promote organic products.

16.6 Facilitate the establishment of organic farm produce outlets in all the districts, with the help of governmental and non-governmental organizations.

16.7 Ensure that the tourism industry, through the Responsible Tourism Initiative, source organic produce from local producers as much as possible for their hotels and resorts.

Strategy 17: Develop a simple certification process in the State for all organic farmers.

ACTIONS

17.1 Encourage through specific scheme the implementation of an internal control system for organic farmer groups.

17.2 Encourage the Participatory Guarantee System of Certification for small and marginal farmers to supply to the domestic market.

17.3 NGOs accredited by the PGS Council of India shall be authorized to help implement and monitor the PGS system in the State.

17.4 The State will develop an Organic Kerala Certification and logo, and "Jaiva Keralam" shall be developed as a brand. Since each country is following different norms, crops aimed at export may go for third-party certification.

17.5 Fix local standards for quality testing and certification.

17.6 Ensure that every organic farmer who is doing organic farming for three years is given the certificate free of cost.

17.7 Include organic livestock rearing (animal husbandry) in the certification system.

Strategy 18: Provide financial incentives for promoting organic farming.

ACTIONS

18.1 Provide interest-free loans to organic farmers, especially small and marginal farmers. Credits linked to banks shall be subsidized through Central/State Governments.

18.2 Set in place production-linked incentive system supports.

18.3 Promote revolving funds system.

18.4 Provide assistance during conversion period; two years for annual crops and three years for perennials.

18.5 Introduce a State-led insurance scheme for small and marginal organic farmers.

18.6 Introduce pension for organic farmers.

Strategy 19: Encourage the use of renewable energy sources.

ACTIONS

19.1 Assistance in terms of expertise and finances should be given for use of bio-gas plants, solar energy, and wind energy units wherever feasible to reduce dependence on external energy sources.

19.2 Develop appropriate small-farm machinery for reducing energy, cost, and drudgery.

Strategy 20: Introduce organic farming in education institutions.

ACTIONS

20.1 Introduce organic farming in educational institutions, prisons, and juvenile homes, through academic inputs. A specific campaign shall be started among students to ensure that they take organically grown food.

20.2 Set up a system in all schools in Kerala to have organic vegetable and fruit gardens as well as paddy, in potential regions, as part of inculcating among the children the love for organic farming and biodiversity conservation and perpetuation in their households. Necessary support schemes may be formulated and implemented through the Local Self Government Institutions.

20.3 Encourage schools to have seed banks and seed farms in the premises, wherever feasible, to produce and supply good quality seeds for use in their nearby regions.

20.4 Promote children-farmer interfaces in each school, which shall include visits to organic farms.

20.5 Encourage schools to link with organic farmers for the supply of rice, vegetables, fruits, milk, egg, and honey as part of the noon-meal and nutritional supplement programs. The ICDS can also be encouraged to supply organic food processed and prepared through SHGs for the Anganwadis.

20.6 Provide suitable incentives to baby food industries that use organic inputs and processes.

20.7 Develop a curriculum for school students on organic farming.

20.8 Publicity through the Farm Information Bureau.

Strategy 21: Reorient research, education, and extension.

ACTIONS

21.1 The KAU would set up a special multi-institutional task force to re-orient the research, education, and extension systems to support the Organic

Farming Policy and the transition of the State's agriculture to organic farming.

21.2 The KAU shall develop a package of practices and model demonstration farms for organic farming in different agro-ecological zones.

21.3 Introduce as part of the course curriculum, both at under- and post-graduate levels, interactions with leading organic farmers, groups, and NGOs promoting organic farming in the state.

21.4 Develop participatory research programs with organic farmers on all aspects of organic farming, ensuring a monthly remuneration for the farmers of the participatory research program.

21.5 Research and inventories so as to recognize and document existing practices of organic farmers.

21.6 Identify and screen native livestock/fish breeds which are locally adaptable and resistant to parasites and diseases.

21.7 Develop herbal remedies for control of diseases and pests of livestock/ crops/ fish.

21.8 To institutionalize the above, an Organic Farming Research Institute (OFRI) may be set up.

Strategy 22: Phase out chemical pesticides and fertilizers from the farming sector.

ACTIONS

22.1 Ensure phased restriction/ban of sale and use of chemical agricultural inputs such as fertilizers, pesticides, fungicides, and weedicides parallel to the implementation of the organic farming policy in the region.

22.2 Through necessary legislation, stop the sale and use of the highly toxic class 1a and 1b pesticides as a preliminary step.

22.3 Declare and maintain ecologically sensitive areas with rich biodiversity and natural resources base (e.g., water bodies), as chemical pesticide and fertilizer-free zones.

22.4 Regulate the sale and use of pesticides through necessary legislations [and] enforcing a prescription-based system, ensuring that pesticides are sold only on a case-to-case basis after obtaining a prescription from the Agriculture Officer.

22.5 Strictly prohibit the sale of pesticides to children, pregnant women, and non-farmers.

22.6 Generate a database on the non-agricultural use of pesticides (e.g., household, storage, food-processing, construction) and regulate their sale and use.

22.7 Review and regulate promotional activities and advertisements of

pesticides as per the FAO Code of Conduct and Guidelines for Pesticide
Use.

22.8 Conduct periodical analyses of water, soil, milk, and crops at the district
level, where pesticides continue to be used, and the data made public.

22.9 Precautionary measures should be taken before using exotic organisms
for bio-control programs.

*Strategy 23: Integrate the programs and activities of various
departments, local self-governments, and organizations.*

ACTION

23.1 Integrate the various government departments, institutions, civil
societies, and their schemes in a harmonious manner duly considering
organic farming principles and local situations. These include government departments such as Agriculture, Animal Husbandry, Forest,
Fisheries, Local Bodies, Finance, Revenue, Industries, Tribal, Khadi
and Village Industries; Financial Institutions, State Corporation Department; institutions such as Kerala Agriculture University [and]
ICAR institutions in the state; Commodity Boards for Spices, Coffee,
Tea, Coconut and Rubber; APEDA, MILMA, and other milk marketing
societies; Farmers' Organizations and Societies, Self Help Groups;
Organic Farming Associations and NGOs promoting organic farming.

Strategy 24: Organizational set-up for promotion of organic farming.

ACTION

24.1 Set up an Organic Kerala Mission to implement the Organic Farming
Policy, Strategy and Action Plan and ensure its success. Since the
coordination of the various departments is vital . . . , a General Council,
to be chaired by the Honourable Chief Minister and, since the policy
has to be implemented by the Agricultural Department, an Executive
Committee to be chaired by the Honourable Minister for Agriculture,
will supervise and guide the functioning of Organic Kerala Mission.

Kerala State Organic Farming Policy,
Strategy and Action Plan
Government of Kerala
2010
Agriculture (P.B.) Department
G.O.(P) no. 39/2010/Agri.   Thiruvananthapuram, 2010 February 10

GLOSSARY

Adivasi	original/tribal inhabitant
block panchayat	local-level administrative area, above the village level
Ezheva	lower-caste Hindu
grama panchayat	local-level administrative unit
grama sabha	local-level voting body
jaiva krishi	organic farming
janman	Hindu landlord under feudal Kerala
kokkarni	pond
kissan	farmer
krishi	farming
krishi bhavan	local-level agriculture office ("agriculture house")
Kudumbashree	women's self-help groups established by the LDF
kulam	water tank
lakh	100,000
lunghi	long, wrap-around cloth tied at one's waist
maharaja	king
Malayalam	Official language of Kerala
Mappila	Muslim
nad	homeland

navara	a red, medicinal rice
padakshera samithi	local-level farmers' committee, established by the LDF
paka	authentic
Palakkadan kattu	Palakkad's wind
panchagavayya	mixture of five products of cow for fertilizer/pesticide
panchayat	local-level administrative area, usually the village-level
rupee	Indian currency
sahai	help
swaraj	home rule, self-rule
vaille	paddy field
vana	jungle, forest
vazha	plantain/banana tree

NOTES

Preface

1. "Fair Trade" refers to a set of ethical production standards. The Fair Trade movement seeks to better the livelihoods of producers located in developing countries with extra, stable income, by formally selling their products at a premium price in markets in developed countries. The Fair Trade movement guarantees this premium to producers and justifies the higher costs to consumers by ensuring (through inspections and certification) that a set of fair and environmentally sustainable standards are being met during production.

Chapter 1

This narration is from an *Incredible !ndia* video called *Timeless India*, designed by India's Ministry of Tourism. The opening scene is based in Kerala.

1. Confederation of Indian Industry, 21.

2. I have translated Sugathakumari's words from Malayalam, the state language of Kerala, into English. I have similarly translated other conversations and interviews throughout this book.

3. Government of Kerala 2010c.

4. Kerala's geographic area encompasses close to fifteen thousand square miles.

5. National Centre of Organic Farming, Ministry of Agriculture. Numbers are based on the latest data, from 2009 to 2010.

6. Food and Agriculture Organization (FAO) of the United Nations 2014b.

7. In 2010, the Government of India developed the National Standards for Organic Production (NSOP), which set the parameters for certified organic agriculture within the country.

8. Osswald and Menon 2013.

9. These numbers exclude areas under "wild forest collection." Between 2003 and 2009, the area under certified organic farming in India grew by almost 2,800 percent (Yadav 2009, 2010). Between 2009 and 2010 there was a 10 percent

decline in the area under organic management. Because little data is currently available for after 2010, it is difficult to discern whether the 2010 decline in area under organic management is part of a long-term trend or was a one time incident. Furthermore, India's National Centre of Organic Farming expects the area under organic production to triple, to over three million hectares, within the next few years (Osswald and Menon 2013).

10. IFOAM 2013.

11. United States Department of Agriculture (USDA), Economic Research Service 2013.

12. Currently, outside of certification meant primarily for organic exports, the Indian government does not regulate the domestic market for organic goods. This absence of regulation has allowed states like Kerala to become more active in developing state-specific organic farming policies.

13. Rupee-dollar conversions in this book are based on a typical exchange rate between 2010 and 2011, when forty-six rupees was about the equivalent of one dollar.

14. Abraham 2008; Garibay and Jyoti 2003.

15. Osswald and Menon 2013.

16. IFOAM 2011b.

17. Osswald and Menon 2013.

18. IFOAM 2011b.

19. Willer 2011.

20. Organic Trade Association 2011; Saltmarsh 2011.

21. *Deutsche Welle* 2007; *Dutch News* 2007; Thompson 2008.

22. Guthman 2004a; Kotz 2011; Smith-Spangler et al. 2012.

23. Tibbetts 2007.

24. Pollan 2006.

25. Smith-Spangler et al. 2012, 359.

26. Chang 2012.

27. Fulton 2012.

28. Cohen 2012.

29. Saltmarsh 2011.

30. Smith-Spangler et al. 2012.

31. FAO 2014a.

32. Seufert et al. 2012.

33. Gilbert 2012.

34. Malthusian ideas about the environment have shaped and continue to influence agricultural interventions and policies within India. Work by the biologist Paul Ehrlich (1975) is a testament to the enduring legacy of Malthusian ideals in the contemporary era, particularly in environmental circles. Ehrlich

argued that India's general unpleasantness and underdevelopment was the result of overpopulation, which was only exacerbated by American food aid in the second half of the twentieth century. These concerns about overpopulation in India served as a major foundation for the introduction in the 1970s of Green Revolution technologies, which dramatically altered social relations and the conditions of India's environment in several destructive ways (Gupta 1998), and which I discuss in the next chapter.

35. J.P. 2012.

36. Buck et al. 1997, 13.

37. Buck et al. 1997. Seven years later, Julie Guthman, a coauthor of this 1997 paper, noted that their piece created a flood of scholarship and debate, which "canonized" their argument as the "conventionalization thesis." Scott et al. (2009) note analogous processes occurring within the Southeast Asian certified organic movement—albeit within the specific cultural and political structures of Thailand, Indonesia, and Vietnam.

38. Jaffee and Howard 2010; McEwan and Bek 2009; Reed 2009; Scott et al. 2009; Valkila 2009.

39. Patel 2012a.

40. Getz and Shreck 2006; Raynolds 2004, 2008.

41. Mutersbaugh 2006.

42. Guthman 2007.

43. Bell 2004, 244.

44. Weiss 2007.

45. Perkins 1997; Shiva 1998.

46. Sahai 2010.

47. George 2012, interview.

48. Sainath 2008, 2011.

49. Holt-Gimenez 2012.

50. Institution of Mechanical Engineers 2013.

51. This issue of compensating farmers for various losses does have precedent in Kerala (for example, for plantains), and continues to be debated among Kerala's policy makers (Manojkumar et al. 2005).

52. My use of the term "countermovement" refers to the political economist Karl Polanyi's (1944) analysis of free markets. Polanyi uses "countermovement" to refer to society's protective response to the marketization of the environment, labor, and money. Countermovements can range from being social movements to government policies. Many scholars of the agro-food system have utilized the analytic of countermovement to make sense of the growing organic and alternative food movements; examples include Bacon (2010), Goodman (2004), Guthman (2007), and Raynolds and Ngcwangu (2010).

53. I rely upon scholarly work from political ecology, a subdiscipline within the fields of geography and ecology, to make these arguments about Kerala's nascent organic farming movement. I am particularly indebted to work by Worster (2008), Foster (2000), and Goodman and Watts (1997), who have written extensively about the dynamism of nature and culture, and the relationship between the two, particularly in local contexts.

Chapter 2

1. Government of Kerala, Kerala Land Use Board, n.d.
2. While no studies to date have been conducted of Wayanad's cancer rate and its correlation to pesticide use, studies from other parts of India, including the northern state of Punjab, have documented that link (Thakur et al. 2008).
3. United States Environmental Protection Agency (EPA), Federal Register, 2009.
4. Eilperin 2008.
5. These figures are based on averages from 1995 and 2008 (Devi 2010). This study also found that the overall usage of pesticides by farmers in Kerala is lower than that of other states and has been declining, but that the reliance on a small number of highly toxic chemicals is growing, to control increasingly virulent pest populations.
6. This figure is from an old World Health Organization (WHO) study from 1990 entitled *Public Health Impact of Pesticides Used in Agriculture.* Pimentel et al. (2013) consider this a low estimate.
7. Perfecto et al. 2009.
8. Davis 2002.
9. Ibid.
10. The enclosure of land refers to the closing off of formerly public lands to locals, who may have relied on resources from this land for traditional subsistence activities, such as hunting or grazing animals. Enclosures became commonplace during the industrial revolution and the advent of private property rights. During this time period, wealthy landowners, royalty, and governments in power would forbid access to lands for a variety of purposes, including the conversion of swaths of areas to large-scale industrial farming and for the setting aside of parkland.
11. Davis 2002.
12. Ibid.
13. Arrighi 1999.
14. Weiss 2007.
15. Chopra 1988; Government of India 1944; Mooij 1999; Sen 1981.

16. Dayal 1968.

17. India's economy is based on five-year planning cycles. India's Second Five Year Plan, from 1956 to 1961, was among the first Five Year Plans to prioritize industrialization.

18. Friedmann 1982.

19. United States Agency for International Development (USAID) 2003.

20. Critics of PL-480 claim that the program was merely instituted to dispose of American grain surpluses that were created by the United States government's farm subsidies. Friedmann (1982) considers PL-480 to be one of the most defining international aid programs of the mid-twentieth century, as the export of surplus grains by America kept the world price of grains and food—particularly in the Third World—low.

21. Perkins 1997; Gupta 1998.

22. Gupta 1998.

23. Perkins 1997.

24. Even though one of the common narratives of the Green Revolution is that the Government of India grasped onto it to reduce food aid dependency from countries like the United States, American agencies were intimately involved in disseminating the Green Revolution. Scholars like Harriss-White et al. (2004), for example, argue that American engagement in food production and distribution in countries like India were shaped overall by geopolitical interests and fears of Communism. Specifically, American policy makers worried that high levels of poverty and hunger in the rural countryside could ignite political unrest, tip the balance of political power, and lead to the rise of Communism in India.

25. The exact beginning and end date of the Green Revolution is debated (Patel 2012b). However, what is important to note is that the Green Revolution normalized market-based, chemical-dependent agriculture that has since been upheld by policy makers and scientists as an ideal way of farming.

26. Many of these subsidies have included direct payments to fertilizer manufacturing companies. The Government of India would set a fixed retail price for subsidies and then pay the difference between the cost of manufacture and the sale of fertilizer back to the manufacturer. However, the Government of India has been reducing the amount of its fertilizer subsidies since joining the World Trade Organization (WTO) in 1992. It then decontrolled the price of certain inputs, such as phosphate. In February 2013, the government announced another 11 percent cut to fertilizer subsidies (FAO 2005; Mehdudia 2013).

27. Chakravarti 1973.

28. Patel 2012b.

29. Sharma and Thaker 2010.

30. Perkins 1997, 39–40.

31. Foster (2000), expounding on Karl Marx's theory of the metabolism of nature and society, utilizes the term "metabolic rift" to theorize this phenomenon.

32. Shiva 1988.

33. Perkins 1997, 258.

34. FAO 2014a.

35. Government of India, Department of Food and Public Distribution 2010.

36. Tharamangalam 2011.

37. Government of Kerala, Second Five Year Plan, Fourth Five Year Plan n.d.

38. Jeromi 2007.

39. Heller 1999.

40. Even before this landmark event, however, the Government of India had been pursuing various economic liberalization policies, such as increased privatization, since the 1980s (Kohli 2006). These reforms of the late twentieth century reflect India's overall "pro-business" stance, have generated increased income and economic inequality within India, and have ushered in a new regime of private accumulation. Agriculture has also become progressively more export-oriented (Corbridge and Harriss 2000; Kohli 2006).

41. Weiss 2007.

42. Government of Kerala 2001.

43. Imported coconut and coconut products can be sold at a lower price in Kerala partially due to lower labor costs in nearby Southeast Asian countries. The minimum wage in Kerala is 200 rupees per day for hard agricultural work, but laborers usually command more compensation for additional, more difficult work (such as picking coconuts from tall trees), as well as meals.

44. Jeromi 2007.

45. Varghese and Sasankan 2007.

46. Kerala's left-leaning parliamentary coalitions, such as the LDF, have typically opposed the Government of India's participation in free trade agreements, including the most recent Association of Southeast Asian Nations (ASEAN) multilateral trade agreement. Yet the LDF has faced opposition on this issue from other political parties within Kerala.

47. Government of India, Ministry of Tourism, n.d.

48. Government of India, Spices Board of India 2010.

49. Singh 2009.

50. Panikkar 1989.

51. Government of Kerala, Second Five Year Plan, 74.

52. Government of India, Directorate of Arecanut and Spices Development 2009.

53. Anandaraj 2000; Vakkayil 2010.

54. Madan et al. 2005.

55. Government of India, Directorate of Arecanut and Spices Development 2009.

56. Vakkayil 2010.

57. Kjosavik and Shanmugaratnam 2007; Tharakan 1998.

58. The story of coffee and pepper is not unique to those crops, though, as Kerala's overall agricultural productivity has been decreasing since the 1970s, reversing early trends. The reasons behind the decline are extensively debated. A summary of these debates can be found in Heller (1999).

59. Daviron and Ponte 2006.

60. Neilson and Pritchard 2009.

61. Oxfam 2012.

62. National Crime Records Bureau of India 2006.

63. Sainath 2011.

64. National Crime Records Bureau of India 2006.

65. Shreyas Social Service Centre.

66. Gupta 1998; Harriss-White et al. 2004; Sainath 2008.

67. Shreyas Social Service Centre.

68. WHO 2006.

69. Sridhar 2008, interview.

70. The work of Carson and others documented how DDT use in agriculture almost led to the extinction of ospreys, birds of prey. Ospreys were being exposed to DDT through their consumption of fish, a staple food for the birds. Fish populations had DDT in their systems as a result of agricultural runoff into waterways. Through their consumption of fish, ospreys would accumulate DDT in their bodies. In turn, DDT affected the shells of the ospreys' eggs, making them very thin. As a result, many chicks did not hatch, threatening the long-term survival of the osprey as a species (Griswold 2012).

71. Government of Kerala, Second Five Year Plan, 70.

72. Kerala's state government later exempted cashew plantations from the ceilings of the 1963 Kerala Land Reforms Act, to encourage the cultivation of cashews (Government of Kerala 2002).

73. Thomas 2010, interview.

74. UNEP 2011.

75. Kulkarni 2011.

76. Nair 2010.

77. *The Hindu* 2010.

78. Vijayan 2010, interview.

79. For example, see Bacon (2010), Goodman (2004), Guthman (2007), and Raynolds and Ngcwangu (2010).

80. Polanyi 1944, 139.

81. Polanyi 1944.

Chapter 3

1. McKibben 1995.

2. McKibben 1999.

3. Mencher 1980.

4. Franke and Chasin 1994, 10.

5. Parayil 2000.

6. Chandy 2005.

7. Kerala's literacy rate is currently about 94 percent, above the overall Indian average (Government of India, Planning Commission, 2011).

8. Ibid.

9. Goodman and Watts 1997.

10. Unfortunately, Polanyi (1944) never fully explains why and how countermovements evolve or emerge in the manner that they do. Nor does he provide deep analysis of the inner workings of countermovements or the specific historical and geographical conditions that produce countermovements (Burawoy 2003). The organic farming literature that refers to countermovements mirrors these shortcomings within Polanyi's analysis, and the dynamics and relationships within and surrounding organic food countermovements have been thus far underanalyzed by scholars or, in the case of Asia, remain unknown. Polanyi's lack of theorization around the inner workings of countermovements help explain why there is such debate in the alternative agriculture literature over what exactly a successful Polanyian countermovement might look like (for example, see Bacon 2010).

11. Panikkar 1989.

12. Conservation biologists have come up with several concepts to identify and preserve key areas of biodiversity, including that of the "hotspot" (Mittermeier et al. 1998). The biodiversity hotspot is a large-scale approach to biodiversity conservation that was identified using plants as indicators of species richness. According to proponents, about 50 percent of the world's biodiversity is found in these hotspots (ibid.). However, as environmental organizations pitch, what makes these areas even more critical for intervention is that this biodiversity is threatened by human activities—nearly 70 percent of the species found in these areas are critically endangered or almost extinct (Conservation International 2007).

13. Daniels and Vencatesan 2008.

14. Additionally, Kerala has one of the most comprehensive Public Distribution Systems (PDS) in the country. The PDS is a social safety net that guarantees commodities such as rice to low-income families. Families are identified by government-issued ration cards.

15. "Caste" refers to the classification of groups of people within Indian society, a classification influenced by Hinduism. Different caste groups are often demarcated by their occupations and the particular rituals they perform according to their place within the caste hierarchy. Typically, and according to cultural norms, members of particular castes tend to marry within their caste; one's caste is hereditary within Indian society. The caste system is not uniform throughout India, and Kerala had a strict caste system before independence. In Kerala, lower-caste communities were regularly discriminated against and barred from several occupations.

16. Desai 2005.

17. This British conquest was the culmination of the East India Company's quest to control the Malabar spice trade, which European powers (French, Dutch, and British) had struggled over for almost three centuries. The British used their influence to gain duty-free access to pepper, cardamom, and sandalwood, disrupting traditional trade (Radhakrishnan 1989). British colonial power came to increasingly depend on the productivity of South India's plantations and forests for infrastructure and trade (Philip 2003).

18. Panikkar 1989; Radhakrishnan 1989.

19. Desai 2005; Sreekumar 2009.

20. Desai 2005; Heller 1999; Panikkar 1989; Radhakrishnan 1989.

21. Herring 1983, 11.

22. About 25 percent of Kerala's population is Muslim, 19 percent is Christian, and 56 percent is Hindu (Government of Kerala and Centre for Development Studies 2005).

23. Government of Kerala, Department of Information and Public Relations.

24. Landowners were compensated by the state government for their loss of land.

25. Herring (1983) states that while Kerala's elected Assembly was receptive to the needs of peasants and laborers, Kerala's courts were controlled by the ruling classes, often comprised of higher-caste Hindus. The courts regularly dismantled the various pieces of land reform legislation that the Assembly would institute. These historical and political factors, argues Herring, shaped Kerala's eventual land redistribution.

26. Excerpts from Kerala's early Five Year Plans are in chapter 2.

27. Herring 1983, 240.

28. For example, based on ethnographic work, historical surveys, and his own household surveys, Ramakumar (2006) argues that benefits from Kerala's land reforms and other public actions are the main reason that the status of life of agricultural workers in the village of Morazha (in Malabar) has improved since the 1950s.

29. The oft-cited Sen (1990) versus Franke and Chasin (1991) debate from the *New York Review of Books* in the early 1990s highlights the fact that other factors, including traditional matriarchal systems of family property inheritance for the Nair caste, have also contributed to Kerala's HDI—particularly around gender relations.

30. Tharamangalam 1998.

31. Isaac and Tharakan 1995.

32. Tharamangalam 1998; 2006.

33. George 1998, 37.

34. Ibid.

35. Communist Party of India (Marxist) 2012.

36. Heller 1999.

37. Heller 1999; Isaac and Tharakan 1995; Williams 2008.

38. Véron 2000.

39. Kerala Sasthra Sahithya Parishad translates into "Kerala People's Science Movement" in English.

40. One visitor included Dr. Salim Ali, a prominent ornithologist and a mentor to one of the first chairs of the Kerala State Biodiversity Board, the government entity that originally spearheaded organic farming in the state, as I explain in chapter 4.

41. Chattopadhyay and Franke 2006; Narayanan and Sajan 2005; Swaminathan 1999.

42. Chattopadhyay and Franke 2006; Narayanan and Sajan 2005.

43. Narayanan and Sajan 2005, 11.

44. Véron 2000, 225.

45. Chattopadhyay and Franke 2006; Véron 2000.

46. Narayanan and Sajan 2005.

47. Although the KSSP has been involved in several government-run and -funded projects, it is a nonpartisan organization. As Prasad himself explained in an interview: "KSSP is a group of people with all varying interests. There are people who belong to all shades of political parties. There are people who are God-fearing, atheists, all kinds of people."

48. Véron 2000.

49. The Kerala Department of Tourism's efforts align with the National Min-

istry of Tourism's Incredible !ndia campaign, in which Kerala's landscapes are heavily featured.

50. Isaac 2010.

51. Kurian 2013.

52. Watts and Peet 2004, 263.

53. Conservation International 2007.

54. Kurian 2013.

55. Devika 2006, 2007; Lukose 2009; Sreekumar 2009; Steur 2009.

56. Reddy et al. 2001.

57. More details about these debates can be found in Heller (1999).

58. Government of Kerala, Kerala Land Use Board, n.d.

59. Chattopadhyay and Franke 2006 and Krishnaprasad 2004.

Chapter 4

1. Kissan Swaraj Yathra translates into "Farmer Self-Rule Journey" in English.

2. Scientific literature has documented that panchagavayya stimulates plant growth and improves soil fertility and plant immunity (Dhama et al. 2005; Prabha and Vasantha 2010; Ravichandran et al. 2011; Sumangala and Patil 2009).

3. The Agriculture Department regulates and implements agriculture policy in the state. Most of the implementation happens at the level of district and panchayat krishi bhavans (village agriculture houses), which oversee administrative details of policies, subsidies, and other programs. The krishi bhavans, as the local-level bodies of the Agriculture Department, also offer advice to farmers about farming methods, technologies, and inputs, relying on information that comes from the Kerala Agricultural University (KAU) system. Many of KAU's recommendations can be found in its annual *Package of Practices*, which offers guidance on how to grow crops. Kerala's Agriculture Department presides over the KAU system, and most bureaucrats and employees of krishi bhavans earn their degrees from KAU before entering civil service.

4. Government of Kerala 2010c, 1.

5. Shiva 2010.

6. Ali was Vijayan's PhD supervisor. Vijayan was also a former researcher at the Salim Ali Foundation, an organization in Tamil Nadu state committed to the conservation of natural resources.

7. Thrissur is both a city and district in central Kerala.

8. Chapter 3 contains more details about the People's Plan and the KSSP.

9. The Convention on Biological Diversity (CBD) is an international treaty created during the 1992 Earth Summit in Rio de Janeiro, where leaders from

various nations recognized the global significance of and threats to biodiversity. The CBD encourages signatories to identify, monitor, and conserve biodiversity through a variety of means. The precise definition of biodiversity remains vague, but the term usually refers to number of species, endemism (species unique to a geographic area), and abundance (Brockington 2001).

10. Chattopadhyay and Franke 2006, 244.

11. National Biodiversity Authority of India 2008.

12. Anuradha et al. 2001; Gadgil 2001.

13. For example, M. K. Prasad, a self-identified Marxist, active environmentalist, and member of the KSSP, sits on the Biodiversity Board and consults for the Kerala State Planning Board (Prasad 2011, interview).

14. When the LDF lost power to the UDF in the parliamentary elections of 2011, Dr. Oommen V. Oommen was appointed by the UDF coalition to succeed Varma.

15. Usha is frequently vocal about her dislike of science and scientists. She downplays her own science background like other staff at Thanal.

16. Fukuoka was a twentieth century Japanese farmer who originally started his career as an agricultural research scientist and inspector. He left that profession to experiment full time with farming techniques that required no chemical inputs. His writings, and the work of other farmers from the developing world, have been influential in Kerala's organic farming movement, which troubles claims that organic farming is "neocolonial" or a north-south movement, arguments I detail in chapter 1. Fukuoka's influence on Kerala's organic farming movement illustrates the fact that what shapes the politics and priorities around sustainable agriculture in developing countries is more complicated than previously analyzed. Finally, Fukuoka's own toning down of his scientific background in agriculture is parallel to Usha's and Sridhar's dismissiveness about their training.

17. Thanal's support for an organic farming policy was not without precedent. In 2002, the Congress-led UDF government attempted to create a more formal organic farming program in the state, to support farmers interested in certification. I explore certification in more detail in chapters 5 and 6.

18. Nair is not his real name. I have changed his name and those of several other informants throughout this book, or I have chosen not to disclose their names, to protect the identities of those who candidly shared their opinions with me and who wished to remain anonymous.

19. Teachers' Association of KAU 2008, 8.

20. Ibid., 6.

21. Nair, as someone straddling two worlds (agricultural extension and the

Biodiversity Board), is a good illustration of how there were sympathizers for the organic farming policy within agricultural extension.

22. *The Hindu* 2008.

23. Government of Kerala, Directorate of Agriculture 2011; Sharma and Thaker 2010.

24. This is the equivalent of 10 million rupees, or just under $200,000. While this may seem small, support for organic farming is growing at the state level (Government of Kerala 2011, 2012, 2013).

25. Varma 2011, interview.

26. Government of Kerala 2010c.

27. Vermicomposting is a method of composting and breaking down food scraps that involves earthworms. The resultant compost is often referred to as "worm castings."

28. In chapters 2 and 3 I provide more details about Kerala's Five Year Plans.

29. Government of Kerala 2010c, 1.

30. Ibid.

31. Ibid., 2–3.

32. Ibid., 3.

33. The Biodiversity Board's and Thanal's critiques of science echo claims by Marxists, feminists, postmodernists, and critical race theorists who have argued that the scientific method, established during the Enlightenment era, is far from objective. They argue that scientific knowledge today has been composed predominantly of information produced by Western elites, typically men, who have historically had the most access to laboratory spaces and other spaces of knowledge production. This "rational" science has therefore produced an incomplete understanding about the world and social and environmental dynamics (Merchant 1980).

34. Abraham 1998; Gupta 1998; Prakash 1999.

35. Braun and Castree 2004; Gupta 1998; Haraway 1988; Latour 1991; Mitchell 2002; Shapin and Schafer 1985.

36. Shiva (1997) points out that many women in India interact more closely with nature on a regular basis, to collect food and fuel (for example, wild plants and firewood) from forests. As a result, women disproportionately bear the negative brunt of changes in resource management, such as the conversion of common lands to private lands.

37. For example, LDF Finance Minister Thomas Isaac's 2010–2011 budget speech (for the year's "Red and Green" budget, as it was named) prominently referred to the importance of environmental protection, signifying the LDF's newfound focus on environmental matters.

38. The tension between the Biodiversity Board and the Agriculture Department confirms that LDF parties still encounter difficulties in pushing their radical agenda at the state level, and that the environment is not a politically neutral issue.

39. See Buck et al. 1997.

40. Scholarly debate around the "agrarian question" highlights how agricultural development around the world has been highly uneven, largely due to the dynamism of people and nature (see Bernstein 1996; Goodman and Watts 1997). Goodman and Watts (1997) rely on the agrarian question to reject totalizing and nondescript notions of globalization as an all-encompassing phenomenon that is erasing geographic differences.

Chapter 5

1. One researcher familiar with the region speculated that Padayetti was chosen to be a model organic farming pilot village because of the political leanings of the former chair of the Biodiversity Board, V. S. Vijayan. "Vijayan is a *paka* [authentic] Communist," he had commented, referring to Vijayan's leftist leanings. Palakkad has historically been a stronghold for the CPI and CPI(M) parties. While this was a side comment by one researcher, it illustrates the implicit leftist political leanings rhizomatous in the organic efforts of the Biodiversity Board.

2. Thanal was also heavily involved in site selection for the pilot. Usha, one of the founders of Thanal and a former agricultural officer in the vicinity, had used her networks to identify Padayetti as a suitable location for the Biodiversity Board's experiment. Thanal had previously conducted educational training programs on seeds and sustainable agriculture for farmers in the area.

3. Block panchayats are a level of government above the village (*grama panchayat*) and below the district. Kerala has fourteen districts. State Agriculture Department offices based at these levels are often referred to as krishi bhavans.

4. Usha 2011, interview.

5. National Centre of Organic Farming, Ministry of Agriculture. Numbers are based on the latest data, from 2009–2010.

6. Government of Kerala 2010b.

7. Ibid.

8. Thanal 2009.

9. Padre 2009.

10. Yields were lower compared to rice grown conventionally, around 2,300 kilograms per acre in the winter harvest (Government of Kerala 2010b).

11. Sridhar 2011, interview.

12. In a 2010 interview with me, Nandan clarified that he and his research-

ers needed more time to assess the long-term effects of organic farming on soil chemistry and microorganisms. Their study consisted of collecting soil core samples from seven test areas (four of which were from organically farmed plots). Researchers analyzed the core samples through multiple means, including microscopic observation.

13. Nandan 2010.

14. Thomas 2010.

15. This study was based on field surveys of twenty-one randomly chosen farmers in Padayetti, to document past and present pesticide usage, as well as direct bird counts (Ganesan 2010).

16. Rice paddy fields are considered wetlands of sorts; rice typically requires submersion in water for some amount of time for growth.

17. The most challenging setback was fully convincing all sixty-six farmers to try organic methods for rice cultivation for three years. As I learned in my visit to Padayetti, a few farmers were reportedly applying chemicals to their soils, despite participating in the pilot. One farmer had also decided to grow ginger in his field instead of rice. Usha acknowledged these issues, reiterating that most participating farmers were farming organically, and that a full conversion of an area to organic agriculture took time.

18. Varma 2011, interview.

19. Government of Kerala 2010a.

20. I received this information from staff at the three block panchayats, who requested that I not use their names.

21. Usha 2011, interview.

22. Nair [1911]2000, 6.

23. Jacob 2006; Kjosavik and Shanmugaratnam 2007; Philip 2003.

24. Herring 1983.

25. Several other political and historical events—such as the national-level Grow More Food campaign, which encouraged cultivation on land classified as "wastelands" to increase domestic food production—stimulated extensive agricultural development in Wayanad because of its sparse population density.

26. Syrian Christians belong to the Eastern Rite of the Catholic Church. Several religious leaders claim that the Syrian Christian lineage commenced with the baptism of Indian families in South India by the apostle Thomas, shortly after the death of Christ. While the exact origins of Syrian Christianity in Kerala are debated by scholars and religious leaders, about 20 percent of Kerala's population is currently Christian (Government of Kerala and Centre for Development Studies 2006). Some of these Christian communities are comprised of recent converts to Christianity, the result of historic Portuguese missionary activity in the state. However, Syrian Christians tend to hold a higher-caste po-

sition in Kerala's society compared to recent converts, many of whom were from lower-caste Hindu families.

27. Patnaik 2006.

28. Government of Kerala and Centre for Development Studies 2006; Government of Kerala, Kerala Land Use Board; Krishnaprasad 2004.

29. Government of Kerala, State Planning Board.

30. A study by Shreyas, a Catholic NGO based in Wayanad, found that 40 percent of the suicide victims in Wayanad were Christians.

31. Kerala Catholic Bishops Council 2014.

32. Franke and Chasin 1994.

33. In fact, many Catholic officials also made it clear to me that they had many disagreements with Kerala's Communist parties.

34. Kerala Catholic Bishops Council 2014.

35. Ibid.

36. Ibid.

37. Jose 2011, interview.

38. Peringarapillil 2011, interview.

39. This is information relayed to me by a staff member at Indocert who wished to remain anonymous. Since 2002, Indocert has also been accredited by several other organizations, which are listed on its website: http://www .indocert.org/accreditations.html. According to its site, Indocert pursues various accreditations "to establish our credibility and competence." Indocert bases its organic certification along the stipulations and conditions of the NPOP (Indocert 2012).

40. Peringarapillil 2011, interview; Vakkayil 2010.

41. This price excludes inspection and travel fees.

42. IFOAM 2004.

43. George 2011, interview.

44. IFOAM n.d.

45. Organic Wayanad is also a certified Fair Trade entity.

46. Before receiving organic certification and the associated price premiums, farmers are required to wait out a three-year conversion period. During this time, they must pay certification and inspection fees.

47. George 2011, interview.

48. The Spices Board subsidizes attendance to Biofach (up to 50 percent for flights and the conference in 2010) and provides a free stall for Indian organic representatives to use. Each year, IOFPCL must apply for this subsidy.

49. Before receiving actual bulk orders, however, IOFPCL has had to ship several samples of products to interested buyers, who would then test the samples for chemical residues and contamination. Chackochan described this

relationship-building time period as nerve wracking, but he proudly stated that IOFPCL now had a trusted reputation within European organic circles.

50. Chackochan did also acquire both public and private loans to build this facility.

51. I have chosen not to reveal the name of this buyer, given that farmers freely shared their opinions with me.

52. This coffee was in the form of dried, husked, and graded green coffee. Coffee is called "green" before it is roasted. The coffee for Organic Wayanad's shipment to Germany was roasted elsewhere, outside the purview of both IOFPCL and Organic Wayanad. Drying, husking, and grading are processes that IOFPCL paid for and arranged once it procured the coffee from farmers in Organic Wayanad. Farmers had the option of dropping off their coffee cherries (which is what coffee is called before it is hulled) at the IOFPCL office in Wayanad or the processing center. They also had the option of coordinating with member farmers and Organic Wayanad to rent a vehicle to have their coffee picked up and dropped off at the IOFPCL office or the processing center. While IOFPCL has member farmers throughout Kerala and South India who produce coffee, IOFPCL decided to procure the majority of the coffee for this order from Organic Wayanad, since IOFPCL's farmers in Wayanad have a greater quantity of coffee in production. Furthermore, the capital of Wayanad District has a processing center where IOFPCL can husk and grade coffee in bulk.

53. Neilson and Pritchard 2009.

54. A staff member of IOFPCL requested that I not disclose the full details of the total amount that IOFPCL received for this order, due to proprietary reasons. However, this advance was the equivalent of 1,600,000 rupees, or $30,000. Some of these funds went toward processing and administrative costs, while the rest went to small farmers. In a meeting, members of Organic Wayanad agreed that small farmers, who supplied less than a hundred kilograms for the order, would receive full payment at the time of procurement. Farmers who supplied greater than a hundred kilograms of coffee cherries received 50 percent of their share of the advance. Because Organic Wayanad is also a certified Fair Trade organization, 3 percent of the entire premium went to Organic Wayanad's Fair Trade activities, which includes scholarships for the children of farmers (Chackochan 2011, interview).

55. Almeida 2013.

56. In 2012, Organic Wayanad exported eighteen tons of coffee to Germany. Farmers received 70 rupees per kilogram (George 2013).

57. I pushed these points with Chackochan on a few occasions, recalling that even the use of certain additives in organic farming was contested in places like the United States. He would relent on some days about the challenges of or-

ganic farming, but only on the point of processing and value-addition activities; Chackochan wished it were easier for Indians to process foods, as opposed to simply being suppliers of raw materials. "Processing standards are difficult," he admitted, and then he stated that even if IOFPCL had access to processing facilities for commodities, the final prices for the outputs would make them unafford-able for most Indian consumers.

58. The experiences of farmers in Kerala do not fit neatly into north-south boundaries or even buyer-seller dualisms of inequality and burden. Instead, cer-tified organic agriculture in Kerala arose out of meaningful global connections, relationships, and ongoing dialogue—such as Peringarapillil's Christian friend-ships in Europe, influence from Fukuoka's writings, and direct conversations Chackochan has had and maintained with buyers at the Biofach conference. Such cross-cultural encounters and influences are not novel to Kerala, as Grove (1995) has documented that the knowledge collected from Keralites by Euro-peans during precolonial and colonial expeditions greatly influenced botanical texts and the classification of species—resources relied upon today by natural-ists and scientists. Kerala has historically maintained such diverse international connections due to several factors, such as its high Syrian Christian population (Dempsey 2001) and coastal trading ports (Parayil 2000). Some theorists have even gone as far to suggest that Kerala's quality of life achievements and political movements may be the result of its historically cosmopolitan nature and inter-actions with other countries and cultures (Franke and Chasin 2000).

59. Another farmer of Organic Wayanad conveyed similar points to me during an interview, and he also reminded me that any of Organic Wayanad's member farmers could sell to whomever whenever they wanted, and were not bound by standards dictating the entirety of their decisions. This farmer him-self, for example, sold his organic coconuts at the conventional market in his town in 2011. He, too, had been farming without chemicals before he pursued certification.

60. These are all various methods of farming without chemicals that can be certified organic. Biodynamic and Vedic farming, for example, revolve around astrological calendars. Zero-budget and natural farming were both promoted by Masanobu Fukuoka and eschew the use of most inputs (including organic ones) and tilling.

61. Part of the reason there has been a lack of organized social groups (re-garding farming) in Wayanad has to do with its historical remoteness, sparse population, and significant influx of migrants. Therefore, certification systems such as ICs's provided a first-time opportunity to organize farmers into groups interested in sustainable agriculture.

62. Here I am again referring to Polanyi (1944), who observed that counter-

movements temper the destructive forces of markets, and reembed them into social relations.

63. These claims align with scholarship that has called attention to the fact that standards (and certification) do not create uniform effects for landscapes and communities (Bingen and Busch 2006; Dunn 2003).

64. In 2011, the Stockholm Convention on Persistent Organic Pollutants Conference of the Parties added endosulfan to Annex A, an action that bans the use of endosulfan by its signatories. Kasaragod's experience with endosulfan in northern Kerala was often cited by delegates as the justification for the global ban (Mathew 2011).

65. The Indian government requires that all approved pesticides have a safety label: Red ("extremely toxic"), yellow ("highly toxic"), blue ("moderately toxic"), and green ("slightly toxic"). Endosulfan had a yellow label.

66. Government of Kerala 2013.

67. IFOAM 2013.

68. IFOAM 2011b.

Chapter 6

1. Subramanian 2013.

2. It is unclear how many of these vegetables were produced out of state, however, as profenofos was banned by Kerala's Agriculture Department in 2011 as a follow-up to the organic farming policy (Martin 2013).

3. In contrast, Osswald and Menon (2013) have suggested that Indian shoppers, as opposed to those in other countries, tend to value personal relationships with and trust in specific producers and shop owners over third-party certified label claims.

4. I describe this confrontation between various stakeholders around the organic farming policy in chapter 4.

5. The division of labor in farming is gendered in Kerala. Men typically cultivate large-scale cash crops, while women tend to vegetables and gardens intended for home consumption.

6. Osswald and Menon (2013) point out that India's organic sector is "largely divided into two strands," including export-oriented and domestic organic farming initiatives (29).

7. Herring 1983.

8. Yadav 2009.

9. Government of Kerala 2010c, 4–5.

10. There are, however, other national schemes that are subsidizing annual organic certification costs, including one by the State Horticultural Mission, a

branch of the National Horticultural Mission, a department under the Ministry of Agriculture. Currently, each eligible farmer receives 150 rupees per acre during each year of the three-year conversion period to organic agriculture.

11. A 10 percent decrease in the number of certified organic farmers throughout India between 2008–2009 and 2009–2010 was officially documented by the National Centre of Organic Farming (NCOF) (Yadav 2010). One possible explanation for the drop could be the global recession, which slowed the growth of organic consumption in places like the United States (Martin and Severson 2008).

12. IFOAM 2011a.

13. India's NCOF and IFOAM have, however, created several guidance documents on the PGS. The NCOF has also developed two PGS-labels (Braganza 2010; Osswald and Menon 2013). Additionally, there is movement within the private sector and international development agencies to develop more structure around the PGS and labels (Osswald and Menon 2013).

14. Government of Kerala 2010c, 15.

15. Ibid.

16. An academic subfield called political ecology, with roots in political economy and several other fields in the social sciences, emerged during this time. It espoused to analyze physical environmental changes and conflicts with tools from these other academic disciplines, and by focusing on historical, social, and political factors. As a result, political ecological explanations of land use struggles depart from traditionally accepted interpretations that have claimed that the source of environmental conflict in developing countries rests in overpopulation or the ignorance of natives in resource management (Robbins 2004; Watts and Peet 2004).

17. Moore 1996, 128.

18. Ibid.

19. Agarwal 1992; Baviskar 1995, 2005; Pandian 2009.

20. Crosby 1972.

21. Cook 2004; Mintz 1985.

22. Countryside Agency 2002.

23. USDA, National Agricultural Statistics Service 2009.

24. Naylor et al. 2005; Pollan 2007.

25. DuPuis and Goodman 2005.

26. Nair [1911] 2000.

27. Drayton 2000.

28. Pandian 2009; Philip 2003.

29. Kjosavik and Shanmugaratnam (2007) provide a more detailed precolonial and colonial history of Wayanad.

30. Philip 2003.

31. The government did not break apart land that was covered under the exemptions to land reform, such as that which was devoted to tea.

32. Perkins 1997.

33. Government of Kerala 2011.

34. Many Syrian Christian families also encroached on Wayanad's "wastelands" during national campaigns such as the Grow More Food campaign. The Grow More Food campaign was initiated by the national government to encourage the cultivation of land throughout India to end food shortages.

35. Many British planters relied heavily on Syrian Christian farmers to manage plantations of cash crops, such as tea, due to shared religious beliefs around Christianity.

36. John 1991; Joseph 1988; Joseph 2003; Mathew 1989; Tharakan 1984; Varghese 1970.

37. Another quarter of the population is Muslim. Hindus, Jains, and members of the Adivasi communities make up the rest of the population (Government of India, Department of Information Technology, n.d.).

38. Although no official numbers exist to document exactly how many certified organic farmers in Kerala are from Syrian Christian backgrounds, George, the coordinator of Organic Wayanad, estimates that the majority of farmers in the ICS are Christian. Furthermore, the other large certified organic ICS in Wayanad, Wayanad Social Service Society, is connected to the Catholic Church, and most of its membership is Christian. Similarly, the pioneer organic certification organizations in Kerala—INFAM, IOFPCL, Indocert, and Organic Wayanad—were all originally set up with assistance from the Catholic Church. Hence, it is accurate to say that the Syrian Christian communities in Kerala have taken an active leadership role in the third-party certified organic export movement.

39. Conservation International 2007.

40. WWF Global n.d.

41. Brookfield and Stocking 1999.

42. The analytic of agrobiodiversity calls attention to the facts that people have been manipulating biodiversity for several generations and that much of the landscape around us has been produced by human labor.

43. Varma 2011, interview.

44. Vijayan 2009, interview.

45. Government of Kerala 2009a, 6–7.

46. Perfecto et al. 2009.

47. In Kerala, political alliances and governments vacillate between the Congress-led UDF and the Communist-led LDF. The Indian National Congress (or Congress party) is colloquially known as the "party of independence"—the

party of many of the national leaders who promoted and negotiated Indian independence from the British Empire. In Kerala, there are several factions of the Congress party, and these tend to be more economically conservative.

48. I emphasize here that my analysis does not attempt to speak for all members of the Syrian Christian community, some of whom are strong supporters of the 2010 organic farming policy and members of Kerala's Communist parties.

49. At the turn of the twentieth century, over half of the schools in Southern Kerala were operated by Christian groups. Their presence in the educational sector influenced the development and expansion of education in Kerala (Centre for Development Studies and Government of Kerala 2005).

50. Joseph 2003.

51. Winter 2003.

52. Massey 1994, 151.

53. Born and Purcell 2006; DuPuis and Goodman 2005; Hinrichs 2003.

54. The election was very close, and the UDF won with a margin of only four seats.

55. Perfecto et al. 2009; Zimmerer 1996.

56. Raman 2010.

Chapter 7

1. IOFPCL 2004.

2. When I asked the students separately what their career aspirations were, most confirmed that they were indeed leaning toward becoming agriculture officers.

3. Sherief 2011, interview.

4. Guthman 2011; Nash 2006.

5. Thottathil et al. 2012.

6. Even the 2012 study by Smith-Spangler et al. noted that a diet of conventional foods could lead to higher levels of pesticides found within the human body, suggesting that organic foods are healthier for consumers.

7. Reuters 2011.

8. While I was conducting field research in India, the price of onions skyrocketed to between 60 to 80 rupees per kilogram at local markets. These prices were well over a dollar per kilogram, expensive even by American standards. Onions are a key component of Indian cuisine, yet many of my friends and informants cut back on their onion purchases, given the high price. A convergence of multiple political and ecological phenomena contributed to India's onion shortage, exemplifying the fact that food security in Kerala and India is not just tied to

yield output but to factors such as national and international politics. Specifically, these factors ranged from unseasonal rains in Maharashtra, an onion-producing state, to a trade dispute with Pakistan.

9. Sahai 2010.

10. The little available data is mostly from gray literature, authored by lobbyists, business interests, and NGOs. Examples include Marwaha (2005) and Tiwari et al. (2005).

11. For example, see the study by Charyulu and Biswas (2010).

12. Ramesh et al. 2005.

13. Furthermore, since many organic products are also sold at premium prices, even if yields decrease with organic production, organic farming can still be very profitable. One study of organic grain production in Wisconsin, for example, measured financial returns up to 110 percent on organic fields, compared to conventional chemical agriculture, in part due to the price premiums associated with organic foodstuffs (Chavas et al. 2009). Other studies of organic agricultural methods in America confirm that economic profits for farmers can be higher with organic systems of farming, even after factoring in costs such as labor (Cavigelli et al. 2009; Delate et al. 2011; Delbridge et al. 2011; Jacobsen et al. 2010; Mahoney et al. 2003). During the period of the Cavigelli et al. (2009) study from 2000 to 2005 in Maryland, researchers found that the prices for conventional grains fluctuated more than organic grain prices, rendering organic agriculture less of a financial risk for farmers. Other sustainable methods of agriculture, such as conservation farming, no-till, and planting erosion barriers, also save farmers money (Hobbs 2007). Additionally, these sustainable systems compensate for the loss of ecosystem services and biodiversity, public health costs, and pesticide resistance associated with heavy pesticide application from conventional agriculture, valued at over $7 billion (Pimentel 2005).

14. Guthman 2007.

15. Studies by David Pimentel and his researchers at Cornell University and the Rodale Institute demonstrate that the question of yields and benefits depend on the types of crops, soil quality, climate, and several other factors.

16. Nitrogen runoff is "suffocating" wildlife (Charles 2013), the world is running out of naturally occurring phosphorous (Philpott 2013), and the price of these inputs continues to rise.

17. Worster 2008, 378.

18. But, readers may ask, is Kerala not the exception, because of its unique politics? My overarching goal has not been to reproduce the abstraction of the "Kerala model," or to replicate fantasies of development policies regarding agriculture, but rather to highlight social transformations that I believe do not

have predetermined trajectories. Kerala illustrates the fact that opportunities for meaningful social changes that immediately impact (and better) the lives of people exist around us.

19. These standards are mandatory food safety requirements that Poland has had to meet before its entry into the European Union. Activists worried that small-scale Polish producers would therefore be squeezed out of the market, unable to compete with those who could more quickly change production practices to comply with these international standards. However, these worries did not materialize (Dunn 2003).

20. Fairfax et al. (2013) define "industrial district" as a place "where focused interactions among those involved in a particular trade or activity create a sense of common enterprise" (22).

21. Funes et al. 2002.

22. Some scholars have argued that ideas about "local" can serve as a proxy for environmental and social sustainability (Fairfax et al. 2013). However, I argue that "local" is a very incomplete proxy and can gloss over many environmental and ethical problems.

23. Roman-Alcalá 2013.

24. Ibid.

25. Patel 2013.

26. A 2011 study released by the Kerala Forest Research Institute concerning pineapple pickers who were losing their fingernails after being exposed to chemical inputs on pineapple farms elicited a firestorm of litigation and claims of libel from pineapple growers. This study had been conducted and released with the support of many organic farming activists and supporters of the 2010 organic farming policy. Pineapple growers complained to the media that radicals in the state were intent on defaming them, in addition to blocking trade and economic opportunities for farmers.

27. Osswald and Menon (2013), who have surveyed the organic retail sector in India, argue that without external financial and marketing support for organic certification, farmers struggle to obtain third-party certification.

28. For example, the new Agriculture Minister praised organic farming in a media-heavy event at a June 2011 state-level workshop on animal husbandry in Wayanad, Kerala.

29. Both sides are also proponents of what I consider Polanyi's (1944) protective countermovement, which aims to subordinate markets back into societal and ecological relations (and bring back an "embeddedness" of markets within society).

30. Furthermore, *how* and *whether* the supporters of Kerala's organic farming policy and certified organic farmers will move ahead with alliance building

within Kerala's organic farming countermovement has yet to be decided. How the tensions of Kerala's agrarian cultural politics will be resolved will be a key determinant in the long-term fate of Kerala's organic farming countermovement. To further grasp whether and how alliances may or may not be built (and how and why) within Kerala's organic farming countermovement, a statewide survey of organic farmers could be conducted. A survey would empirically and better capture the political leanings, cultural identities, and practices of various organic farmers, so that more concrete assertions about various organic farming groups and their practices throughout Kerala could be made. Additionally, survey results juxtaposed with maps of multiple ecologies of Kerala would also provide insight into the relationship between different agrarian practices and Kerala's biodiversity, as well as the effects of agricultural policies on the environment. While I originally envisioned executing a statewide survey during my fieldwork in Kerala, and even developed a draft of a survey with the assistance of faculty at Berkeley and Thanal, the obstacles of limited time and resources prevented me from conducting such research. The only existing survey of organic farmers in Kerala is a 2004 unpublished working paper from the research institute Centre for Development Studies in Thiruvananthapuram, Kerala, entitled "Future in the Past: A Study on the Status of Organic Farming in Kerala," by V. Balachandran. His work consists of analysis of a mail-in questionnaire of 151 respondents. However, not all of the respondents were organic farmers; nor were the geographical regions of Kerala represented in a statistically accurate manner.

31. Kerala's PDS has come under criticism by Keralites in the past few years for supplying poor-quality rice (much of which is procured from outside of the state). Sourcing rice and other staples from within Kerala might mitigate some of these concerns.

Afterword

1. Government of Kerala 2013.
2. Martin 2013.
3. Western Ghats Ecology Expert Panel 2011, 40.
4. *The Times of India* 2013.
5. UNCTAD 2013.

INTERVIEWS

Between 2009 and 2013, I conducted interviews
with the following people featured in this book.
Several others requested anonymity,
so they are not listed below.

P. J. Chackochan

K. V. Dayal

K. M. George

K. Jayakumar

P. A. Jose

Bijoy Nandan

Anthony Panakal

Joseph Varghese Peringarapillil

M. K. Prasad

A. K. Sherief

R. Sridhar

George Thomas

S. Usha

R. V. Varma

V. S. Vijayan

BIBLIOGRAPHY

Abraham, Ansu. 2008. Organic farming: Key elements and characteristics. *Vikas Vani Journal*, January 1.

Abraham, Itty. 1998. *The Making of the Indian Atomic Bomb: Science, Secrecy and the Postcolonial State*. New Delhi: Orient Longman Limited.

Agarwal, Bina. 1992. The gender and environment debate: Lessons from India. *Feminist Studies* 18 (1): 119–58.

Almeida, Isis. 2013. Goldman lowers Arabica coffee price forecasts on Brazil crop. *Bloomberg News*, April 23.

Altieri, M., L. Ponti, and C. I. Nicholls. 2012. Soil fertility, biodiversity and pest management. In *Biodiversity and Insect Pests: Key Issues for Sustainable Management*, eds. Geoff M. Gurr, Stephen D. Wratten, and William E. Snyder. New York: John Wiley and Sons.

Anandaraj, M. 2000. *Diseases of Black Pepper*. Indian Institute of Spices Research, Kozhikode, Kerala. Reading, UK: Harwood Academic Publishers.

Anuradha, R. V., Bansuri Taneja, and Ashish Kothari. 2001. *Experiences with Biodiversity Policy-Making and Community Registers in India*. Participation in Access and Benefit-Sharing Policy Case Study no. 3, the Convention on Biological Diversity, United Nations Environment Programme.

APEDA. 2007–2008. Organic Products. http://www.apeda.gov.in/apeda website/organic/Organic_Products.htm.

Arrighi, Giovanni. 1999. The global market. *Journal of World-System Research* 2.

Bacon, Chris. 2010. Who decides what is fair in Fair Trade? Agri-environmental governance of standards, access, and price. *Journal of Peasant Studies* 37 (1): 111–47.

Balachandran, V. 2004. Future in the past: A study on the status of organic farming in Kerala. Discussion Paper no. 82, Kerala Research Programme on Local Level Development, Thiruvananthapuram, India: Centre for Development Studies.

Baviskar, Amita. 1995. *In the Belly of the River. Tribal Conflicts over Development in the Narmada Valley*. New York: Oxford University Press.

———. 2005. Red in Tooth and Claw? Looking for Class in Struggles Over Nature. In *Social Movements in India: Poverty, Power, and Politics*, eds. Raka

Ray and Mary Fainsod Katzenstein. Lanham, MD: Rowman and Littlefield Publishers.

Bernstein, H. 1996. Agrarian questions then and now. *Journal of Peasant Studies* 24 (1/2): 22–57.

Bingen, Jim, and Lawrence Busch, eds. 2006. *Agricultural Standards: The Shape of the Global Food and Fiber System*. Dordrecht: Springer.

Born, Branden, and Mark Purcell. 2006. Avoiding the local trap: Scale and food systems in planning research. *Journal of Planning Education and Research* 26:195–207.

Braganza, Miguel. 2010. Report on stakeholder consultation meetings of the new national PGS program in India. *Organic News* 2 (2): 1–2.

Braun, Bruce, and Noel Castree. 2004. The construction of nature and the nature of construction. In *Remaking Reality, Nature at the Millennium*, eds. Bruce Braun and Noel Castree. New York: Routledge.

Brockington, Dan. 2001. *Fortress Conservation: The Preservation of the Mkomazi Game Reserve, Tanzania*. Oxford: James Currey.

Brookfield, Harold, and Michael Stocking. 1999. Agrodiversity: Definition, description and design. *Global Environmental Change* 9:77–80.

Buck, D., C. Getz, and J. Guthman. 1997. From farm to table: The organic vegetable commodity chain of Northern California. *Sociologia Ruralis,* 37 (1): 3–20.

Burawoy, M. 2003. For a sociological Marxism: The complementary convergence of Antonio Gramsci and Karl Polanyi. *Politics and Society* 31 (2): 193–261.

Carson, Rachel. 1962. *Silent Spring.* Boston: Houghton Mifflin Company.

Cavigelli, Michael A., Beth L. Hima, James C. Hanson, John R. Teasdale, Anne E. Conklin, and Yao-chi Lu. 2009. Long-term economic performance of organic and conventional field crops in the mid-Atlantic region. *Renewable Agriculture and Food Systems* 24 (2): 102–19.

Central Coffee Research Institute. 2006. *Package of Practices for Organic Coffee,* ed. Dr. Jayarama, Director of Research, Central Coffee Research Institute.

Chakravarti, A. K. 1973. Green revolution in India. *Annals of the Association of American Geographers* 63 (3): 319–30.

Chandy, Oommen. 2005. Foreword. In *Human Development Report 2005, Kerala,* eds. Government of Kerala and Centre for Development Studies. Thiruvananthapuram, Kerala: State Planning Board, Government of Kerala.

Chang, Kenneth. 2012. Stanford scientists cast doubt on advantages of organic meat and produce. *The New York Times,* September 3.

Charles, Dan. 2013. Fertilized world, a mixed blessing. *National Geographic,* May.

Charyulu, Kumara D., and Subho Biswas. 2010. *Economics and Efficiency of Organic Farming vis-à-vis Conventional Farming in India.* IIMA Working Papers Series, no. WP2010-04-03, Indian Institute of Management Ahmedabad, Research and Publication Department.

Chasin, Barbara, and Richard Franke. 1991. The Kerala difference. *New York Review of Books,* October 24.

Chattopadhyay, Srikumar, and Richard Franke. 2006. *Striving for Sustainability.* New Delhi: Concept Publishing Company.

Chavas, Jean-Paul, Joshua L. Posner, and Janet L. Hedtcke. 2009. Organic and conventional production systems in the Wisconsin integrated cropping systems trial: II. Economic and risk analysis 1993–2006. *Agronomy Journal* 101 (2): 288–95.

Chopra, R. N. 1981. *Evolution of Food Policy in India.* New Delhi: Macmillan India Limited.

———. 1988. *Food Policy in India, A Survey.* New Delhi: Intellectual Publishing House.

Cohen, Roger. 2012. The organic fable. *The New York Times,* September 6.

Communist Party of India (Marxist). 2012. People's planning. Kerala State Committee. http://cpimkerala.org/eng/peoples-planning-31.php.

Confederation of Indian Industry, *Vision 2025 for the State of Kerala.* http://www. cii.in/PublicationDetail.aspx?enc=tagxijDliEcUoCTAWa3Rvw==

Conservation International. 2007. *Biodiversity Hotspots.* Western Ghats and Sri Lanka. http://www.biodiversityhotspots.org/xp/Hotspots/ghats/Pages /default.aspx.

Cook, Ian. 2004. Follow the thing: Papaya. *Antipode* 36 (4): 642–64.

Corbridge, S., and J. Harriss. 2000. *Reinventing India: Liberalization, Hindu Nationalism, and Popular Democracy.* Oxford: Blackwell.

Countryside Agency. 2002. *Eat the View: Promoting Sustainable Local Products.* Wetherby, UK: Countryside Agency Publications.

Crosby, A. W. 1972. *The Columbian Exchange: Biological and Cultural Consequences of 1492.* Westport, CT: Greenwood Press.

Daniels, R. J. Ranjit, and Jayshree Vencatesan. 2008. *Western Ghats, Biodiversity, People, Conservation.* New Delhi: Rupa and Co.

Daviron, Benoit, and Stefano Ponte. 2006. *The Coffee Paradox: Global Markets, Commodity Trade and the Elusive Promise of Development.* London: Zed Books.

Davis, Mike. 2002. *Late Victorian Holocausts: El Niño Famines and the Making of the Third World.* New York: Verso.

Dayal, Rajeshwar. 1968. *India's New Food Strategy.* New Delhi: Metropolitan Book Co.

Delate, Kathleen, Daniel Cwach, and Craig Chase. 2011. Organic no-tillage system effects on soybean, corn and irrigated tomato production and economic performance in Iowa, USA. *Renewable Agriculture and Food Systems* 27 (1): 49–59.

Delbridge, Timothy A., Jeffrey A. Coulter, Robert P. King, Craig C. Sheaffer, and Donald L. Wyse. 2011. Economic performance of long-term organic and conventional cropping systems in Minnesota. *Agronomy Journal* 103 (5): 1372–82.

Dempsey, Corinne G. 2001. *Kerala Christian Sainthood: Collisions of Culture and Worldview in South India.* New York: Oxford University Press.

Desai, Manali. 2005. Indirect British rule, state formation, and welfarism in Kerala, India, 1860–1957. *Social Science History* 29 (3): 457–88.

Deutsche Welle. 2007. Food crunch as German appetite for organic grows. May 2007.

Devi, Indira P. 2010. Pesticides in agriculture—a boon or a curse? A case study of Kerala. *Economic and Political Weekly* 45 (26 and 27): 199–207.

Devika, J. 2006. Negotiating women's social space: public debates on gender in early modern Kerala, India. *Inter-Asia Cultural Studies,* 7 (1): 43–61.

———. 2007. Fears of contagion? Depoliticisation and recent conflicts over politics in Kerala. *Economic and Political Weekly,* 42 (25): 2464–70.

Dhama, K., Rajesh Rathore, R. S. Chauhan, and Simmi Tomar. 2005. Panchgavya (cowpathy): An overview. *International Journal of Cow Science* 1 (1): 1–15.

Drayton, Richard. 2000. *Nature's Government: Science, Imperial Britain, and the "Improvement" of the World.* New Haven, CT: Yale University Press.

Dunn, Elizabeth C. 2003. Trojan pig: Paradoxes of food safety regulation. *Environment and Planning A,* 35:1493–1511.

DuPuis, Melanie E., and David Goodman. 2005. Should we go "home" to eat?: Toward a reflexive politics of localism. *Journal of Rural Studies* 21:359–71.

Dutch News. 2007. Supermarkets face organic food shortage. December 5.

Ehrlich, Paul R. 1975. *The Population Bomb.* Rivercity, MA: Rivercity Press.

Eilperin, Juliet. 2008. In surprise move, EPA bans carbofuran residue on food. *The Washington Post,* July 25. http://www.washingtonpost.com/wp-dyn/content/story/2008/07/24/ST2008072403523.html.

EPA (US). 2009. *Carbofura; Final Tolerance Revocations.* http://www.epa.gov/fedrgstr/EPA-PEST/2009/May/Day-15/p11396.htm.

Estabrook, Barry. 2011. *Tomatoland: How Industrial Farming "Destroyed" the Tasty Tomato,* Kansas City, MO: Andrews McMeel Publishing.

Fairfax, Sally K., Louise Nelson Dyble, Greig Tor Guthey, Lauren Gwin, Monica Moore, and Jennifer Sokolove. 2013. *California Cuisine and Just Food.* Cambridge, MA: MIT Press.

FAO. 2005. *Fertilizer Use by Crop in India*, eds. R. K. Tewatia and T. K. Chanda. Rome: Land and Plant Nutrition Management Service Land and Water Development Division, FAO.

———. 2014a. *Hunger Statistics.* http://www.fao.org/hunger/en.

———. 2014b. What are certified organic products? FAQ. http://www.fao .org/organicag/oa-faq/oa-faq2/en.

Foster, John Bellamy. 2000. *Marx's Ecology: Capitalism and Nature.* New York: Monthly Review Press.

Franke, Richard W., and Barbara H. Chasin. 1994. *Kerala: Radical Reform as Development in an Indian State.* Oakland, CA: Food First.

———. 2000. Is the Kerala model sustainable? Lessons from the past, prospects for the future. In *Kerala: The Development Experience*, ed. Govidan Parayil. London: Zed Books.

Friedmann, Harriet. 1982. The political economy of food: The rise and fall of the postwar international food order. *American Journal of Sociology* 88:248–86.

Fulton, April. 2012. When it comes to buying organic, science and beliefs don't always mesh. National Public Radio, September 7. http://www.npr.org /blogs/thesalt/2012/09/07/160681396/when-it-comes-to-buying-organic -science-and-beliefs-dont-always-mesh.

Funes, Fernando, Luis García, Martin Bourque, Nilda Pérez, and Peter Rosset, eds. 2002. *Sustainable Agriculture and Resistance. Transforming Food Production in Cuba.* Food First Books and ACTAF (Cuban Association of Agricultural and Forestry Technicians) and CEAS (Center for the Study of Sustainable Agriculture, Agrarian University of Havana).

Gadgil, Madhav. 2001. *Ecological Journeys, the Science and Politics of Conservation in India.* Delhi: Permanent Black.

Ganesan, K. 2010. *Monitoring of Pesticide Residue in Select Components of an Agro-Ecosystem Adopting Organic and Chemical Farming in Padayetti Village, Palakkad District, Kerala.* Report submitted to the Kerala State Biodiversity Board.

Garibay, Salvador V., and Katke Jyoti. 2003. Market Opportunities and Challenges for Indian Organic Products. Research Institute of Organic Agriculture (FIBL), ACNielsen ORG-MARG, Swiss State Secretariat (SECO).

George, K. K. 1998. Historical roots of the Kerala model and its present crisis. *Bulletin of Concerned Asian Scholars* 30 (4): 35–40.

George, Nirmala. 2011. India's wheat left to rot due to lack of storage. Associated Press, May 10.

Getz, Christy, and Aimee Shreck. 2006. What organic and fair trade labels do not tell us: Towards a place-based understanding of certification. *International Journal of Consumer Studies*, 30 (5): 490–501.

Gilbert, Natasha. 2012. Organic Farming is Rarely Enough. *Nature*, April 25. http://www.nature.com/news/organic-farming-is-rarely-enough-1.10519.

Goodman, David, and Michael Watts, eds. 1997. *Globalising Food: Agrarian Questions and Global Restructuring.* London: Routledge.

Goodman, Michael. 2004. Reading Fair Trade: Political ecological imaginary and the moral economy of Fair Trade foods. *Political Geography* 23: 891–915.

Government of India. Department of Food, New Delhi. 1944. *Food Situation in India.*

———. Department of Agriculture and Cooperation, Ministry of Agriculture, Directorate of Arecanut and Spices Development. 2009. *Black Pepper Guide.*

———. Department of Food and Public Distribution. 2010. *Country-wise Status of Export of Rice and Wheat on Diplomatic Basis.* http://dfpd.nic.in/fcamin/impex/file6.pdf.

———. Spices Board of India. 2010. *Black Pepper* (extension pamphlet).

———. Planning Commission. 2011. *India Human Development Report 2011.*

———. 2013. Department of Information Technology. *Wayanad District Profile.* http://wayanad.nic.in/profile.htm.

———. Ministry of Tourism. n.d. Incredible !ndia campaign. http://www.incredibleindia.org/.

Government of Kerala. 2001. *Impact of WTO on Kerala Agriculture,* G.O. (MS) no.163/2001/AD dated 31.07-2001. Thiruvananthapuram: Agriculture Department.

———. 2002. The Kerala Land Reforms (Amendment) Bill. http://www.kerala.gov.in/docs/pdf/land_reforms.pdf.

———. 2009a. Department of Environment and Kerala State Biodiversity Board. *Kerala State Environment Policy.*

———. 2009b. Kerala Agricultural University. *Ad-hoc Package of Practices, Recommendations for Organic Farming: Crops.*

———. 2010a. Agriculture Department. Agriculture Department circular dated August 26, 2010, Subject: Annual Plan 2010–11 Organic Farming Programme-guidelines.

———. 2010b. Kerala State Biodiversity Board, Agro-biodiversity Restoration Programme Team. *Agro-biodiversity Restoration Project, Padayetti, Erimayur Panchayat, Palakkad.*

———. 2010c. Kerala State Biodiversity Board. *Kerala State Organic Farming Policy, Strategy and Action Plan.*

———. 2011. *Kerala Budget 2011–2012.* Finance Department. http://www.kerala.gov.in/index.php?option=com_content&view=article&id=3764&Itemid=2150.

————. State Planning Board. Directorate of Agriculture. 2011. *Selected Indicators of Agricultural Development in Kerala (2008–2009 and 2009–2010)*.

————. Finance Department. 2012. *Kerala Budget 2012–2013*. http://www
.kerala.gov.in/index.php?option=com_content&view=article&id=3996
&Itemid=3178.

————. Finance Department. 2013. *Kerala Budget 2013–2014*. http://www
.kerala.gov.in/index.php?option=com_content&view=article&id=4613
&Itemid=3312.

————. Department of Information and Public Relations. n.d. *Political Background*. http://www.kerala.gov.in/index.php?option=com_content&view
=article&id=3064&Itemid=2378.

————. Kerala Land Use Board. n.d. http://kslub.kerala.gov.in.

————. State Planning Board. n.d. *Fourth Five Year Plan, 1969–1974*.

————. State Planning Board. n.d. *Second Five Year Plan, 1956–1961*.

————. State Planning Board. n.d. Wayanad. Department of Economics and Statistics. http://www.ecostat.kerala.gov.in.

Government of Kerala and Centre for Development Studies. 2005. *Human Development Report 2005, Kerala*. State Planning Board. http://www.undp.org
/content/dam/india/docs/human_develop_report_kerala_2005_full
_report.pdf.

Gupta, Akhil. 1998. *Postcolonial Developments, Agriculture in the Making of Modern India*. Durham, NC: Duke University Press.

Guthman, Julie. 2004a. *Agrarian Dreams: The Paradox of Organic Farming in California*, Berkeley: University of California Press.

————. 2004b. The trouble with "organic lite" in California: A rejoinder to the conventionalisation" debate. *Sociologia Ruralis* 44 (3): 301–16.

————. 2007. The Polanyian way? Voluntary food labels as neoliberal governance. *Antipode* (39) 3: 456–78.

————. 2011. *Weighing In, Obesity, Food Justice, and the Limits of Capitalism*. Berkeley: University of California Press.

Griswold, Eliza. 2012. How "Silent Spring" ignited the environmental movement. *The New York Times*, September 21. http://www.nytimes.com
/2012/09/23/magazine/how-silent-spring-ignited-the-environmental
-movement.html?pagewanted=all&_r=0.

Grove, Richard. 1995. *Green Imperialism: Colonial Expansion, Tropical Island Edens and the Origins of Environmentalism, 1600–1860*. Cambridge: Cambridge University Press.

Haraway, Donna. 1988. Situated knowledges: The science question in feminism and the privilege of partial perspectives. *Feminist Studies* 4 (3): 575–99.

Harriss-White, Barbara, S. Janakarajan, and Diego Colatei. 2004. Introduction: Heavy agriculture and light industry in South India villages. In *Rural India Facing the 21st Century*, eds. Barbara Harriss-White and S. Janakarajan. London: Anthem Press.

Heller, Patrick. 1999. *The Labor of Development: Workers and the Transformation of Capitalism in Kerala, India*. Ithaca, NY: Cornell University Press.

Herring, Ronald. 1983. *Land to the Tiller: The Political Economy of Agrarian Reform in South Asia*. New Haven, CT: Yale University Press.

Hindu, The. 2008. Kerala cabinet okays organic farming policy. October 16. http://www.thehindubusinessline.in/bline/2008/10/16/stories/20081016 50862300.htm.

———. 2010. 2,836 Endosulfan victims identified. December 30.

———. 2011. Flagrant use of chemicals to ripen fruits on the rise. March 31.

Hinrichs, C. Clare. 2003. The practice and politics of food system localization. *Journal of Rural Studies* 19 (1): 33–45.

Hobbs, P. R. 2007. Conservation agriculture: What is it and why is it important for future sustainable food production? Profitability of organic cropping systems in Southwestern Minnesota. *Journal of Agricultural Science*, 145:127–37.

Holt-Gimenez, Eric. 2012. We already grow enough food for 10 billion people—and still can't end hunger. *The Huffington Post*, May 2. http://www.huffingtonpost.com/eric-holt-gimenez/world-hunger_b_1463429.html.

IFOAM. 2004. *Smallholder Group Certification Guidance Manual for Producer Organizations.*http://www.imo.ch/portal/pics/documents/ics_guidance _manual.pdf.

———. 2011a. *Participatory Guarantee Systems (PGS).* http://www.ifoam.org /about_ifoam/standards/pgs.html.

———. 2011b. *The World of Organic Agriculture, Statistics and Emerging Trends 2011*, eds. Helga Willer and Lukas Kilcher. Frick, Switzerland: FiBL; Bonn: IFOAM.

———. 2013. *Statistics 2013: Sales Now Top US $60 Billion for the First Time.* Press release. http://ifoam.org/public/Press_Release_IFOAM_FiBL _final_EN.pdf.

———. n.d. Internal Control Systems (ICS) for Group Certification. http:// www.ifoam.org/en/internal-control-systems-ics-group-certification.

Indian Council of Agricultural Research. 2011. *Dr Swaminathan Calls an Evergreen Revolution in India.* http://www.icar.org.in/en/node/2826.

Indocert. 2012. *Accreditations.* http://www.indocert.org/accreditations.html.

http://iofpcl.com/index.php?option=com_content&task=view&id=74 &Itemid=54.

Institution of Mechanical Engineers. 2013. *Global Food. Waste Not, Want Not.* http://www.imeche.org/knowledge/themes/environment/global-food.

International Competence Centre for Organic Agriculture (ICCOA). *About Organic Sector.* http://www.iccoa.org/About_Organic_sector.php.

IOFPCL. 2004. *News and Events.* Linking the farmers with the end user directly.

Isaac, T. M. Thomas. 2010. 2010–2011 Introductory Budget Speech for the Annual Budget for the State of Kerala, March 5.

Isaac, T. M. Thomas, and Tharakan, P. K. Michael. 1995. Kerala: Towards a new agenda. *Economic and Political Weekly,* 30 (31 and 32): 1993–2004.

Jacob, T. G. 2006. *Wayanad, Misery in an Emerald Bowl.* Mumbai: Vikas Adhyayan Kendra.

Jacobsen, K. L., C. L. Escalante, and C. F. Jordan. 2010. Economic analysis of experimental organic agricultural systems on a highly eroded soil of the Georgia Piedmont, USA. *Renewable Agriculture and Food Systems,* 25 (4): 296–308.

Jaffee, Daniel, and Philip H. Howard. 2010. Corporate cooptation of organic and fair trade standards. *Agriculture and Human Values,* 27: 387–99.

Jeromi, P. D. 2007. Farmers' indebtedness and suicides. Impact of agricultural trade liberalisation in Kerala. *Economic and Political Weekly,* 42 (31): 3241–47.

John, K. C. 1991. *Kerala the Melting Pot. A Political History.* New Delhi: Nunes Publishers.

Joseph, Brigit, and K. J. Joseph. 2005. Commercial agriculture in Kerala after the WTO. *South Asia Economic Journal,* 6 (1): 37–57.

Joseph, K. V. 1988. *Migration and Economic Development of Kerala.* New Delhi: Mittal Publications.

Joseph, Shally. 2003. *Entrepreneurs of Kerala.* New Delhi: Northern Book Centre.

J.P. 2012. Harvests and Farmland. *The Economist,* December 19. http://www.economist.com/blogs/feastandfamine/2012/12/harvests-and-farmland.

Kabir, M. 2010. On the periphery: Muslims and the Kerala model. In *Development, Democracy and the State,* ed. K. Ravi Raman. London: Routledge Contemporary South Asia.

Kerala Catholic Bishops Council. 2014. *Overview, Origin of the INFAM.* http://kcbc.in/content/indian-farmers-movement .

Kinver, Mark. 2006. *Britain Now "Eating the Planet."* BBC News. April 15. http://news.bbc.co.uk/2/hi/science/nature/4897252.stm.

Kjosavik, Darley Jose, and Nadarajah Shanmugaratnam. 2007. Property rights
    dynamics and indigenous communities in highland Kerala, South India:
    An institutional-historical perspective. *Modern Asian Studies,* 41 (6):
    1183–1260.

Kohli, Atul. 2006. Politics of economic growth in India, 1980–2005. *Economic
    and Political Weekly* 41 (43): 1251–59.

Kosek, Jake. 2006. *Understories: The Political Life of Forests in Northern New
    Mexico.* Durham, NC: Duke University Press.

Kotz, Deborah. 2011. Organic produce from China: Can you trust it? *Boston
    Globe,* December 14.

Krishnaprasad, P. 2004. *Mounting Suicides: Urgent Need to Save Wayanad
    Farmers.* www.countercurrents.org/gl-prasad200704.htm.

Kulkarni, Kausubh. 2011. Endosulfan makers rise on reports top court
    OKs export of chemical. Reuters. http://in.mobile.reuters.com/article
    /businessNews/idININdia-59636820110930.

Kumar, A. M. Sunil, ed. 2010. *Jaiva Krishi Sahai.* Farm Information Bureau,
    Agriculture Department, Government of Kerala.

Kurian, Vinson. 2013. Welfare, green and sustainability themes to fore in Ker-
    ala deficit budget. *The Hindu,* March 15. http://www.thehindubusinessline
    .com/news/states/welfare-green-and-sustainability-themes-to-fore-in
    -kerala-deficit-budget/article4512684.ece.

Latour, Bruno. 1991. *We Have Never Been Modern.* Cambridge, MA: Harvard
    University Press.

Lukose, Ritty. 2009. *Liberalization's Children: Gender, Youth, and Consumer
    Citizenship in Globalizing India.* Durham, NC: Duke University Press.

Madan, M. S., Y. R. Sarma, K. V. Peter, K. Sivaraman, S. Varma, V. Srinivasan,
    and P. Singh. 2005. Impact assessment of improved management practices
    for phytophthora foot rot disease in black pepper. In *Impact of Agricultural
    Research, Post-Green Revolution Evidence from India,* eds. P. K. Joshi, Suresh
    Pal, P. S. Birthal, and M. C. S. Bantilan. New Delhi: National Centre for Ag-
    ricultural Economic and Policy Research and International Crops Research
    Institute for the Semi-Arid Tropics.

Mahoney, Paul R., Kent D. Olson, Paul M. Porter, David R. Huggins, Cather-
    ine A. Perillo, and R. Kent Crookston. 2003. Profitability of organic crop-
    ping systems in southwestern Minnesota. *Renewable Agriculture and Food
    Systems* 19 (1): 35–46.

Manojkumar, K., B. Sreekumar, and G. S. Ajithkumar. 2005. Crop insurance
    scheme: A Case Study of Banana Farmers in Wayanad District. Discussion
    Paper no. 54, Kerala Research Programme on Local Level Development.
    Thiruvananthapuram, India: Centre for Development Studies.

Martin, Andrew, and Kim Seversen. 2008. Sticker shock in the organic aisles. *The New York Times*, April 18.

Martin, K. A. 2013. Banned pesticide residues found in vegetable samples. *The Hindu*, June 18. http://www.thehindu.com/news/cities/Kochi/banned -pesticide-residues-found-in-vegetable-samples/article4824152.ece.

Marwaha, B. C. 2005. Is India in a position to switch over to pure organic farming in totality? *Indian Journal of Fertilisers* 1 (7): 47–52.

Mathew, George. 1989. *Communal Road to a Secular Kerala*. New Delhi: Concept Publishing Company.

Mathew, Roy. 2011. Tension at Stockholm Convention meeting over endosulfan. *The Hindu*, April 27. http://www.thehindu.com/news/national/kerala /tension-at-stockholm-convention-meeting-over-endosulfan/article 1772488.ece.

Massey, Doreen. 1994. *Space, Place, and Gender*. Minneapolis: University of Minnesota Press.

McEwan, Cheryl, and David Bek. 2009. The political economy of alternative trade: Social and environmental certification in the South African wine industry. *Journal of Rural Studies* 25 (3): 255–66.

McKibben, Bill. 1995. The enigma of Kerala: One state in India is proving development experts wrong. *UTNE Reader*. http://www.utne.com/community /theenigmaofkerala.aspx.

———. 1999. Kerala India. *National Geographic Traveler*. Reprinted at KeralaKerala.com, http://www.keralakerala.com/national-geographic -traveller-Bill-McKibben-Kerala.html.

McMichael, Philip David. 2009. A food regime analysis of the world food crisis. *Agriculture and Human Values*, 4:281–95.

Mehdudia, Sujay. 2013. Major cut in fuel, food, fertilizer subsidies. *The Hindu*, February 28. http://www.thehindu.com/news/national/major-cut-in -fuel-food-fertilizer-subsidies/article4462708.ece.

Mencher, Joan. 1980. The lessons and non-lessons of Kerala: Agricultural labourers and poverty. *Economic and Political Weekly* 15 (41, 42, 43).

Merchant, Carolyn. 1980. *The Death of Nature: Women, Ecology, and the Scientific Revolution*. New York: Harper.

Mintz, Sidney W. 1985. *Sweetness and Power*. Penguin Press.

Mitchell, Timothy. 2002. *Rule of Experts: Egypt, Techno-Politics, Modernity*. Berkeley: University of California Press.

Mittermeier, Russell A., Norman Meyers, Jorgen B. Thomsen, Gustavo A. B. da Fonseca, and Silvio Olivieri. 1998. Biodiversity hotspots and major tropical wilderness areas: Approaches to setting conservation priorities. *Conservation Biology* 12 (13): 516–20.

Mooij, Jos. 1999. *Food Policy and the Indian State: The Public Distribution System in South India*. New York: Oxford University Press.

Moore, Donald. 1996. Marxism, culture, and political ecology. Environmental struggles in Zimbabwe's Eastern Highlands. In *Liberation Ecologies*, eds. Richard Peet and Michael Watts. London: Routledge.

Mutersbaugh, Tad. 2006. Certifying biodiversity: Conservation networks, landscape connectivity, and certified agriculture in southern Mexico. In *Globalization and New Geographies of Conservation*, ed. Karl S. Zimmerer. Chicago: University of Chicago Press.

Nair, C. Gouridasan. 2010. Kerala imposes ban on endosulfan use. *The Hindu*, November 20.

Nair, Gopalan. 1911 (2000). *Wynad, Its Peoples and Traditions*. Madras: Higginbotham and Co.

Nandan, Bijoy. 2010. Progress report, agrobiodiversity enhancement programme—study on benthic fauna and soil chemistry of selected wetlands in Palakkad, Kerala. Report submitted to the Kerala State Biodiversity Board.

Narayanan, N. C., and Sajan, G. 2005. Civil society in an overtly partisan political context: What enables/constrains the Kerala Sastra Sahitya Parishad (KSSP)? Working Paper no. 189. Anand: Institute of Rural Management (IRMA).

Nash, Linda. 2007. *Inescapable Ecologies: A History of Environment, Disease, and Knowledge*. Berkeley: University of California Press.

National Biodiversity Authority of India. 2008. *People's Biodiversity Register*. http://nbaindia.org/content/105/30//pbr.html.

National Centre of Organic Farming, Ministry of Agriculture. 2010. *Organic Certification Area and Production Statistics Year 2009–10*. Government of India. http://ncof.dacnet.nic.in/OrganicFarmingStatistics/Organic%20Area%20and%20Production%20statistics%202009-10.pdf.

National Crime Records Bureau of India. 2006. Suicides in India. In *Accidental Deaths and Suicides in India—2006*. Government of India. http://ncrb.nic.in/adsi/data/adsi2006/home.htm.

Naylor, Rosamond, Henning Steinfeld, Walter Falcon, James Galloway, Vaclav Smil, Eric Bradford, Jackie Alder, and Harold Mooney. 2005. Losing the links between livestock and land. *Science* 310 (5754): 1621–22.

Neilson, Jeff, and Bill Pritchard. 2009. *Value Chain Struggles*. London: John Wiley and Sons.

Organic Trade Association. 2011. *Industry Statistics and Projected Growth*. http://www.ota.com/organic/mt/business.html.

Osswald, Nina, and Manoj K. Menon. 2013. *Organic Food Marketing in Urban*

Centres of India. International Competence Centre for Organic Agriculture (ICCOA).

Oxfam. 2012. *Food Crises Doomed to Repeat Until Leaders Find Courage to Fix Problems*. http://www.oxfam.org/sites/www.oxfam.org/files/food-price -crisis-oxfam-media-advisory-aug2012.pdf.

Padre, Shree. 2009. Kokkarni, saviour of paddy. *India Together*, April 12. http:// www.indiatogether.org/2009/apr/env-padayetti.htm.

Pandian, Anand. 2009. *Crooked Stalks: Cultivating Virtue in South India*. Durham, NC: Duke University Press.

Panikkar, K. N. 1989. *Against Lord and State. Religion and Peasant Uprisings in Malabar, 1836–1921*. Oxford: Oxford University Press.

Parayil, Govindan, ed. 2000. *Kerala: The Development Experience*, London: Zed Books.

Patel, Raj. 2012a. *Organic vs. Industrial Agriculture Rematch*. http://rajpatel .org/2012/05/03/organic-vs-industrial-agriculture-rematch.

———. 2012b. The Long Green Revolution. *Journal of Peasant Studies* 40 (1): 1–63.

———. 2013. *Raj Patel on Food Sovereignty, Localism, and Markets*. Interview in Farmtogethernow.org, May 11. http://farmtogethernow.org/2013/05/11 /raj-patel-on-food-sovereignty-localism-and-markets.

Patnaik, Utsa. 2006. Theorizing food security and poverty in the era of economic reforms. *Social Scientist* 33 (4): 50–81.

Perfecto, Ivette, John Vandermeer, and Angus Wright. 2009. *Nature's Matrix. Linking Agriculture, Conservation and Food Sovereignty*. London: Earthscan.

Perkins, John H. 1997. *Geopolitics and the Green Revolution, Wheat, Genes, and the Cold War*. Oxford: Oxford University Press.

Philip, Kavita. 2003. *Civilizing Natures: Race, Resources, and Modernity in Colonial South India*. New Brunswick, NJ: Rutgers University Press.

Philpott, Tom. 2013. A brief history of our deadly addiction to nitrogen fertilizer. *Mother Jones*, April 19. http://www.motherjones.com/tom-philpott /2013/04/history-nitrogen-fertilizer-ammonium-nitrate.

Pimentel, D., T. W. Culliney, and T. Bashore. 2013. Public health risks associated with pesticides and natural toxins in foods. In *Radcliffe's IPM World Textbook*, eds. E. B. Radcliffe and W. D. Hutchison. St. Paul: University of Minnesota College of Food, Agricultural and Natural Resource Sciences.

Pimentel, David. 2005. Environmental and economic costs of the application of pesticides primarily in the United States. *Environment, Development and Sustainability* 7:229–52.

Polanyi, Karl. 1944. *The Great Transformation: The Political and Economic Origins of Our Time*. Boston: Beacon Press.

Pollan, Michael. 2006. *The Omnivore's Dilemma: A Natural History of Four Meals*. New York: Penguin Press.

Prabha, M. R. and K. Vasantha. 2010. Effect of organic fertilizer and Panchagavya spray on the growth and biomass of *Cassia angustifolia Vahl. Plant Archives* 10 (1): 279–80.

Prakash, Gyan. 1999. *Another Reason: Science and the Imagination of Modern India*. Princeton, NJ: Princeton University Press.

Radhakrishnan, P. 1989. *Peasant Struggles, Land Reforms and Social Change, Malabar, 1836–1982*. London: Sage.

Ramakumar, R. 2006. Public action, agrarian change and the stand of living of agricultural workers: A study of a village in Kerala. *Journal of Agrarian Change* 6 (3): 306–45.

Raman, K. Ravi. 2010. The Kerala model: Situating the critique. In *Development, Democracy and the State,* ed. K. Ravi Raman. London: Routledge Contemporary South Asia.

Ramesh, P., Mohan Singh, and Subha A. Rao. 2005. Organic farming: Its relevance to the Indian context. *Current Science* 88 (4): 561–68.

Ravichandran, G., N. Natarajan, K. Manorama, and K. Vanangamudi. 2011. Effect of organic sprays on storage behaviour of seed potatoes. *Indian Journal of Horticulture* 68(3): 399–407.

Raynolds, Laura T. 2004. The Globalization of Organic Agro-Food Networks. *World Development* 32 (4): 725–43.

———. 2008. The organic agro-export boom in the Dominican Republic: Maintaining tradition or fostering transformation? *Latin American Research Review* 43 (1): 161–84.

Raynolds, Laura T., and Siphelo Unathi Ngcwangu. 2010. Fair Trade Rooibos tea: Connecting South African producers and American consumer markets. *Geoforum* 41 (1): 74–83.

Reddy, Srinivasa V., C. Thamban, C. V. Sairam, Bindu Chandran, S. R. Prabhu, A. S. Sukumaran, and M. R. Hegde. 2001. Participatory research in paddy cultivation in Kasaragod District of Kerala: A case study. *Journal of Tropical Agriculture* 39:42–46.

Reed, Matt. 2009. For whom?—The governance of organic food and farming in the UK. *Food Policy* 34 (3): 280–86.

Reuters. 2011. *India's Projected Food Supply and Demand*. http://www.sify.com.

Robbins, Paul. 2004. *Political Ecology*. London: Routledge.

Roman-Alcalá, Antonio. 2013. From food security to food sovereignty. *Civil Eats*, May 29.

Sahai, Suman. 2010. Rs 60,000 crore is the cost of rotting food grain every year. Yet, millions go hungry. *Tehelka Magazine* 7 (31).

Sainath, P. 2008. *Everybody Loves a Good Drought, Stories from India's Poorest district*. London: Penguin Books.

———. 2011. In 16 years, farm suicides cross a quarter million. *The Hindu*, October 29. http://www.thehindu.com/opinion/columns/sainath/in-16 -years-farm-suicides-cross-a-quarter-million/article2577635.ece.

Saltmarsh, Matthew. 2011. Strong sales of organic foods attract investors. *The New York Times*, May 23. http://www.nytimes.com/2011/05/24/business /global/24organic.html.

Scott, Steffanie, Peter Vandergeest, and Mary Young. 2009. Certification standards and the governance of green foods in Southeast Asia. In *Corporate Power in Global Agrifood Governance*, eds. Jennifer Clapp and Doris Fuchs. Cambridge, MA: MIT Press.

Sen, Amartya. 1981. *Poverty and Famines: An Essay on Entitlements and Deprivation*. Oxford: Clarendon Press.

———. 1990. More than a hundred million women are missing. *New York Review of Books*, December 20.

Seufert, Verena, Navin Ramankutty, and Jonathan A. Foley. 2012. Comparing the yields of organic and conventional agriculture. *Nature* 485:229–32.

Shapin, Steven, and Simon Schafer. 1985. *Leviathan and the Air Pump: Hobbes, Boyle, and the Experimental Details*. Princeton, NJ: Princeton University Press.

Sharma, Vijay Paul, and Hrima Thaker. 2010. Fertilizer subsidy in India: Who are the beneficiaries? *Economic and Political Weekly* 45 (12): 68–76.

Shiva, Vandana. 1988. *Staying alive: Women, ecology, and development*. London: Zed Books.

———. 1997. *Biopiracy*. Cambridge, MA: South End Press.

———. 2010. Closing speech at the Indian Biodiversity Conference in Thiruvananthapuram, Kerala, India.

Shreyas Social Service Centre. n.d. *Increasing Suicides in Wayanad, A Study Report, Wayanad Series—2*. Wayanad, Kerala: Research and Documentation Wing of Shreyas Social Service Centre.

Singh, Gorakh. 2009. Foreword. In *Black Pepper Guide*, ed. Directorate of Arecanut and Spices Development, Department of Agriculture and Cooperation. Calicut: Government of India, Ministry of Agriculture.

Smith-Spangler, Crystal, Margaret L. Brandeau, Grace E. Hunter, Clay J. Bavinger, Maren Pearsen, Paul J. Eschbach, Vandana Sundaram, Hau Liu, Patricia Schirmer, Christopher Stave, Ingram Olkin, and Dena M. Bravata. 2012. Are organic foods safer or healthier than conventional alternatives? A systematic review. *Annals of Internal Medicine* 157:348–66.

Smukler, S. M., L. E. Jackson, L. Murphree, R. Yokota, S. T. Koike, and R. F.

Smith. 2008. Transition to large-scale organic vegetable production in the Salinas Valley, California. *Agriculture, Ecosystems and Environment* 126: 168–88.

Sreekumar, Sharmila. 2009. The land of "gender paradox"? Getting past the commonsense of contemporary Kerala. *Inter-Asia Cultural Studies* 8 (1): 34–54.

Sridhar, R. 2008. *Endosulfan Poisoning and the Struggle of the Community in Kasaragod to Regain Life and the Living Land*. Power Point presentation on behalf of Thanal and Pesticide Action Network-Asia, Kerala, India.

Steur, Luisa. 2009. Adivasi mobilisation: "Identity" versus "class" after the Kerala model of development? *Journal of South Asian Development* 4 (1): 25–44.

Subramanian, Meera. 2013. Bihar's school deaths highlight India's struggle with pesticides. *The New York Times*, July 30.

Sumangala, K., and M. B. Patil. 2009. Panchagavya—an organic weapon against plant pathogens. *Journal of Plant Disease Sciences* 4 (2): 147–51.

Swaminathan, M. S. 1999. Silent Valley National Park—A biological paradise. In *Silent Valley, Whispers of Reason*, eds. T. M. Manoharan, S. D. Biju, T. S. Nayar, and P. S. Easa. Thiruvananthapuram, India: Kerala Forest Department, in association with Kerala Forest Research Institute.

Teachers' Association of KAU. 2008. *Can Organic Agriculture Replace Conventional Agriculture? Reflections on the Organic Agricultural Policy proposed by the Bio Diversity Board of Kerala*.

Thakur, J. S., B. T. Rao, A. Rajwanshi, H. L. Parwana, and K. Kumar. 2008. Epidemiological study of high cancer among rural agricultural community of Punjab in northern India. *International Journal of Environmental Research and Public Health* 5 (5): 399–407.

Thanal. 2009. Report of the agro-diversity restoration programme, Padayetti, Erimayur Panchayath, Palakkad, (December 2008–March 2009). Submitted by Thanal to the Kerala State Biodiversity Board.

Tharakan, P.K.M. 1984. Intra-regional differences in agrarian systems and internal migration: A case study of the migration of farmers from Travancore to Malabar, 1930–1950. Working Paper no. 194. Thiruvananthapuram, India: Centre for Development Studies.

———. 1998. *Coffee, Tea or Pepper? Factors Affecting Choice of Crops by Agro-Entrepreneurs in Nineteenth Century South-West India*. Thiruvananthapuram, India: Centre for Development Studies.

Tharamangalam, Joseph. 2006. Understanding Kerala's paradoxes: The problematic of the Kerala model of development. In *Kerala, the Paradoxes of Pub-*

lic Action and Development, ed. Joseph Tharamangalam. Hyderabad, India: Orient Longman Private Limited.

———. 2011. *Agrarian Class Conflict*. Vancouver: UBC Press.

Thomas, Sabu K. 2010. Diversity and community structure of ground surface dwelling arthropods in the agroecosystems of Kerala. Progress report submitted to the Kerala State Biodiversity Board.

Thompson, James. 2008. UK organic market held back by supply shortage. *Retail Week*, January 25. http://www.retail-week.com/uk-organic-food -market-held-back-by-supply-shortage/541544.article.

Thottathil, Sapna, Michelle Gottlieb, and Lucia Sayre. 2012. Green and clean. *Greenhealth* Magazine, Practice Greenhealth. http://greenhealthmagazine .org/green-and-clean-2/.

Tibbetts, Graham. 2007. Organic food "air miles" are catastrophic. *The Telegraph*, July 17. http://www.telegraph.co.uk/earth/agriculture/foodmiles /3300679/Organic-food-air-miles-are-catastrophic.html.

Times of India, The. 2013. Kasturirangan report: Govt equivocates on main issues. October 22. http://articles.timesofindia.indiatimes.com/2013-10-22 /thiruvananthapuram/43287124_1_hlwg-oommen-chandy-wgeep-report.

Tiwari, K.N., Gavin Sulewski, and Sam Portch. 2005. Challenges of meeting nutrient needs in organic farming. *Indian Journal of Fertilisers* (4): 41–48, 51–59.

UNCTAD. 2013. *Wake Up Before It Is Too Late*. United Nations. http://unctad .org/en/PublicationsLibrary/ditcted2012d3_en.pdf.

UNEP. 2011. United Nations targets widely used pesticide endosulfan for phase out. Press release, Stockholm Convention on Persistent Organic Pollutants (POPs), Fifth Meeting of the Conference of the Parties.

———. n.d. Signatures and ratifications. Stockholm Convention on Persistent Organic Pollutants (POPs). http://www.pops.int/documents/signature.

USAID. 2003. *Celebrating Food for Peace, 1954–2004*. http://foodaid.org/news /wp-content/uploads/2011/01/FFP_50thAv_Brochure.pdf.

USDA, Economic Research Service. 2013. *Organic Production*. http://www.ers .usda.gov/data-products/organic-production.aspx#.UnlvKBDjW4E

USDA, National Agricultural Statistics Service. 2009. *Trends in US Agriculture*. http://www.nass.usda.gov/Publications/Trends_in_U.S._Agriculture.

Upendranadh, C. 2010. Coffee conundrum: Whither the future of small grower in India? NRPPD Discussion Paper 3.

Vakkayil, Jacob D. 2010. INFAM in Wayanad, Kerala. In *Inclusive Value Chains: A Pathway Out of Poverty*, ed. Malcolm Harper. Singapore: World Scientific Publishing Co.

Valkila, Joni. 2009. Fair Trade organic coffee production in Nicaragua—Sustainable development or a poverty trap? *Ecological Economics* 68 (12): 3018–25.

Varghese, T. C. 1970. *Agrarian Change and Economic Consequences: Land Tenures in Kerala 1850–1960.* New Delhi: Allied Publishers.

Varghese, Thomas, and I. V. Sasankan. 2007. Unfretted marketing, regulation how? *Kerala Calling* 27 (5): 14–15.

Watts, Michael. 2005. Nature/culture: A natural history. In *Spaces of Geographical Thought,* eds. R. Johnston and P. Cloke. London: Sage.

Watts, Michael, and Richard Peet. 2004. Liberating political ecology. In *Liberation Ecologies,* eds. Richard Peet and Michael Watts. 2nd edition. London: Routledge.

Western Ghats Ecology Expert Panel. 2011. Report of the Western Ghats Ecology Expert Panel. Submitted to the Ministry of Environment and Forests, Government of India. http://moef.nic.in/downloads/public-information /wg-23052012.pdf.

Weiss, Tony. 2007. *The Global Food Economy.* London: Zed Books.

Willer, Helga. 2011. Organic agriculture worldwide—The results of the FiBL/ IFOAM survey. In *The World of Organic Agriculture, Statistics and Emerging Trends 2011,* eds. Helga Willer and Lukas Kilcher. FiBL and IFOAM.

Williams, Michelle. 2008. *The Roots of Participatory Democracy: Democratic Communists in South Africa and Kerala, India.* New York: Palgrave Macmillan.

Williams, Raymond. 1980. Ideas of nature. In *Problems in Materialism and Culture,* London: Verso.

Winter, Michael. 2003. Embeddedness, the new food economy and defensive localism. *Journal of Rural Studies* 19 (1): 23–32.

WHO. 2006. Pesticides are a leading suicide method. http://www.who.int /mediacentre/news/notes/2006/np24/en.

WWF Global. n.d. *Priority Places: Western Ghats, India.* http://wwf.panda.org /what_we_do/where_we_work/western_ghats.

Worldwatch Institute. 2013. *Global Food Prices Continue to Rise.* http://www .worldwatch.org/global-food-prices-continue-rise-0.

Worster, Donald. 2008. The ecology of order and chaos. In *Ecology,* ed. Carolyn Merchant. 2nd edition. Amherst, NY: Humanity Books.

Yadav, A. K. 2009. *Organic Status in India.* Regional Centre of Organic Farming (RCOF), India.

———. 2010. *Organic Farming Newsletter* 6 (4).

Zimmerer, Karl S. 1996. *Changing Fortunes: Biodiversity and Peasant Livelihood in the Peruvian Andes.* Berkeley: University of California Press.

INDEX